THIS BOOK IS DEDICATED TO...

My mom, Irene; my dad, Jack; my twin sister, Nancy;
and my wonderful friend who gives me inspiration and guidance, Kim.

AND A VERY SPECIAL THANKS TO...

Dick & Jeannie Patchin of Delta Publishing... I just can't thank you enough for your support of my products since I first showed up on your "distribution doorstep." You can't imagine how much I appreciate your kindness, enthusiasm, and friendship over these many years. It's with the most heartfelt gratitude that I say, *Thank you!!*

The uber-"fantabulous," hilarious and talented Monica Mauro... one big mega *Thank you!* for letting me dig deep into the recesses of your brain and pull out some of the most creative and wonderful suggestions which have been implemented in this book!

Ken Estep... *Thank you!* for always being so open to my questions and sharing your years of experience working with students. You gave me insight that I simply didn't have before which helped to make this new version of my book something I'm so proud of!

Dominque Valentino and her eagle eye to detail! I can't begin to tell you how much your comments and suggestions were invaluable to me...and to those who will be using this book. You definitely helped to make this a better and more exciting project!

Cover Idiom: "to tie the knot"

Book Design and Production: Slangman Publishing
Copy Editor: Christine Cantera
Front Cover Illustration: Ty Semaka
Inside Illustrations: Ty Semaka

Copyright © 2018 by David Burke
Published by Slangman Publishing
Email: info@slangman.com
Website: http://www.slangman.com

Slangman is a trademark of David Burke. All rights reserved.

Reproduction or translation of any part of this work beyond that permitted by section 107 or 108 of the 1976 United States Copyright Act without the permission of the copyright owner is unlawful. Requests for permission or further information should be addressed to the Permissions Department, Slangman Publishing, Inc.

This publication is designed to provide accurate and authoritative information in regard to the subject matter covered. It is sold with the understanding that the publisher is not engaged in rendering legal, accounting, or other professional services. If legal advice or other expert assistance is required, the services of a competent professional should be sought.

The persons, entities and events in this book are fictitious. Any similarities with actual persons or entities, past and present, are purely coincidental.

ISBN: 9781891888663

Printed in the United States of America
10 9 8 7 6 5 4 3 2 1

TOEFL® iBT is a registered trademark of the Educational Testing Service (ETS), Princeton New Jersey, USA.

A WORD FROM SLANGMAN...

TO TEACHERS & STUDENTS

Welcome to the first book in *Slangman's Street Speak* series! This new and completely updated book is **40% larger** than the original book, in full color, and contains **free audio & video links** to give you more "inside" information about the way Americans *really* speak. And best of all...the videos will **automatically update weekly** to give you the newest and most popular slang and idioms *used by everyone!*

Each book in *Slangman's Street Speak* series will equal years of actually living here in the U.S. So *fasten your seat belt* ("Get ready for something exciting!") and *check out* ("take a look at") all the words you may not have been able to understand before... *until now!*

FREE AUDIO & VIDEO PROGRAMS!

To stream the *free audio programs*, simply scan the SLANGMAN QR Code to the right. Next to each exercise that has an audio program, you'll notice the ![SOUNDCLOUD] icon indicating which track to play in the collection.

The tracks for all the chapters can be quickly found at:
bit.ly/Speak1-SOUNDCLOUD

To download all of the audio tracks onto your computer, go to:
bit.ly/StreetSpeak1-ALLTRACKS

SCAN ME!

┌ Now playing on ┐
SOUNDCLOUD

SCAN ME!

┌ Now playing on ┐
SLANGMAN

To access the *free videos*, simply scan the SLANGMAN QR Code at the end of each chapter using your favorite QR Code Reader. Or, scan the QR Code to the left and you'll find all the videos in one place!

The videos for all the chapters can also be easily found at:
bit.ly/Speak1-SLANGMANTV

USING THE VIDEOS

Autoplay	⬤	0.25
Speed	Normal >	0.5
Subtitles/CC	Off >	0.75
Quality	Auto 1080p >	Normal
		1.25
		1.5
		2

CC ⚙HC ▭ 🔲 ⛶

One of the great things about using YouTube® with the Slangman videos is that you can slow down the video and audio. That way you can clearly understand every new word and all those typical reductions and contractions. Then, play it back again faster... and faster until you understand everything easily! The diagram above shows you how.

LEGEND

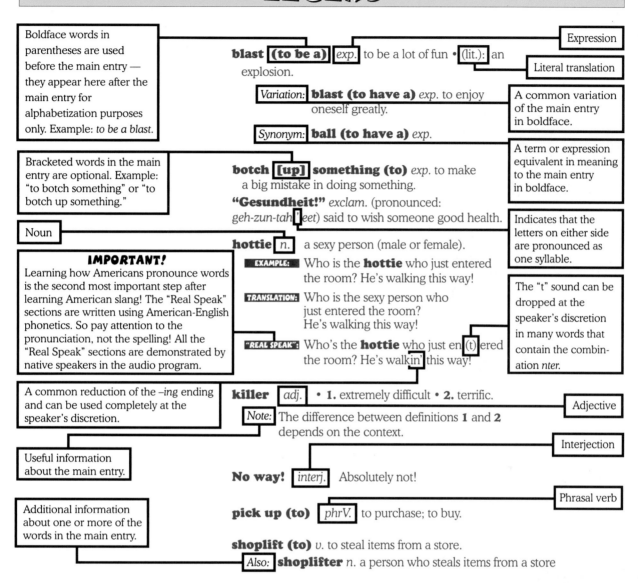

Boldface words in parentheses are used before the main entry — they appear here after the main entry for alphabetization purposes only. Example: *to be a blast.*

blast (to be a) *exp.* to be a lot of fun • (lit.): an explosion.

Expression

Literal translation

Variation: **blast (to have a)** *exp.* to enjoy oneself greatly.

A common variation of the main entry in boldface.

Synonym: **ball (to have a)** *exp.*

A term or expression equivalent in meaning to the main entry in boldface.

Bracketed words in the main entry are optional. Example: "to botch something" or "to botch up something."

botch [up] something (to) *exp.* to make a big mistake in doing something.

"Gesundheit!" *exclam.* (pronounced: geh-zun-tah·eet) said to wish someone good health.

Indicates that the letters on either side are pronounced as one syllable.

Noun

hottie *n.* a sexy person (male or female).

IMPORTANT!
Learning how Americans pronounce words is the second most important step after learning American slang! The "Real Speak" sections are written using American-English phonetics. So pay attention to the pronunciation, not the spelling! All the "Real Speak" sections are demonstrated by native speakers in the audio program.

EXAMPLE: Who is the **hottie** who just entered the room? He's walking this way!

TRANSLATION: Who is the sexy person who just entered the room? He's walking this way!

"REAL SPEAK": Who's the **hottie** who just en·(t)·ered the room? He's walkin' this way!

The "t" sound can be dropped at the speaker's discretion in many words that contain the combination *nter.*

A common reduction of the –ing ending and can be used completely at the speaker's discretion.

killer *adj.* • **1.** extremely difficult • **2.** terrific.

Note: The difference between definitions **1** and **2** depends on the context.

Adjective

Useful information about the main entry.

Interjection

No way! *interj.* Absolutely not!

Additional information about one or more of the words in the main entry.

Phrasal verb

pick up (to) *phrV.* to purchase; to buy.

shoplift (to) *v.* to steal items from a store.

Also: **shoplifter** *n.* a person who steals items from a store

EXPLANATION OF ICONS

These exercises reinforce visual recognition of the slang terms and idioms presented throughout this book.

These exercises include fill-ins, crossword puzzles, word matches and many other fun word games to help you use the new terms in context.

These oral exercises are designed to help you to begin speaking and thinking like a native.

SOUNDCLOUD

One of the most important parts of any language is to be able to understand what you hear. These exercises can be found on the audio program.

MORE ON... SLANGMAN

More information about this topic is in the video segment. See the last page of each chapter for a QR Code to the episode or go to **bit.ly/ Speak1-SLANGMANTV**

TABLE OF CONTENTS

ACTIVITIES	FROM THE SLANGMAN FILES

ACTIVITIES

KEY TO "REAL SPEAK"
Did You = Did 'Ja

LET'S USE "REAL SPEAK!"
READING
A. Wha'did they say?
SPEAKING
B. Did'ja or Didn'chu?

LET'S PRACTICE!
READING
A. Context Exercise
READING
B. Choose the Right Word
WRITING
C. Complete the Phrase
SPEAKING
D. Is it "Yes" or is it "No"?

POPULAR IDIOMS, SLANG & JARGON HAVING TO DO WITH:

A PARTY

— IDIOMS AND SLANG FOR —

"DRUNK"
"SOBER"

KEY TO "REAL SPEAK"
"T" = "D" • ...ED = 'D, 'T, or 'ID?

LET'S USE "REAL SPEAK!"
SPEAKING
A. "T" Pronounced Like "D"

LET'S PRACTICE!
WRITING
A. TV Commercial
WRITING
B. You're the Author
READING
C. True or False
READING
D. Crossword Puzzle

POPULAR IDIOMS, SLANG & JARGON HAVING TO DO WITH:

SHOPPING

KEY TO "REAL SPEAK"
Must Have = Must'a • Would'a, Should'a, Could'a

LET'S USE "REAL SPEAK!"
WRITING
A. Should'a, Could'a Would'a, Must'a

LET'S PRACTICE!
WRITING
A. I Know the Answer, But What's the Question?
READING
B. Find Your Perfect Match
SPEAKING
C. Imagine That...

POPULAR IDIOMS, SLANG & JARGON HAVING TO DO WITH:

ENTERTAINMENT

TOP 30 MOVIE QUOTES USED IN CONVERSATIONS

KEY TO "REAL SPEAK"
And = 'N • In = 'N

LET'S USE "REAL SPEAK!"
SPEAKING
A. Put the Pairs Back Together

LET'S PRACTICE!
WRITING
A. Find the Missing Words
READING
B. Match the Sentences

POPULAR IDIOMS, SLANG & JARGON HAVING TO DO WITH:

TRAVEL

— IDIOMS AND SLANG FOR —

"RELAX"
"TENSE"

KEY TO "REAL SPEAK"
To = Ta or Da

LET'S USE "REAL SPEAK!"
WRITING
A. "Across" Word Puzzle
SPEAKING
B. "Ta Be" or not "Ta Be"

LET'S PRACTICE!
WRITING
A. Complete the Fairy Tale
READING
B. Context Exercise
WRITING
C. Complete the Phrase

POPULAR IDIOMS, SLANG & JARGON HAVING TO DO WITH:

FLYING

— IDIOMS AND SLANG FOR —

"SLEEP"

TABLE OF CONTENTS (CONTINUED)

ACTIVITIES		**FROM THE SLANGMAN FILES**
KEY TO "REAL SPEAK" Going To = Gonna **LET'S USE "REAL SPEAK!"** **SPEAKING** A. Now You're Gonna Do a "Gonna" Exercise **READING** B. Is it *Gonna* or *Going to*?	**LET'S PRACTICE!** **READING** A. Choose the Right Word **WRITING** B. Crossword Puzzle **READING** C. Match the Column	POPULAR IDIOMS, SLANG & JARGON HAVING TO DO WITH: **A RESTAURANT**
KEY TO "REAL SPEAK" Want To = Wanna **LET'S USE "REAL SPEAK!"** **SPEAKING** A. Wanna or Wansta	**LET'S PRACTICE!** **READING** A. Correct or Incorrect **WRITING** B. Blank-Blank **READING** C. True or False	POPULAR IDIOMS, SLANG & JARGON HAVING TO DO WITH: **THE ROAD**
KEY TO "REAL SPEAK" He='E • Him='Im • His='Is Her='Er • Them = 'Em **LET'S USE "REAL SPEAK!"** **WRITING** A. Should'a, Could'a Would'a, Must'a **SPEAKING & WRITING** A. Change 'Em to Real Speak	**LET'S PRACTICE!** **READING** A. Truth or Lie **WRITING** B. Find the Definition **WRITING** C. Find-The-Word Grid	POPULAR IDIOMS, SLANG & JARGON HAVING TO DO WITH: **SCHOOL**
KEY TO "REAL SPEAK" You=Ya • Your=Yer You're=Yer • Yours=Yers **LET'S USE "REAL SPEAK!"** **WRITING** A. Unscramble	**LET'S PRACTICE!** **WRITING** A. Unfinished Conversation **READING** B. Choose the Right Word **WRITING** C. Complete the Story	POPULAR IDIOMS, SLANG & JARGON HAVING TO DO WITH: **HEALTH**
KEY TO "REAL SPEAK" Have To = Hafta • Has To = Hasta **LET'S USE "REAL SPEAK!"** **SPEAKING & WRITING** A. Now You Hafta Do a "Hafta" Exercise	**LET'S PRACTICE!** **WRITING** A. Create Your Own Story *(Part 1)* **SPEAKING** B. Create Your Own Story *(Part 2)* **READING** C. What Would You Do If Someone Said...?	POPULAR IDIOMS, SLANG & JARGON HAVING TO DO WITH: **DATING**

AT THE PARTY

LET'S WARM UP!

MATCH THE PICTURES *(Answers on p. 213)*

As a fun way to get started, see if you can guess the meaning of the idioms and slang words in red by reading each sentence below along with its corresponding numbered illustration.

1. Don't get so upset! **Get a grip**!
   "get a grip" means: . . . . ☐ leave me alone . . . . ☐ get control of your emotions

2. I can't believe Nancy **crashed my party**!
   "crashed my party" means: . . . . . ☐ drove to my party . . . . ☐ came to my party uninvited

3. Rob seems a little upset. **What's up with** him?
   "what's up with" means: . . . . . . ☐ what's wrong with . . . . . . ☐ who is that

4. Why did you invite Joe to your party? He's such a **party pooper**!
   "party pooper" means:. . . . . ☐ negative person . . . . ☐ happy person

5. Steve is such a **party animal**! He goes to a different party every night!
   "party animal" means:. . . . . ☐ animal who wears party hats . ☐ lover of parties

6. David is very muscular because he's been working out for years. He's a real **hottie**!
   "hottie" means:. . . . . ☐ crazy person . . . . ☐ sexy person

7. You drove down that one-way street against traffic?! **No way**!
   "no way" means:. . . . . ☐ that's wonderful . . . . ☐ that's impossible

8. That story can't be true. Are you **messing with me**?
   "messing with me" means: . . . . . ☐ disagreeing with me. . . . . . ☐ kidding me

9. What a great party! I'm **having a blast**!
   "having a blast" means: . . . . ☐ terribly bored . . . . ☐ having a great time

10. **Check out** that dress. Isn't it ugly?
    "check out" means:. . . . . ☐ look at . . . . ☐ don't look at

11. I'm not inviting Diane to my party. I **can't stand** her.
    "can't stand" means:. . . . . ☐ really like . . . . ☐ really dislike

12. I'm not inviting Paul to my party. He really **bugs me**!
    "bugs me" means: . . . . ☐ makes me laugh . . . . ☐ annoys me

LET'S TALK!

A. DIALOGUE USING SLANG & IDIOMS

The words introduced on the previous two pages are used in the following dialogue and illustrated in the long picture above. Can you understand the conversation and find the illustration that corresponds to the slang? *Note:* The translation of the words in boldface is on the right-hand page.

— *Debbie and Becky are attending a party* —

Debbie: I don't know why I let you convince me to come here. I hate parties.

Becky: Would you **get a grip**? Don't be such a **party pooper**! This is going to be a **blast**!

Debbie: Oh, I forgot… you're such a **party animal**! Oh, no. **Check out** who just **crashed the party**. Sheila Hampton. I **can't stand** her. She always criticizes me about the way I dress. That girl really **bugs me**!

Becky: She should look in the mirror some time! I mean, **what's up with** her hair?!

Debbie: **No way**! Isn't that Ernie Milton?!

Becky: Are you **messing with me**? That's Ernie Milton?! He's turned into such a **hottie**! I can't believe how much he has changed in just a year!

LET'S TALK!

B. DIALOGUE TRANSLATED INTO STANDARD ENGLISH

LET'S SEE HOW MUCH YOU REMEMBER!
Just for fun, bounce around in random order to the words and
expressions in boldface below. See if you can remember their
slang equivalents without looking at the left-hand page!

— Debbie and Becky are attending a party —

Debbie: I don't know why I let you convince me to come here. I hate parties.

Becky: Would you **get control of your emotions**? Don't be such a **negative person**!
This is going to be a **great time**!

Debbie: Oh, I forgot… you're such a **partier**! Oh, no. **Take a look at** who just **came to the
party without an invitation**. Sheila Hampton. I can't **tolerate** her. She always
criticizes me about the way I dress. That girl really **annoys me**!

Becky: She should look in the mirror some time! I mean, **what's wrong with** her hair?!

Debbie: **That's impossible**! Isn't that Ernie Milton?

Becky: Are you **teasing me**! That's Ernie Milton?! He's turned into such a **sexy person**! I can't
believe how much he has changed in just a year!

C. DIALOGUE USING "REAL SPEAK"

The dialogue below demonstrates how the slang conversation
on the previous page would *really* be spoken by native speakers!

— *Debbie 'n Becky'er attending a pardy* —

Debbie: I dunno why I letchu convince me da come here. I hate pardies.

Becky: Would'ja **ged a grip**? Don't be such a **pardy pooper**! This'ez gonna be a **blast**!

Debbie: Oh, I fergot… y'r such a **pardy animal**! Oh, no. **Check oud** 'oo jus' **crashed the pardy**. Sheila Hampton. I **can't stand** her. She ahways cridicizes me about the way I dress. That girl really **bugs me**!

Becky: She should look 'n the mirrer some time! I mean, **what's up w'th** 'er hair?!

Debbie: **No way**! Isn't that Ernie Milton?!

Becky: Are you **messing w'th me**? That's Ernie Milton?! He's turned inta such a **hoddie**! I can't b'lieve how much 'e's changed 'n just a year!

DID YOU = DID'JA

In the above dialogue using "Real Speak," the phrase "Would you get a grip" became "**Would'ja** get a grip." In everyday pronunciation, the personal pronoun **you** is pronounced a few different ways as seen below:

RULES

D + Y = J

When a word ending in **d** is followed by a word beginning with **y**, the **y** often takes the sound of **j**.

did you = *did'ju* or *did'ja*
would you = *would'ju* or *would'ja*

T + Y = CH

When a word ending in **t** is followed by a word beginning with **y**, the **y** often takes the sound of **ch**.

let you = *let'chu* or *let'cha*
what you = *what'chu* or *what'cha*

HOW DOES IT WORK?

Did you eat yet?

*Did **y**ou eat **y**et?*
↓   ↓
*Did **j**ou eat **ch**et?*
} In this sentence, the **y** in **you** follows a **d** and takes the sound of **j**. The **y** in **yet** follows a **t** and takes the sound of **ch**.

*Did **j**ou eat **ch**et?*
↓
*Did **juh** eat **ch**et?*
} The unstressed vowel combination **ou** in **you** is commonly pronounced **uh** (often seen written as **'a**). Therefore, **you** becomes **ya** or, in this case, **ja** since the letter **y** is preceded by a **d**.

↓
*Did'**ja** eat'**ch**et?*

BUT!

When **you** *is* stressed (meaning that the voice goes up), it is pronounced *ju*:

*No. Did you? = No. Did'**ju**?*

Also, when **you** is preceded by **did** and is part of
a compound subject, it is pronounced *ju*:

*Did you and Nancy have fun at the party? = Did'**ju** and Nancy have fun at the party?*

LET'S USE "REAL SPEAK!"

A. WHA'DID THEY SAY? *(Answers on p. 213)*

Match the sentence in "Real Speak" with the standard English
translation by checking the appropriate box.

1. **What did'ja do?**
   - [ ] a. What do you do?
   - [ ] b. What did you do?

2. **I want'cha to leave.**
   - [ ] a. I want you to leave.
   - [ ] b. I want to chew a leaf.

3. **Didn'cha finish your homework? Not'chet.**
   - [ ] a. Didn't you finish your homework? Not yet.
   - [ ] b. Didn't you finish your homework? No Chet.

4. **Why don'cha get'cher car fixed?**
   - [ ] a. Why don't you get your car fixed?
   - [ ] b. Why don't you get her car fixed?

5. **Is that'cher book?**
   - [ ] a. Is that your book?
   - [ ] b. Is that chair broken?

6. **Did'ja eat'chet? No, did'ju?**
   - [ ] a. Did you eat yet? No, did you?
   - [ ] b. Did you cheat, Chet? No, did you?

B. DID'JA OR DIDN'CHU?

Read the question or statement out loud from Column 1 with
the response from Column 2. Then start again using the short
version response from Column 3.

Column 1		Column 2		Column 3 *(short version)*
*Did '**ja** go?*	▶	*No. Did '**ju** go?*	OR	*No. Did '**ju**?*
*I thought '**cha** left yesterday.*	▶	*Really? I thought '**chu** left yesterday!*	OR	*Really? I thought '**chu** did!*
*Did '**ja** finish your homework?*	▶	*Yeah. Did '**ju** finish your homework?*	OR	*Yeah. Did '**ju**?*
*Could '**ja** help Steve?*	▶	*No, could '**ju** help him?*	OR	*No, could '**ju**?*

LET'S LEARN!

VOCABULARY

The following words and expressions were used in the previous dialogues. Let's take a closer look at what they mean.

blast (to have a) *exp.* to have a great time.

EXAMPLE:	We **had a blast** at the amusement park! We stayed there all day and night!
TRANSLATION:	We **had a great time** at the amusement park! We stayed there all day and night!
"REAL SPEAK":	We **had a blast** 'it the amusement park! We stayed there all day 'n night!
Variation:	**blast (to be a)** *exp.* to be a lot of fun, to be exciting.
Synonym:	**ball (to have a)** *exp.*

NOW DO IT. COMPLETE THE PHRASE ALOUD:
It was a blast going to...

bug someone (to) *exp.* to annoy someone.

EXAMPLE:	Every time my aunt comes to visit, she criticizes me about the way I wear my hair. She really **bugs me**!
TRANSLATION:	Every time my aunt comes to visit, she criticizes me about the way I wear my hair. She really **annoys me**!
"REAL SPEAK":	Ev'ry time my aunt comes ta visit, she cridicizes me about the way I wear my hair. She really **bugs me**!
Synonym 1:	**drive someone crazy (to)** *exp.*
Synonym 2:	**get on someone's nerves (to)** *exp.*
Synonym 3:	**get under someone's skin (to)** *exp.*
Synonym 4:	**rub someone the wrong way (to)** *exp.*
Synonym 5:	**work someone's last good nerve (to)** *exp.*

NOW YOU DO IT. COMPLETE THE PHRASE ALOUD:
It really bugs me when...

check out someone/something (to) *exp.* to look at someone/something unusual or interesting.

EXAMPLE:	**Check out** the new dress Irene is wearing! I've never seen anything like it!
TRANSLATION:	**Look at** the new dress Irene is wearing! I've never seen anything like it!
"REAL SPEAK":	**Check out** the new dress Irene's wearing! I've never seen anything like it!
Synonym 1:	**get a load of someone/something (to)** *exp.*
Synonym 2:	**feast one's eyes on something (to)** *exp.* (upon presenting a delicious food) • *Feast your eyes* on this!

NOW YOU DO IT. COMPLETE THE PHRASE ALOUD:
Check out that...

crash a party (to) *exp.* to go to a party (wedding, concert, or any other event) without an invitation.

EXAMPLE: I don't recognize those people over there. I can't believe they **crashed my party**!

TRANSLATION: I don't recognize those people over there. I can't believe they **came to my party without an invitation**!

"REAL SPEAK": I don't recognize those people over there. I can't believe they **crashed my pardy**!

Variation: **party crasher** *exp.* one who goes to a party uninvited.

Note: The movie entitled **Wedding Crashers** (2005) and its sequel, **Wedding Crashers 2** (2017), are about two men who go to wedding receptions without an invitation.

NOW YOU DO IT. COMPLETE THE PHRASE ALOUD:
Last week, I crashed a...

get a grip (to) *exp.* to get control of one's emotions.

EXAMPLE: I've never seen you so upset! If you don't **get a grip**, you're going to get an ulcer!

TRANSLATION: I've never seen you so upset! If you don't **get control of your emotions**, you're going to get an ulcer!

"REAL SPEAK": I've never seen you so upset! If ya don't **ged a grip**, yer gonna ged 'n ulcer!

Note: This expression refers to someone who is so upset that he/she needs "to get a grip" on his/her emotions.

Variation: **get a grip on oneself (to)** *exp.*

Synonym 1: **a hold of oneself (to get)** *exp.*

Synonym 2: **chill / chill out / take a chill pill (to)** *exp.*

Synonym 3: **get it together (to)** *exp.*

Synonym 4: **get one's act together (to)** *exp.*

Synonym 5: **pull oneself together (to)** *exp.*

Synonym 6: **simmer down (to)** *exp.*

NOW YOU DO IT. COMPLETE THE PHRASE ALOUD:
Get a grip and stop...

hottie *n.* sexy person (either male or female).

EXAMPLE: David used to be very thin and weak. Now he's become a real **hottie**!

TRANSLATION: David used to be very thin and weak. Now he's become a real **sexy person**!

"REAL SPEAK": David usta be very thin 'n weak. Now 'e's become a real **hoddie**!

Synonym 1: **he-man** *n.*

Synonym 2: **hunk** *n.*

Synonym 3: **macho-man** *n.*

Synonym 4: **stud** *n.* / **muscle stud** *n.*

NOW YOU DO IT. COMPLETE THE PHRASE ALOUD:
...is a real hottie!

mess with someone (to) *exp.* to tease or kid someone.

EXAMPLE:	I think Joe was **messing with you** when he said he has ten children. He just wanted to see your reaction.
TRANSLATION:	I think Joe was **teasing you** when he said he has ten children. He just wanted to see your reaction.
"REAL SPEAK":	I think Joe w'z **messing w'th ya** when 'e said 'e has ten children. He jus' wan'ed ta see yer reaction.
Synonym 1:	**blow smoke (to)** *exp.*
Synonym 2:	**fake someone out (to)** *exp.*
Synonym 3:	**play head games with someone (to)** *exp.*
Synonym 4:	**play with someone (to)** *exp.*
Synonym 5:	**pull someone's leg (to)** *exp.*
Synonym 6:	**toy with someone (to)** *exp.*
Synonym 7:	**yank/pull someone's chain (to)** *exp.*

NOW YOU DO IT. COMPLETE THE PHRASE ALOUD:
Susan was messing with me when she said...

"No way!" *interj.* • **1.** Absolutely not! • **2.** That's impossible!

EXAMPLE 1:	Lend you money? **No way!** The last time you borrowed money from me, you never paid me be back!
TRANSLATION:	Lend you money? **Absolutely not!** The last time you borrowed money from me, you never paid me back!
"REAL SPEAK":	Lend'ja money? **No way!** The las' time ya borrowed money fr'm me, ya never paid me back!
EXAMPLE 2:	Todd just bought a new BMW?! **No way!** He doesn't have any money!
TRANSLATION:	Todd just bought a new BMW?! **That's impossible!** He doesn't have any money!
"REAL SPEAK":	Todd jus' bawd a new BMW?! **No way!** He doesn' have any money!
Note:	The difference between definitions **1.** and **2.** simply depends on the context.
Synonym:	**"Get real!"** *interj.*

NOW YOU DO IT. COMPLETE THE PHRASE ALOUD:
You just found ...?! No way!

party animal *exp.* one who loves to go to parties often.

EXAMPLE:	I don't know how Don functions at work. He's such a **party animal** and never sleeps!
TRANSLATION:	I don't know how Don functions at work. He's such a **lover of parties** and never sleeps!
"REAL SPEAK":	I dunno how Don functions 'it work. He's such a **pardy animal** 'n never sleeps!

NOW YOU DO IT. COMPLETE THE PHRASE ALOUD:
The biggest party animal I know is...

party pooper *exp.* someone who is generally negative and ruins everyone else's fun.

EXAMPLE:	You invited Chad to your birthday party? Why?! He's such a **party pooper**!
TRANSLATION:	You invited Chad to your birthday party? Why?! He's such a **negative person**!
"REAL SPEAK":	You invided Chad ta yer birthday pardy? Why?! He's such a **pardy pooper**!

Synonym 1: **buzzkill** *exp.* Note that *buzzed* is slang for a mild state of inebriation where you're just starting to feel carefree. So, a **buzzkill** is someone who ruins your joyful state.

Synonym 2: **downer** *n.* (Note that a variation is **Debbie Downer**. Although it's a girls name, it can be said when referring to a guy when used in jest.)

Synonym 3: **killjoy** *exp.*

NOW YOU DO IT. COMPLETE THE PHRASE ALOUD:
...is such a party pooper because...

unable to stand **someone (to be)** *exp.* to be unable to tolerate someone; to dislike.

EXAMPLE:	I **can't stand** our new math teacher. She always gives us homework on the weekend.
TRANSLATION:	I **can't tolerate** our new math teacher. She always gives us homework on the weekend.
"REAL SPEAK":	I **can't stand** 'ar new math teacher. She always gives us homework on the weekend.

Synonym: **unable to stomach someone (to be)** *exp.*

NOW YOU DO IT. COMPLETE THE PHRASE ALOUD:
I can't stand Carl because...

"What's up with...?" *exp.* "What's the problem with..." "What's wrong with..."

EXAMPLE:	**What's up with** your brother? He looks really upset about something!
TRANSLATION:	**What's the problem with** your brother? He looks really upset about something!
"REAL SPEAK":	**What's up with** yer brother? He looks really upsed about something!

Synonym 1: **"What's with...?"** *exp.*

Synonym 2: **"What's the deal with...?"** *exp.* / *Also:* **"What's his/her deal?"**

NOW YOU DO IT. COMPLETE THE PHRASE ALOUD:
What's up with...?

LET'S PRACTICE!

(Answers on p. 213)

A. CONTEXT EXERCISE

Read the short conversations. Decide whether the slang used makes sense or doesn't make sense. Circle your answer.

READING
TRACK 6
SOUNDCLOUD

– Did you have fun at the party?
– Yes. I had a blast!

MAKES SENSE   DOESN'T MAKE SENSE

– I'm so upset!
– Get a grip. You need to relax.

MAKES SENSE   DOESN'T MAKE SENSE

–Bob is so unattractive!
–I know. He's such a hottie!

MAKES SENSE   DOESN'T MAKE SENSE

– Is David your best friend?
– Yes! He really bugs me!

MAKES SENSE   DOESN'T MAKE SENSE

– My mother is a skydiver.
– You're messing with me!

MAKES SENSE   DOESN'T MAKE SENSE

– I don't recognize that woman.
– I think she crashed our party!

MAKES SENSE   DOESN'T MAKE SENSE

– I can't stand Harriet!
– I like her, too!

MAKES SENSE   DOESN'T MAKE SENSE

– What's up with Steve?
– He's nervous about his grades.

MAKES SENSE   DOESN'T MAKE SENSE

– Check out that clown fish!
– I can't. I don't have a library card.

MAKES SENSE   DOESN'T MAKE SENSE

B. CHOOSE THE RIGHT WORD *(Answers on p. 213)*
Underline the word that best completes the phrase.

1. Why are you so (**happy**, **relaxed**, **upset**)? I think you need to get a grip!

2. David is so (**thin**, **muscular**, **fat**). What a hottie!

3. You won a million dollars? Are you (**cussing**, **fussing**, **messing**) with me?

4. I had a (**bang**, **blast**, **boom**) at the party. It was so much fun!

5. What's (**up**, **down**, **over**) with the boss? He's been screaming at people all morning.

6. Did you check (**in**, **out**, **up**) that guy's haircut? It looks terrible.

7. Ed looks tired all the time because he's such a party (**fish**, **bird**, **animal**).

8. I can't stand Susan. She's always so (**nice**, **helpful**, **mean**) to me.

9. My little sister asks me questions all the time! Sometimes she really (**bugs**, **insects**, **rodents**) me!

10. That's your father? (**Yes**, **No**, **Maybe**) way! He looks so young!

C. COMPLETE THE PHRASE
Complete the phrase by choosing the appropriate words from the list below. Use each answer only once.

(Answers on p. 213)

get a grip	**blast**	**pooper**
messing with me	**no way**	**what's up**
bugs	**can't stand**	**hottie**

1. _____ with Tom? He's been in a bad mood all day.

2. I've never seen you so upset! _____!

3. Nancy gave birth to twins and she didn't even know she was pregnant?! I don't believe it. Are you _____?

4. My brother borrowed my car again without asking. That really _____ me!

5. I had a _____ at the amusement park!

6. I _____ our new math teacher. She gives us so much homework every weekend!

7. Carol asked you if she could borrow money again? _____! She borrows money from you every week!

8. You never want to go with us anywhere! Sometimes you're such a party _____ .

9. Mike used to be so ugly, but he's turned into a real _____ .

D. IS IT "YES" OR IS IT "NO"? *(Answers on p. 213)*

Read Person A's questions aloud followed by the correct response from Person B. Use the suggested words to create your answer.

PERSON A	PERSON B
1. Do you think that Joe works out at the gym often?	Yeah. [use: **hottie**]
2. Do you like Stephanie?	Nah. [use: **can't stand**]
3. Did you stay home and study last night?	Nah. [use: **crashed a party**]
4. You won a million dollars?! Are you serious?	Nah. [use: **messing with you**]
5. Did you notice how upset Jim is today?	Yeah. [use: **get a grip**]
6. Did the teacher give you homework over the weekend?	Yeah. [use: **bugs me**]
7. Did you see that diamond necklace Cindy is wearing?	Yeah. [use: **check it out**]
8. Did you know Kim is pregnant?	Nah. [use: **no way**]
9. Did you have a good time at the carnival?	Yeah. [use: **had a blast**]
10. Did you notice what happened to Steve's eye?	Yeah. [use: **what's up with**]

TRACK 10
SOUNDCLOUD

EXERCISES FOR THIS SECTION ARE IN THE WORKBOOK.

Popular Idioms, Slang & Jargon
Having to do with: A PARTY

bring down a party (to) exp. said of a person who is so negative and depressing that he/she lowers the energy and excitement of a party.

> **EXAMPLE:** During the party, Lee kept talking about how she quit her job, crashed her car, and lost her dog. She sure knows how **to bring down a party**!
>
> **TRANSLATION:** During the party, Lee kept talking about how she quit her job, crashed her car, and lost her dog. She sure knows how **to lower the energy and excitement of a party**!
>
> **"REAL SPEAK":** During the pardy, Lee kep' talking about how she quid 'er job, crashed 'er car, an' lost 'er dog. She sher knows how **da bring down a pardy**!
>
> *Note:* The name "Lee" can be used for a man or woman.

costume party exp. a social gathering where the guests dress in costume.

> **EXAMPLE:** At Joe's **costume party**, I went as Frankenstein.
>
> **TRANSLATION:** At Joe's **social gathering where everyone came in costume**, I went as Frankenstein.
>
> **"REAL SPEAK":** At Joe's **costume pardy**, I wen' 'ez Frankenstein.
>
> *Synonym:* **masquerade party** exp.

dance the night away (to) exp. to dance all night.

> **EXAMPLE:** Kristen's birthday party was great! Everyone had the best time! We all **danced the night away**!

> **TRANSLATION:** Kristen's birthday party was great! Everyone had the best time! We all **danced all night**!
>
> **"REAL SPEAK":** Kristen's birthday pardy w'z great! Ev'ryone had the bes' time! We all **dance' the nide away**!

MORE ON... SLANGMAN

drink up (to) phrV. to drink as much as one wants.

> **EXAMPLE:** **Drink up**! It's your birthday!
>
> **TRANSLATION:** **Drink all you want**! It's your birthday!
>
> **"REAL SPEAK":** **Drink up**! It's yer birthday!

farewell party exp. a party in honor of someone who is leaving (such as on a vacation, after quitting a job, etc.).

> **EXAMPLE:** John is going to be so surprised when he finds out we're giving him a **farewell party**! I hope he enjoys retirement!
>
> **TRANSLATION:** John is going to be so surprised when he finds out we're giving him a **party because he's leaving**! I hope he enjoys retirement!
>
> **"REAL SPEAK":** John's gonna to be so saprised when 'e fin's out w'r givin' 'im a **farewell pardy**! I hope 'e enjoys retirement!
>
> *Synonym:* **goodbye party** exp.

guilty party *exp.* a person (or people) responsible for doing something illegal or unkind.

> **EXAMPLE:** Someone broke Michelle's computer at her party. And I think I know who the **guilty party** is!

> **TRANSLATION:** Someone broke Michelle's computer at her party. And I think I know who the **person responsible** is!

> **"REAL SPEAK":** Someone broke Michelle's c'mpuder ad 'er pardy. An' I think I know who the **guilty pardy** is!

hangover *n.* a severe headache caused by drinking an excess of alcohol.

> **EXAMPLE:** Shhh! Not so loud! I have the worst **hangover** from the party last night!

> **TRANSLATION:** Shhh! Not so loud! I have the worst **headache from drinking** at the party last night!

> **"REAL SPEAK":** Shhh! Not so loud! I 'ave the worst **hangover** fr'm the pardy las' night!

housewarming party *exp.* a celebration in honor of someone's new home.

> **EXAMPLE:** Now that you've moved into your new home, we should invite all your friends over for a **housewarming party**!

> **TRANSLATION:** Now that you've moved into your new home, we should invite all your friends over for a **party to celebrate your new home**!

> **"REAL SPEAK":** Now th't chu've moved inda yer new home, we should invide all yer frenz over fer a **housewarming pardy**!

> *Variation:* **home warming** *n.*

in full swing (to be) *exp.* said of a party that is at the height of activity.

> **EXAMPLE 1:** You want to leave now?! But the party is **in full swing**!

> **TRANSLATION:** You want to leave now?! But the party is **at the height of activity**!

> **"REAL SPEAK":** Ya wanna leave now?! B't the pardy's **'n full swing**!

invite *n.* short for "invitation."

> **EXAMPLE 1:** If you're free next Saturday, I'd love for you to come to my party. I'll send you an **invite**!

> **TRANSLATION:** If you're free next Saturday, I'd love for you to come to my party. I'll send you an **invitation**!

> **"REAL SPEAK":** If y'r free nex' Sadurday, I'd love fer ya da come da my pardy. A'll sen' ja 'n **invite**!

let one's hair down (to) *exp.* to behave in an uninhibited manner.

> **EXAMPLE:** You're always working. You need to go out with us and dance! **Let your hair down**!

> **TRANSLATION:** You're always working. You need to go out with us and dance! **Behave in an uninhibited manner**!

> **"REAL SPEAK":** Y'r ahways working. Ya need da go out w'th us 'n dance! **Let cher hair down**!

> *Synonym:* **to cut loose (to)** *exp.*

life of the party (to be the) *exp.* A lively, amusing person who is the center of attention at a social gathering.

> **EXAMPLE:** We should invite Stewart to dinner. He's always **the life of the party**!

> **TRANSLATION:** We should invite Stewart to dinner. He's always **such an amusing person at social events**!

> **"REAL SPEAK":** We should 'nvite Stewart ta dinner. He's ahways **the life 'a the pardy**!

> *Note:* **The Life of the Party** – a 2018 movie about a middle-aged mother (Melissa McCarthy) who returns to college to complete her degree.

party (to) *v.* **1.** to go to parties; **2.** to do drugs.

> EXAMPLE: Do you like to **party**? I do it every chance I get!
>
> TRANSLATION: Do you like to **go to parties / do drugs**? I do it every chance I get!
>
> "REAL SPEAK": Do you like to **party**? I do it every chance I get!
>
> *Note:* This is a dangerous word because it has two *very* different meanings! The difference all depends on the delivery, and intention, of the speaker. If you're not sure about the meaning or implication, *ask!*
>
> *Synonym 1:* **party hard (to)** *exp.*
>
> *Synonym 2:* **party hardy (to)** *exp.* Note that *hardy* is actually an American "Real Speak" spelling of *hearty* (meaning "enthusiastically") in order for the two words to rhyme. The rhyme wouldn't exist using a British accent!

party of [number] *exp.* group of (used to indicate the number of seats that will be occupied at a location).

> EXAMPLE: *Host:* Welcome to David's Eatery. How many are in your party?
> *Customer:* We're a **party of** six.
> *Host:* The wait time will be twenty minutes.
>
> TRANSLATION: *Host:* Welcome to David's Eatery. How many are in your party?
> *Customer:* We're a **group of** six.
> *Host:* The wait time will be twenty minutes.
>
> "REAL SPEAK": *Host:* Welcome ta David's Eadery. How many 'er in yer pardy?
> *Customer:* We're a **pardy 'ev** six.
> *Host:* The wait time'll be twen'y minutes.

"Party's over!" *exp.* "Your illegal activity is over!" (used in televison crime shows).

> EXAMPLE: *Freeze!* Put down your guns! **Party's over**!
>
> TRANSLATION: *Don't move!* Put down your guns! **Your illegal activity is over**!
>
> "REAL SPEAK": *Freeze!* Put down yer guns! **Pardy's over**!

Note: *"Freeze!"* is a popular slang command meaning "Don't move!"

pool party *exp.* a gathering where everyone is invited to eat and swim.

> EXAMPLE: Now that you got your pool installed, are you going to have a **pool party**?
>
> TRANSLATION: Now that you got your pool installed, are you going to have a **gathering where people can eat and swim**?
>
> "REAL SPEAK": Now th't chu've got cher pool installed, ya gonna have a **pool pardy**?

ring in the new year (to) *exp.* to celebrate the beginning of the new year.

> EXAMPLE: Let's all get together on New Year's Eve and **ring in the new year** together!

> TRANSLATION: Let's all get together on New Year's Eve and **celebrate the beginning of the new year** together!
>
> "REAL SPEAK": Let's all get tagether on New Year's Eve 'n **ring in the new year** dagether!

R.S.V.P. or **RSVP** *exp.* initials added to the bottom of an invitation which stand for the French phrase, *Répondez s'il vous plaît,* meaning "Respond please" – this informs the guest to let the host know whether or not he/she will be attending the event.

> EXAMPLE: Make sure to add an **RSVP** at the bottom of your wedding invitations, so that you know exactly how many people will be coming.

TRANSLATION: Make sure to add a **confirmation of attendance** at the bottom of your wedding invitations, so that you know exactly how many people will be coming.

"REAL SPEAK": Make sher da add 'n **RSVP** 'it the boddom 'ev yer wedding invitations, so th't cha know exac'ly how many people'll be coming.

Note 1: **RSVP** is also used as a verb meaning, "to let the host know whether or not you'll be attending the event."

EXAMPLE: I forgot to **RSVP** to Carol's party!

TRANSLATION: I forgot to **send a confirmation of attendance** to Carol's party!

"REAL SPEAK": I fergot ta **RSVP** da Carol's pardy!

shindig n. an informal but elaborate party or dance.

EXAMPLE: Wow! This is some **shindig**! Jessica really knows how to throw a party!

TRANSLATION: Wow! This is some **elaborate event**! Jessica really knows how to throw a party!

"REAL SPEAK": Wow! This 'ez some **shindig**! Jessica really knows how da throw a pardy!

shower n. (a shortened version of *bridal shower*) a pre-wedding celebration in honor of the bride where female guests bring gifts.

EXAMPLE: Irene got some great gifts at her **shower**! It's hard to believe she'll be married in just two days!

TRANSLATION: Irene got some great gifts at her **pre-wedding celebration**! It's hard to believe she'll be married in just two days!

"REAL SPEAK": Irene got s'm great gifts ad 'er **shower**! It's hard da believe she'll be married 'n jus' two days!

Also: **baby shower** exp. a party for an expectant mother where she is given presents for her or for her baby.

slumber party exp. a party, most commonly held by children or teenagers, where guests are invited to spend the night, usually in sleeping bags.

EXAMPLE: Were you invited to Nancy's **slumber party**? Her living room can fit twenty sleeping bags!

TRANSLATION: Were you invited to Nancy's **party where everyone is going to spend the night**? Her living room can fit twenty sleeping bags!

"REAL SPEAK": Were you invided ta Nancy's **slumber pardy**? Her living room c'n fit twen'y sleeping bags!

Note: The noun **slumber** means "sleep" but typically only used in the expression above.

snooze fest exp. a bore (said of a really boring event such as a party, lecture, movie, person, etc.)

EXAMPLE: Cindy is a real **snooze fest**! She never has anything interesting to say!

TRANSLATION: Cindy is a real **bore**! She never has anything interesting to say!

"REAL SPEAK": Cindy is a real **snooze fest**! She never has anything interesting to say!

Variation: **snoozer** n.

Note: **snooze (to)** v. slang for "to sleep" / **snooze** n. nap.

Synonym: **crashing bore** exp.

social butterfly exp. a very outgoing person who loves going to events to socialize and meet people.

EXAMPLE: Karen is such a **social butterfly**! If there's a big event somewhere, she'll be there!

TRANSLATION: Karen is such an **outgoing person who loves going to events to socialize and meet people**! If there's a big event somewhere, she'll be there!

"REAL SPEAK": Karen's such a **social budderfly**! If there's a big event somewhere, she'll be there!

Variation: Also seen as **quite the social butterfly**: *Karen goes from party to party every night. She's **quite the social butterfly**! Remember, when modifying a noun, **such** is followed by the indefinite article **a** and **quite** is followed by the definite article **the**.

stag party *exp.* a celebration held for a man shortly before his wedding day, attended by his male friends only.

EXAMPLE: Can you believe Emily *crashed* her fiancé's **stag party**? He must have been so embarrassed!

TRANSLATION: Can you believe Emily *went without being invited* to her fiancé's **pre-wedding party for men only**? He must have been so embarrassed!

"REAL SPEAK": C'n ya b'lieve Emily *crashed* 'er fiancé's **stag pardy**? He must'a been so embarrassed!

Synonym: **bachelor party** *exp.*

surprise party *exp.* a party that is secretly planned for someone.

EXAMPLE: My wife gave me a **surprise party** for my birthday! All my friends were there!

TRANSLATION: My wife gave me a **party that was planned secretly** for my birthday! All my friends were there!

"REAL SPEAK": My wife gay'me a **saprise pardy** fer my birthday! All my friends were there!

tailgate party *exp.* a social event where food and drinks are served from the open tailgate of a car.

EXAMPLE: Before the football game, we all had a **tailgate party** in the parking lot. It was a *blast*!

TRANSLATION: Before the football game, we all had a **party where food and drinks were served from the open tailgate of our car** in the parking lot. It was a *so much fun*!

"REAL SPEAK": B'fore the football game, we all had a **tailgate pardy** 'n the parking lot. It w'z a *blast*!

throw a party (to) *exp.* to hold a social gathering with music, drinks, and dancing.

EXAMPLE: Let's **throw a party** for Nick to congratulate him on his new job!

TRANSLATION: Let's **hold a social gathering with music, drinks, and dancing** for Nick to congratulate him on his new job!

"REAL SPEAK": Let's **throw a pardy** fer Nick ta c'ngradjalade 'im on 'is new job!

whoop it up (to) *phrV.* to go to a party and celebrate with complete abandon.

EXAMPLE: Vicki loves to **whoop it up** on the weekends!

TRANSLATION: Vicki loves to **party with complete abandon** on the weekends!

"REAL SPEAK": Vicki loves ta **whoop id up** on the weekenz!

IDIOMS & SLANG FOR "DRUNK"

as drunk as a skunk *exp.*

blasted *adj.*

blitzed *adj.*

bombed *adj.*

buzzed *adj.*

cooked *adj.*

dead drunk *exp.*

feeling no pain *exp.*

fried *adj.*

had a few too many *exp.*

hammered *adj.*

hosed *adj.*

krunk / crunk *adj.* comes from "crazy drunk."

liquored up *exp.*

loaded *adj.*

messed up *adj.*

plastered *adj.*

ripped *adj.*

toasted *adj.*

trashed *adj.*

wasted *adj.*

wrecked *adj.*

under the influence *exp.* comes from "under the influence of alcohol."

> *Note:* **DUI** (pronounced D-U-I) a serious criminal offense received when one is found "**D**riving **U**nder the **I**nfluence."

> *Variation:* **DWI** (pronounced D-W-I) meaning "**D**riving **W**hile **I**ntoxicated."

IDIOMS & SLANG FOR "SOBER"

cold sober *exp.* totally sober.
> *Also:* **stone cold sober** *exp.* completely and totally sober.

designated driver *exp.* the person who volunteers not to drink so he/she can drive friends to a destination safely.

on the wagon (to be) *exp.* said of a person who no longer drinks alcohol.

> *Antonym:* **fall off the wagon (to)** *exp.* to start drinking again after quitting.

sworn off alcohol (to be) *exp.* to have permanently stopped drinking alcohol.

teetotaler *n.* a person who does not drink alcohol.

SLANGMAN Explains More idioms & Slang for...
—AT THE PARTY—

SCAN ME!

CHAPTER 1

SCAN THE QR CODE OR GO TO: bit.ly/StreetSpeak1-Chapter1

THIS VIDEO EPISODE CONTAINS...

MORE ON... TV SLANGMAN

Key to "REAL SPEAK"
- **Did you** = *Did'ja*
  - The 3 common ways to reduce "you"

MORE ON... TV SLANGMAN

dance'
- When the sound of three consonants are together, the second one is typically silent:
  - I coo**ked th**e be**st d**inner la**st n**ight! = *I cook' the bes' dinner las' night!*

REGULAR UPDATES! CHECK BACK OFTEN!

Teen Slang
- Newest teen slang used at parties

REGULAR UPDATES! CHECK BACK OFTEN!

Idioms & slang used on TV this week plus the latest Teen Slang!
- Slangman gives you his TOP 5 LIST of the latest idioms and slang from the most popular TV shows in the U.S. plus the newest slang teens are using today!

REGULAR UPDATES! CHECK BACK OFTEN!

Newest American slang just entered into the dictionary

LET'S WARM UP!

READING

MATCH THE PICTURES *(Answers on p. 214)*

As a fun way to get started, see if you can guess the meaning of the idioms and slang words in red by reading each sentence below along with its corresponding numbered illustration.

1. Did you taste this blueberry pie? It's **to die for**!

2. Why did you pay so much for that TV? What **a rip-off**!

3. If you're ready, I can **ring up** your purchases.

4. This store has **rock-bottom** prices.

5. My local grocery store **carries** the best chocolates!

6. The market is **slashing** its prices.

7. My mother always says I need to eat more **veggies**.

8. These pastries are **making my mouth water**.

9. My mother made a cake **from scratch**.

10. I need to **pick up** some milk at the market.

A. thievery

B. buy

C. absolutely fantastic

D. making me drool

E. add up

F. provides customers with

G. extremely low

H. from the very beginning (using fresh ingredients)

I. vegetables

LET'S TALK!

A. DIALOGUE USING SLANG & IDIOMS

The words introduced on the previous two pages are used in the following dialogue and illustrated in the long picture above. Can you understand the conversation and find the illustration that corresponds to the slang? *Note*: The translation of the words in boldface is on the right-hand page.

— Bill and Liz are shopping for dinner —

Bill: I sure hope they **carry** organic chicken in this market.

Liz: It's right over here. Wow! It's only twenty-nine cents a pound!

Bill: Talk about **rock-bottom** prices!

Liz: I know. They've been **slashing** their prices all week.

Bill: I have an idea. Along with the chicken, let's **pick up** some **veggies** and make a big salad tonight. We could also buy a cake for dessert.

Liz: Great idea! Look at this pastry section. It's **to die for**! Just look at all these cakes! The smell of these pastries is **making my mouth water**.

Bill: Wait! Did you see the price of these cakes? They cost more than the chicken! What a **rip-off**! Let's just make one **from scratch**. It'll be a lot cheaper.

Liz: I think you're right. Let's hurry and get the cashier to **ring up** our purchases. I'm starving!

LET'S TALK!

B. DIALOGUE TRANSLATED INTO STANDARD ENGLISH

LET'S SEE HOW MUCH YOU REMEMBER!
Just for fun, bounce around in random order to the words and
expressions in boldface below. See if you can remember their
slang equivalents without looking at the left-hand page!

— *Bill and Liz are shopping for dinner* —

Bill: I sure hope they **provide customers with** organic chicken in this market.

Liz: It's right over here. Wow! It's only twenty-nine cents a pound!

Bill: I'm surprised about the **extremely low** prices!

Liz: I know. They've been **significantly reducing** their prices all week.

Bill: I have an idea. Along with the chicken, let's **buy** some chicken and **vegetables** and make a big salad tonight. We could also buy a cake for dessert.

Liz: Great idea! Look at this pastry section. It's **fantastic**! Just look at all these cakes! The smell of these pastries is **making me drool**.

Bill: Wait! Did you see the price of these cakes? They cost more than the chicken! What **thievery**! Let's just make one **from the beginning using fresh ingredients**. It'll be a lot cheaper.

Liz: I think you're right. Let's hurry and get the cashier to **add up** our purchases. I'm starving!

C. DIALOGUE USING "REAL SPEAK"

The dialogue below demonstrates how the slang conversation on the previous page would *really* be spoken by native speakers!

— Bill 'n Liz 'er shopping fer dinner —

Bill: I sher hope they **carry** organic chicken 'n th's market.

Liz: It's ride over here. Wow! It's only twen'y-nine cents a pound!

Bill: Talk about **rock-boddom** prices!

Liz: I know. They' been **slashing** their prices all week.

Bill: I 'av 'n idea. Along w'th the chicken, let's **pick up** s'm **veggies** 'n make a big salad tanight. We could also buy a cake fer dessert.

Liz: Grade idea! Look 'it th's pastry section. It's **ta die for**! Jus' look ad all these cakes! The smell 'a these pastries 'ez **making my mouth wader**.

Bill: Wait! Did'ja see the price 'a these cakes? They cos' more th'n the chicken! Whad a **rip-off**! Let's jus' make one **fr'm scratch**. Id'll be a lot cheaper.

Liz: I think y'r right. Let's hurry 'n get the cashier da **ring up** 'ar purchases. I'm starving!

"T" = "D"

In the above dialogue using "Real Speak," "water" became "wader." Unlike British English, Americans commonly pronounce the letter "t" like a "d" in certain cases.

RULES

When a "t" is between two voiced vowels, the "t" is often pronounced like a soft "d" whether in a single word such as "city" (ci*d*y) or within a phrase such as "What a beautiful city!" (Wh*ad* *a* beau*d*iful ci*d*y).

HOW DOES IT WORK?

Look *at* this pastry section.
Ok, bu*t* let's hurry.
Did you le*t* the dog out?

} In these sentences, the "t" retains its sound. Why? Because in each case, there is a vowel on only one side of the "t."

(Gre*at* idea!)
Grea*d* idea!

(Did you inv*it*e Ellen to the party?)
Did you invi*d*e Ellen to the party?

} In these sentences, the "t" is pronounced as a "d" because in each case, there is a vowel on both sides of the "t."

BUT!

In many cases, when "t" is between an "n" and an "e," the "t" is often silent, as seen in the "Real Speak" dialogue where "twenty" is pronounced "**twen'y**." Below are more common examples:

prin*t*er = **prin'er**
cen*t*er = **cen'er**
en*t*ertainment = **en'ertainment**

complemen*t*ed = **complemen'ed**
coun*t*ed = **coun'ed**
presen*t*ed = **presen'ed**

...ED = 'D, 'T, OR 'ID?

When "ed" is added to a regular verb to form the past tense, the "ed" is pronounced **'d**, **'t**, or **'id** depending on what precedes it:

HOW DOES IT WORK?

...ed = 'd	...ed = 't	...ed = 'id
(after a voiced sound, meaning that you are making a sound which causes your vocal chords to vibrate rather than making a sound such as "sh" where your vocal chords do not move.)	*(after an unvoiced sound such as the sound of "sh," "k," "ss," etc. which do not involve your vocal chords.)*	*(after a "t" or "d")*
play**ed** tennis travel**ed** to Paris order**ed** lunch deliver**ed** pizza happen**ed** yesterday	slash**ed** prices talk**ed** to him dress**ed** nicely reduc**ed** cost increas**ed** sales	decid**ed** to go add**ed** salt want**ed** money need**ed** rest visit**ed** Tokyo

LET'S USE "REAL SPEAK!"

A. "T" PRONOUNCED LIKE "D" *(Answers on p. 214)*

STEP 1: Underline all instances where "t" is pronounced like "d."
STEP 2: Repeat the sentence aloud in "Real Speak."

1. What a beautiful sweater! Did you get it when you went shopping last Saturday?

2. My parents ordered a bottle of champagne for their anniversary.

3. My laptop computer is battery-operated.

4. What a great car! Is it an automatic?

5. Let's go to the party later. Betty said there's going to be a lot of good food there.

6. What city do you live in?

7. Would you like a soft drink or a bottle of water?

8. Did you invite that pretty girl to your house for a little dinner?

9. I just bought a potted plant. It's a beautiful bonsai tree.

10. What a pity about your little sister's babysitter. I heard she got into a car accident!

LET'S LEARN!

SPEAKING

TRACK 13
SOUNDCLOUD

VOCABULARY

The following words and expressions were used in the previous dialogues. Let's take a closer look at what they mean.

carry something (to) *exp.* to provide customers with something they can buy or use.

> **EXAMPLE:** From now on, I'm only eating healthy foods. I hope this market **carries** organic products!
>
> **TRANSLATION:** From now on, I'm only eating healthy foods. I hope this market **provides customers with** organic products!
>
> **"REAL SPEAK":** Fr'm now on, I'm only eading healthy foods. I hope th's market **carries** organic produc's!
>
> **NOW YOU DO IT. COMPLETE THE PHRASE ALOUD:**
> *I always go to this market because they carry...*

from scratch (to make something) *exp.* • **1.** when used in reference to cooking, it means "to start or make something from the very beginning using fresh ingredients • **2.** (in general) to start something from the very beginning.

> **EXAMPLE 1:** Your daughter made this cake **from scratch**? When I was her age, I was using package mixes!
>
> **TRANSLATION:** Your daughter made this cake **starting from the very beginning using fresh ingredients**? When I was her age, I was using package mixes!
>
> **"REAL SPEAK":** Yer dauder made this cake **fr'm scratch**? When I w'z her age, I w'z using package mixes!
>
> **EXAMPLE 2:** I made a mistake on this drawing. Now I have to start over **from scratch**.
>
> **TRANSLATION:** I made a mistake on this drawing. Now I have to start over **from the very beginning**.
>
> **"REAL SPEAK":** I made a mistake on this drawing. Now I hafta stard over **fr'm scratch**.
>
> **NOW YOU DO IT. COMPLETE THE PHRASE ALOUD:**
> *My mother makes ...from scratch.*

make one's mouth water (to) *exp.* said of something that makes one drool.

> **EXAMPLE:** The smell of that fresh bread is **making my mouth water**!
>
> **TRANSLATION:** The smell of that fresh bread is **making me drool**!
>
> **"REAL SPEAK":** The smell 'a that fresh bread's **making my mouth wader**!
>
> **NOW YOU DO IT. COMPLETE THE PHRASE ALOUD:**
> *The smell of ...makes my mouth water!*

pick up (to) *phrV.* when in reference to going to the store, it means "to buy" or "to get."

EXAMPLE: I'm going to the market. Can I **pick up** something for you?

TRANSLATION: I'm going to the market. Can I **buy** something for you?

"REAL SPEAK": I'm going ta the market. C'n I **pick up** something for ya?

Synonym: **grab (to)** *v.* (lit.): to take.

NOW YOU DO IT. COMPLETE THE PHRASE ALOUD:
The last thing I picked up at the store was...

ring up (to) *phrV.* (said of a cashier) to add up, to tally.

EXAMPLE: I'm going to find a cashier **to ring up** my groceries.

TRANSLATION: I'm going to find a cashier **to add up** my groceries.

"REAL SPEAK": I'm gonna find a cashier **da ring up** my gros'ries.

Synonym: **check out (to)** *phrV.* • **1.** to add up a customer's purchases • **2.** to settle one's account at a grocery store or hotel • **3.** *(as seen earlier)* to look at; to observe.

EXAMPLE 1: My checkstand is open. I can **check you out** over here.

TRANSLATION: My checkstand is open. I can **add up your purchases** over here.

"REAL SPEAK": My checkstand's open. I can **check ya oud** over here.

EXAMPLE 2: We need to **check out** of the hotel early.

TRANSLATION: We need to **settle our account** at the hotel early.

"REAL SPEAK": We need ta **check oud** 'a the hotel early.

EXAMPLE 3: **Check out** that beautiful new car!

TRANSLATION: **Take a look at** that beautiful new car!

"REAL SPEAK": **Check out** that beaudiful new car!

NOW YOU DO IT. COMPLETE THE PHRASE ALOUD:
The cashier rang up my order of...

rip-off *n.* (said of something overpriced) thievery, theft.

EXAMPLE: You paid a thousand dollars for that television? What a **rip-off**! I saw an identical television yesterday for a hundred dollars!

TRANSLATION: You paid a thousand dollars for that television? What **thievery**! I saw an identical television yesterday for a hundred dollars!

"REAL SPEAK": You paid a thousan' dollers fer that TV? Whad a **rip-off**! I saw 'n idenical TV yesterday fer a hundred dollers!

Variation: **rip** *n.* a shortened version of: *rip-off.*

Also: **rip someone off (to)** *exp.*

NOW YOU DO IT. COMPLETE THE PHRASE ALOUD:
Having to pay ...dollars for ... is a rip-off!

rock-bottom

adj. (said of a price) extremely inexpensive.

EXAMPLE: I'm going to buy a new car today. The dealer is selling them at **rock-bottom** prices!

TRANSLATION: I'm going to buy a new car today. The dealer is selling them at **extremely low** prices!

"REAL SPEAK": I'm gonna buy a new car taday. The dealer's selling 'em at **rock-boddom** prices!

Synonym: **dirt-cheap** *adj.*

NOW YOU DO IT. COMPLETE THE PHRASE ALOUD:
My grocery store charges rock-bottom prices for...

slash prices (to) *exp.* to reduce prices significantly.

EXAMPLE: Do you want to go with me to the dress shop? They're **slashing their prices** today!

TRANSLATION: Do you want to go with me to the dress shop? They're **significantly reducing their prices** today!

"REAL SPEAK": Do ya wanna go with me da the dress shop? They're **slashing their prices** taday!

Synonym: **cut prices (to)** *exp.*

NOW YOU DO IT. COMPLETE THE PHRASE ALOUD:
The new market is slashing their prices on...

to die for *exp.* used to describe something that is wonderful (usually in reference to food or things).

EXAMPLE: I've never tasted such a wonderful pie in my life! It's **to die for**!

TRANSLATION: I've never tasted such a wonderful pie in my life! It's **absolutely fantastic**!

"REAL SPEAK": I've never tasted such a wonderful pie 'n my life! It's **ta die for**!

Variation: **to die from** *exp.*

NOW YOU DO IT. COMPLETE THE PHRASE ALOUD:
...is to die for!

veggies

n.pl. a popular shortened version of "vegetables."

EXAMPLE: My mother made a great dinner last night. She served chicken, rice, **veggies**, and a wonderful dessert.

TRANSLATION: My mother made a great dinner last night. She served chicken, rice, **vegetables**, and a wonderful dessert.

"REAL SPEAK": My mom made a great dinner las' night. She served chicken, rice, **veggies**, an' a wonderful dessert.

NOW YOU DO IT. COMPLETE THE PHRASE ALOUD:
My favorite veggies are...

LET'S PRACTICE!

TRACK 14
SOUNDCLOUD

WRITING

A. TV COMMERCIAL *(Answers on p. 214)*

Read the commercial and answer each question using a complete sentence *and* with the words from the Vocabulary section.

Welcome to David's Market where we **carry** the largest selection of products in the city! In our produce department, we're **slashing our prices** on all our fruit and **veggies**! Make sure to visit our bakery where you can **pick up** our famous lemon cake. It's **to die for**! We also have everything you need to make wonderful desserts **from scratch**! And best of all, we have ten cashiers waiting **to ring up** your order. So, come to David's market...your first choice in grocery shopping.

QUESTIONS:

1. **At David's Market, what do they have in the produce department?**

   Answer:

2. **Why won't you have to wait in line?**

   Answer:

3. **What did the announcer suggest that you pick up from the bakery?**

   Answer:

4. **Are they raising or lowering prices on vegetables at David's Market?**

   Answer:

5. **How is the lemon cake in the bakery department?**

   Answer:

6. **If you prefer to make the cake yourself, does the market have what you need?**

   Answer:

B. YOU'RE THE AUTHOR

Complete the following dialogue using the word(s) from the list below.

(Answers on p. 214)

carry	mouth water	up	rock	to die for
scratch	pick up	rip-off	slashed	veggies

Joe: We need to _____ some _____ like lettuce, cucumber, and tomatoes for our salad tonight. You're going to love this store. They _____ the best organic products and they've _____ their prices on everything this week.

Kim: You're right! I've never seen such _____-bottom prices. At my store, everything is so expensive. Yesterday I paid five dollars for a loaf of bread! What a _____!

Joe: You're not kidding! Hey, I have an idea. Instead of buying dessert, let's make one from _____...something with chocolate. I have a recipe that's _____!

Kim: You're making my _____! Let's buy the ingredients quickly so we can have the cashier ring _____ our order before I faint from hunger!

C. TRUE OR FALSE *(Answers on p. 215)*

Decide if the sentence is either true or false by checking the appropriate box.

1. If a market **carries** the product you are looking for, it is not sold there.
   ❏ True ❏ False

2. A hundred dollars for a candy bar is a **rip-off**.
   ❏ True ❏ False

3. If you paid a lot more this week for the same item last week, the market is **slashing** its prices.
   ❏ True ❏ False

4. The smell of bread cooking in the oven will **make your mouth water**.
   ❏ True ❏ False

5. A cake that doesn't taste good is **to die for**.
   ❏ True ❏ False

6. People who hate to bake prefer to make cakes **from scratch**.
   ❏ True ❏ False

7. People prefer to shop at stores that have **rock-bottom** prices.
   ❏ True ❏ False

8. A person who never eats carrots, corn, broccoli, or celery prefers to eat **veggies**.
   ❏ True ❏ False

9. A bank teller will **ring up** your order.
   ❏ True ❏ False

10. You can **pick up** a loaf of fresh bread at the bakery.
    ❏ True ❏ False

D. CROSSWORD PUZZLE

Fill in the crossword puzzle by choosing the correct word(s) from the list below.

	ring		bottom		pick
carry		mouth		scratch	

DOWN

1. My horse loves ____, especially carrots.

3. The smell of this soup is making my ____ water!

5. This store is known for having rock- ____ prices. You can always find some great deals here!

8. Do you ____ organic products at this market?

10. Before we leave the market, I have to remember to ____ up some milk.

Page 32 Correction

ACROSS

1. You paid five hundred dollars for a pair of shoes? What a ____-off!

4. My horse loves ____, especially carrots.

8. This cake is delicious! Did you make it from ____?

9. That dress is beautiful! It's to ____ for!

DOWN

1. If you've finished shopping, I'd be happy to ____ up your order for you.

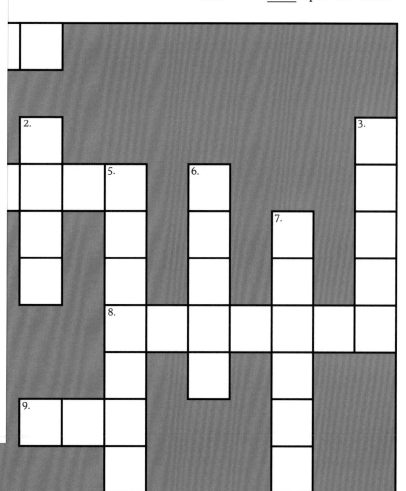

 **FROM THE SLANGMAN FILES**

 TRACK 18 SOUNDCLOUD

EXERCISES FOR THIS SECTION ARE IN THE WORKBOOK.

Popular Idioms, Slang & Jargon
Having to do with: **SHOPPING**

bargain hunting (to go) *exp.* to go to several different stores in order to find the best prices.

> EXAMPLE: Jenn and I **went bargain hunting** today and found some great deals!

> TRANSLATION: Jenn and I **went looking for the best prices in several different stores** today and found some great deals!

> "REAL SPEAK": Jenn 'n I **went bargain hunting** taday 'n foun' s'm great deals!

big box store *exp.* a physically large retail establishment that offers lower prices because they buy products in high volume.

> EXAMPLE: I buy groceries and clothing in **big box stores**. I get a much better deal than I do in typical stores!

> TRANSLATION: I buy groceries and clothing in **large retail establishments that buy products in high volume**. I get a much better deal than I do in typical stores!

> "REAL SPEAK": I buy groc'ries 'n clothing 'n **big box stores**. I ged a much bedder deal th'n I do 'n typical stores!

Synonym 1: **megastore** *n.*

Synonym 2: **superstore** *n.*

Black Friday *exp.* the day after Thanksgiving, which is always Friday, when most stores have a huge sale.

> EXAMPLE: Let's get up early in the morning after Thanksgiving. I don't want to miss all the items that go on sale during **Black Friday**!

> TRANSLATION: Let's get up early in the morning after Thanksgiving. I don't want to miss all the items that go on sale during **the big Friday sale day after Thanksgiving**!

> "REAL SPEAK": Let's ged up early 'n the morning after Thanksgiving. I don't wanna miss all thee idems th't go on sale during **Black Friday**!

brick-and-mortar store *exp.* a physical store as opposed to an online store.

> EXAMPLE: I haven't been to a **brick-and-mortar store** in years. I do all my shopping online to get the best prices!

> TRANSLATION: I haven't been to a **physical store** in years. I do all my shopping online to get the best prices!

> "REAL SPEAK": I haven' been do a **brick-'n-morder store** 'n years. I do all my shopping online ta get the bes' prices!

> *Note:* *Mortar* is a mixture of sand, water, and cement used to attach bricks to each other when building walls.

bull in a china shop (to be like a) *exp.* said of someone who breaks things or who often says the wrong things without thinking first.

> EXAMPLE: I told Susan it was a delicate situation, but she said all the wrong things and insulted everyone! She was **like a bull in a china shop**!

TRANSLATION: I told Susan it was a delicate situation, but she said all the wrong things and insulted everyone! She was **clumsy and awkward in every way**!

"REAL SPEAK": I told Susan it w'z a delicate situation, b't she said all the wrong things an' insulted ev'ryone! She w'z **like a bull 'n a china shop**!

check out (to) *phrV.* to pay for one's items in a store.

EXAMPLE: I think that's all we need. Where do we **check out**?

TRANSLATION: I think that's all we need. Where do we **pay for our items**?

"REAL SPEAK": I think that's all we need. Where do we **check out**?

chop shop *exp.* a place where stolen cars are chopped up into car parts for resale.

EXAMPLE: I can't believe my new car was stolen! It's probably sitting in a **chop shop** somewhere!

TRANSLATION: I can't believe my new car was stolen! It's probably sitting in a **place where stolen cars are chopped up into car parts for resale** somewhere!

"REAL SPEAK": I can't b'lieve my new car w'z stolen! It's prob'ly sidding in a **chop shop** somewhere!

close up shop (to) *exp.* to close the shop (for the day or permanently depending on the context).

EXAMPLE: Let's **close up shop** early and get something to eat.

TRANSLATION: Let's **close the shop** early and get something to eat.

"REAL SPEAK": Let's **close up shop** early 'n get something da eat.

cold cuts *exp.* slices of cold cooked or processed meats.

EXAMPLE: What kind of **cold cuts** do you want on your sandwich? How about turkey?

TRANSLATION: What kind of **cooked and sliced meat** do you want on your sandwich? How about turkey?

"REAL SPEAK": What kind 'a **col' cuts** do ya wan' on yer san'wich? How about turkey?

condiment *n.* a spice or sauce added to a food such as ketchup, mustard, mayonnaise, etc.

EXAMPLE: I love going to this baseball stadium because of the food! We can buy hotdogs over there and then put any kind of **condiment** you want on them!

TRANSLATION: I love going to this baseball stadium because of the food! We can buy hotdogs over there and then put any kind of **spice or sauce** you want on them!

"REAL SPEAK": I love goin' da th's baseball stadium b'cuz 'a the food! We c'n buy hotdogs over there an' then pud any kind'a **condiment** ya wan' on 'em!

Synonym: **topping** *n.*

cost an arm and a leg (to) *exp.* to be very expensive.

EXAMPLE: Those shoes **cost me an arm and a leg** but I just love them!

TRANSLATION: Those shoes **were very expensive** but I just love them!

"REAL SPEAK": Those shoes **cos' me 'n arm 'n a leg bud I jus' love 'em**!

MORE ON...
TV
SLANGMAN

end cap *exp.* a special display on the end of an aisle to highlight sale items or seasonal products.

EXAMPLE: During Thanksgiving, all the markets have turkey stuffing in their **end caps**.

TRANSLATION: During Thanksgiving, all the markets have turkey stuffing in their **special displays on the end of the aisles**.

"REAL SPEAK": During Thanksgiving, all the markets have turkey stuffing in their **en' caps**.

enter one's PIN (to) *exp.* to enter one's **P**ersonal **I**dentification **N**umber when using a debit card.

EXAMPLE: Make sure to change your **PIN** often so it's harder to steal.

TRANSLATION: Make sure to change your **Personal Identification Number** often so it's harder to steal.

"REAL SPEAK": Make sher da change yer **PIN** of'en so it's harder da steal.

express lane *exp.* a special cashier line for people with few items to make purchases faster.

EXAMPLE: Why are you waiting in this long line? You can use the **express lane** because you only have four items!

TRANSLATION: Why are you waiting in this long line? You can use the **fast line** because you only have four items!

"REAL SPEAK": Why 'er ya waiding 'n th's long line? You c'n use the **express lane** b'cuz ya only have four idems!

flea market *exp.* an outdoor shopping area where people rent space to sell merchandise at negotiable prices.

EXAMPLE: I love going to **flea markets** because you can always negotiate a good price.

TRANSLATION: I love going to **outdoor markets** because you can always negotiate a good price.

"REAL SPEAK": I love going da **flea markets** b'cuz ya c'n ahways negoshiade a good price.

fresh out of something (to be) *exp.* to have recently sold the last of something.

EXAMPLE: I'm sorry. We're **fresh out of** chicken but we're offering steaks at half price.

TRANSLATION: I'm sorry. We're **recently sold our last** chicken but we're offering steaks at half price.

"REAL SPEAK": I'm sorry. W'r **fresh oudda** chicken b't w'r offering steaks 'it half price.

garage sale *exp.* a sale of used household items, often held in the garage or front yard of one's house.

EXAMPLE: We're moving into a smaller home next month, so we're going to have a **garage sale** and get rid of as much stuff as we can!

TRANSLATION: We're moving into a smaller home next month, so we're going to have a **sale in our yard of used items** and get rid of as much stuff as we can!

"REAL SPEAK": W'r moving into a smaller home nex' month, so w'r gonna have a **garage sale** 'n get rid 'ev 'ez much stuff 'ez we can!

Synonym 1: **lawn sale** *exp.*

Synonym 2: **yard sale** *exp.*

generic *adj.* (short for **generic brand**) a consumer product that does not have the name of a famous manufacturer on it and is consequently less expensive but often of equal value.

EXAMPLE: I always buy **generic**, especially when I go to the pharmacy. The pills are just as good but so much less expensive!

TRANSLATION: I always buy **products that aren't made by a famous manufacturer**, especially when I go to the pharmacy. The pills are just as good but so much less expensive!

"REAL SPEAK": I ahways buy **generic**, espesh'ly when I go da the pharmacy. The pills'er just 'ez good b't so much less expensive!

haggle (to) *v.* to negotiate over the price of something.

EXAMPLE: At flea markets, you can always **haggle** and get the best deal.

TRANSLATION: At flea markets, you can always **negotiate** and get the best deal.

"REAL SPEAK": At flea markets, you c'n ahways **haggle** 'n get the bes' deal.

Synonym 1: **barter (to)** *v.*

Synonym 2: **dicker (to)** *v.*

Synonym 3: **wheel and deal (to)** *exp.*

hit the stores (to) *exp.* to shop at multiple stores.

EXAMPLE: Let's **hit the stores** early. I want to be sure we get there before all the good stuff is sold!

TRANSLATION: Let's **shop at multiple stores** early. I want to be sure we get there before all the good stuff is sold!

"REAL SPEAK": Let's **hit the stores** early. I wanna be sher we get there b'fore all the good stuff 'ez sold!

impulse item *exp.* an inexpensive and alluring product a customer wasn't planning on buying.

EXAMPLE: My grocery store always has tons of **impulse items** like candy at the cashier. I always end up buying something!

TRANSLATION: My grocery store always has tons of **inexpensive and alluring products** like candy at the cashier. I always end up buying something!

"REAL SPEAK": My groc'ry store ahways has tons 'ev **impulse idems** like candy 'it the cashier. I ahways end up buying something!

kid in a candy store/shop (to be like a) *exp.* said of someone who has complete access to whatever he/she wants.

EXAMPLE: My father said he'd buy me any car from this dealership as a graduation present! I'm **like a kid in a candy store**!

TRANSLATION: My father said he'd buy me any car from this dealership as a graduation present! I **have complete access to anything I want**!

"REAL SPEAK": My father said 'e'd buy me any car fr'm this dealership 'ez a gradjuation present! I'm **like a kid 'n a candy store**!

killer deal *exp.* a purchase made at an excellent price.

EXAMPLE: I just got a **killer deal** on a new TV! It was marked down to half price!

TRANSLATION: I just got a **great low price** on a new TV! It was marked down to half price!

"REAL SPEAK": I jus' godda **killer deal** on a new TV! It w'z mark' down da half price!

mom-and-pop shop *exp.* a small, independent business.

EXAMPLE: I always support the local **mom-and-pop shops**. It's not easy starting your own business!

TRANSLATION: I always support the local **small, independent shops**. It's not easy starting your own business!

"REAL SPEAK": I ahways support the local **mom-'n-pop shops**. It's nod easy starding yer own bizness!

name brand *exp.* a product made by a famous maker or manufacturer.

EXAMPLE: I only buy **name brands** because I trust their products.

TRANSLATION: I only buy **products made by famous manufacturers** because I trust their products.

"REAL SPEAK": I only buy **name bran's** b'cuz I trust their produc's.

off (to be ___% or $___) *exp.* to be ___% or $___ less expensive than the original price.

EXAMPLE: They're having a huge sale at the computer store next week. I'll be able to get the computer I want at **50% off**! Imagine! **$400 off** the original price!

TRANSLATION: They're having a huge sale at the computer store next week. I'll be able to get the computer I want at **50% less**! Imagine! **$400 less** than the original price!

"REAL SPEAK": They're having a huge sale 'it the c'mpuder store next week. A'll be able da get the c'mpuder I wan' 'it **fifdy percen' off**! Imagine! **Four hundred dollers off** the original price!

outlet mall *exp.* a group of stores that sell everything at reduced prices.

EXAMPLE: It's far, but if we drive to the **outlet mall**, we'll save a lot of money on clothing!

TRANSLATION: It's far, but if we drive to the **group of stores where everything is cheaper**, we'll save a lot of money on clothing!

"REAL SPEAK": It's far, b'd 'ef we drive ta thee **outlet mall**, w'll save a lodda money on clothing!

overpriced (to be) *adj.* to be too expensive.

EXAMPLE: Those paper towels are way **overpriced**! The generic ones are a much better deal!

TRANSLATION: Those paper towels are way **too expensive**! The generic ones are a much better deal!

"REAL SPEAK": Those paper towels 'er way **overpriced**! The generic ones 'er a much bedder deal!

penny pincher (to be a) *exp.* to be a person who is unwilling to spend.

EXAMPLE: My brother is rich but never treats anyone to dinner. He's such a **penny pincher**!

TRANSLATION: My brother is rich but never treats anyone to dinner. He's such a **person who is unwilling to spend**!

"REAL SPEAK": My brother is rich but never treats anyone to dinner. He's such a **penny pincher**!

Synonym 1: **cheapskate** *n.*

Synonym 2: **pinchpenny** *n.*

Synonym 3: **stingy** *adj.*

Synonym 4: **tightwad** *n.*

pricey (to be) *adj.* to be expensive; carry a high price.

EXAMPLE: I always make my own coffee in the morning. A cup of coffee is just too **pricey** at coffee shops.

TRANSLATION: I always make my own coffee in the morning. A cup of coffee is just too **expensive** at coffee shops.

"REAL SPEAK": I ahways make my own coffee 'n the morning. A cup 'a coffee 'ez jus too **pricey** 'it coffee shops.

produce *n.* (pronounced: *PRO-duce*) fruits and vegetables that have been produced or grown, especially by farming.

EXAMPLE 1: They have delicious **produce** in this market. The apples are so sweet!

TRANSLATION: They have delicious **fruits and vegetables** in this market. The apples are so sweet!

"REAL SPEAK": They have delicious **produce** 'n th's market. The apples'er so sweet!

Note: When the accent is on the second syllable (pronounced *pro-DUCE*), it becomes a verb meaning "to create." With that in mind, how do you pronounce the following? *The **produce** is **produced** in California.*

rain check *exp.* a coupon issued to a customer, guaranteeing that a sale item that is out of stock may be purchased at a later date at the same reduced price.

EXAMPLE: I'm so sorry but the sale item you want is sold out! But don't worry. I'll give you a **rain check**.

TRANSLATION: I'm so sorry but the sale item you want is sold out! But don't worry. I'll give you a **coupon that will give you the same reduced price when the item is back in stock**.

"REAL SPEAK": I'm so sorry b't the sale idem ya wan' 'ez sold out! B't don't worry. A'll give ya a **rain check**.

retail therapy *exp.* shopping to make oneself feel happier.

EXAMPLE: I had such a hard week at work! I definitely need a weekend of **retail therapy**! Do you want to go with me?

TRANSLATION: I had such a hard week at work! I definitely need a weekend of **shopping to make me feel happier**! Do you want to go with me?

"REAL SPEAK": I had such a hard week 'it work! I def'nitely need a weekend 'ev **retail therapy**! Do you wanna go with me?

Synonym: **shopping therapy** *exp.*

set up shop (to) *exp.* to open a business.

EXAMPLE: Since we're selling surfboards, it makes the most sense **to set up shop** near the beach.

TRANSLATION: Since we're selling surfboards, it makes the most sense **to open our business** near the beach.

"REAL SPEAK": Since w'r selling surfboards, it makes the mos' sense **ta sed up shop** near the beach.

shop around (to) *phrV.* to go from store to store in search of the best price for a particular item.

EXAMPLE: I need to find a new couch. I'm going to **shop around** for one on Saturday.

TRANSLATION: I need to find a new couch. I'm going to **go from shop to shop** for one on Saturday.

"REAL SPEAK": I need da find a new couch. I'm gonna **shop aroun'** fer one on Sadurday.

shop till you drop (to) *exp.* to keep shopping until you're too exhausted to do any more.

EXAMPLE: Look at all these great sales! Let's **shop till we drop**!

TRANSLATION: Look at all these great sales! Let's **shop until we're too exhausted to do any more**!

"REAL SPEAK": Look 'id all these great sales! Let's **shop till we drop**!

shopaholic *n.* a person who is addicted to shopping.

EXAMPLE: Jill spends a thousand dollars a week on new clothes! I've never seen such a **shopaholic** before!

TRANSLATION: Jill spends a thousand dollars a week on new clothes! I've never seen such a **person addicted to shopping** before!

"REAL SPEAK": Jill spen'z a thousan' dollers a week on new cloze! I've never seen such a **shopaholic** b'fore!

shoplift (to) *v.* to steal items from a store.

EXAMPLE: Where did you get that expensive watch? Did you **shoplift** it?!

TRANSLATION: Where did you get that expensive watch? Did you **steal it from a store**?!

"REAL SPEAK": Where'd ja get thad expensive watch? Did'ja **shoplift** it?!

Also 1: **shoplifter** *n.* a person who steals items from stores.

Also 2: **shoplifting** *v.* the act of stealing items from a store.

Synonym: **five-finger discount** *exp. I got the five-finger discount on this necklace;* I stole this necklace.

shopping spree *exp.* a short period of time in which someone buys a lot of items.

> EXAMPLE: For your birthday, let's go on a **shopping spree**. My treat!
>
> TRANSLATION: For your birthday, let's go **buy lots of items in a short period of time**. My treat!
>
> "REAL SPEAK": Fer yer birthday, let's go on a **shopping spree**. My treat!

steal (to be a) *exp.* to be an incredibly low price.

> EXAMPLE: That grand piano is only two hundred dollars! You should buy it! That's **a steal**!
>
> TRANSLATION: That grand piano is only two hundred dollars! You should buy it! That's **an incredibly low price**!
>
> "REAL SPEAK": That gran' piano's only two hundred dollers! You should buy it! That's **a steal**!

swipe one's card (to) *exp.* to pay by passing one's credit card through a narrow slot in a special machine that reads information on the card's magnetic strip.

> EXAMPLE: Your total is thirty-four dollars. When you see the light, please **swipe your card**.
>
> TRANSLATION: Your total is thirty-four dollars. When you see the light, please **pass your credit card through the narrow slot in the machine**.
>
> "REAL SPEAK": Yer todal's thirdy-four dollers. When ya see the light, please **swipe yer card**.

talk shop (to) *exp.* to talk about one's work.

> EXAMPLE: I hate going to events with your work friends. All they ever do is **talk shop**!
>
> TRANSLATION: I hate going to events with your work friends. All they ever do is **talk about work**!
>
> "REAL SPEAK": I hate going do events w'th yer work friends. All they ever do 'ez **talk shop**!

"That comes to ___ dollars" *exp.* "Your total is ___ dollars."

> EXAMPLE: Two sweaters and one pair of pants… **that comes to** one hundred fifty dollars.
>
> TRANSLATION: Two sweaters and one pair of pants… **your total is** one hundred fifty dollars.
>
> "REAL SPEAK": Two sweaders 'n one pair 'ev pants… **that comes ta** one hundred fifdy dollers.

window shopping (to go) *exp.* to look at the items displayed in shop windows, especially without intending to buy anything.

> EXAMPLE: I can't afford to buy any new clothes. So for now, I'm just **going window shopping**.

> TRANSLATION: I can't afford to buy any new clothes. So for now, I'm just **going to look at the items in the store windows**.
>
> "REAL SPEAK": I can' afford da buy any new cloze. So fer now, I'm jus' **gonna go window shopping**.

worth every penny (to be) *exp.* said of something that is worth the money you spent on it.

> EXAMPLE: My new laptop was expensive, but it was **worth every penny**. It's really fast! Now I'm super productive!
>
> TRANSLATION: My new laptop was expensive, but it was **worth all the money I spent on it**. It's really fast! Now I'm super productive!
>
> "REAL SPEAK": My new laptop w'z expensive, b'd it w' **worth ev'ry penny**. It's really fast! Now I'm super praductive!

SLANGMAN
Explains More idioms & Slang for...
~AT THE MARKET~

SCAN ME!

CHAPTER 2

SCAN THE QR CODE OR GO TO: bit.ly/StreetSpeak1-Chapter2

THIS VIDEO EPISODE CONTAINS...

Talk about...
- When to use it to indicate surprise.

shopping
- Slangman presents his TOP 5 LIST of shopping slang and idioms

'n
- When 'n = **an**, **and**, or **in**

can'
- When **can** = *cannot* and **c'n** = *can*
  - *I can' afford to buy any new clothes.* = I cannot afford to buy any new clothes.

Idioms & slang used on TV this week plus the latest Teen Slang!
- Slangman gives you his TOP 5 LIST of the latest idioms and slang from the most popular TV shows in the U.S. plus the newest slang teens are using today!

Newest American slang just entered into the dictionary

LET'S WARM UP!

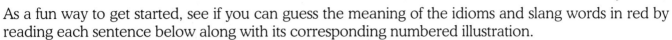

MATCH THE PICTURES *(Answers on p. 215)*

As a fun way to get started, see if you can guess the meaning of the idioms and slang words in red by reading each sentence below along with its corresponding numbered illustration.

1. What a horrible actor! He **can't act his way out of a paper bag**.

   Definition: "is an excellent actor"

   ☐ True   ☐ False

2. What a great movie! It's going to be a real **blockbuster**!

   Definition: "failure"

   ☐ True   ☐ False

3. This is my first movie **premiere**! I hope I see some celebrities!

   Definition: "closing"

   ☐ True   ☐ False

4. That was the worst movie I've ever seen. What a **bomb**!

   Definition: "success"

   ☐ True   ☐ False

5. When's this movie going to begin?! Let's **get the show on the road**!

   Definition: "hurry and get started"

   ☐ True   ☐ False

6. Did you read the **write-up**? It's supposed to be a great movie.

   Definition: "review"

   ☐ True   ☐ False

7. The movie is going to be very popular. It's being **plugged** all over the world!

   Definition: "promoted"

   ☐ True   ☐ False

8. That unpopular movie surprised everyone. It turned out to be a **sleeper**!

   Definition: "surprisingly successful movie"

   ☐ True   ☐ False

9. There are no tickets left. It's a **sellout**.

   Definition: "performance for which all of the tickets have been sold"

   ☐ True   ☐ False

10. My role is too large! I have too many **lines** to memorize!

    Definition: "words in a script"

    ☐ True   ☐ False

11. I was just invited to a **red carpet event**! I don't know what to wear!

    Definition: "an event with important people"

    ☐ True   ☐ False

12. Dan loves being **in the limelight**! He certainly isn't the shy type!

    Definition: "an electrician"

    ☐ True   ☐ False

LET'S TALK!

A. DIALOGUE USING SLANG & IDIOMS

The words introduced on the previous two pages are used in the following dialogue and illustrated in the long picture above. Can you understand the conversation and find the illustration that corresponds to the slang? *Note:* The translation of the words in boldface is on the right-hand page.

— George and David are at the movies —

George: It's a good thing we got tickets early. The movie is a **sellout**!

David: I'm not surprised. The **premiere** was a real **red carpet event** and they've been **plugging** this movie for weeks! So, of course it's a **blockbuster**!

George: The critics must have been surprised it turned out to be such a **sleeper**!

David: I'll say. They said it was going to be a **bomb** and the performers **couldn't act their way out of a paper bag**.

George: Well, yesterday I saw a **write-up** and the reviewer said there were a lot of funny **lines** with great performances.

David: I can't imagine being **in the limelight** all the time like those actors.

George: Well, those actors better get on stage soon or their audience is going to leave. Let's **get the show on the road**!

LET'S TALK!

B. DIALOGUE TRANSLATED INTO STANDARD ENGLISH

LET'S SEE HOW MUCH YOU REMEMBER!
Just for fun, bounce around in random order to the words and
expressions in boldface below. See if you can remember their
slang equivalents without looking at the left-hand page!

— George and David are at the movies —

George: It's a good thing we got tickets early. The movie **doesn't have any tickets left**!

David: I'm not surprised. The **opening** was a real **big event with important people** and they've been **promoting** this movie for weeks! So, of course it's a **huge success**!

George: The critics must have been surprised it turned out to be such a **success after starting slowly**!

David: I'll say. They said it was going to be a **complete failure** and the performers **were terrible actors**.

George: Well, yesterday I saw a **review** where the reviewer said there were a lot of funny **phrases in the script** with great performances.

David: I can't imagine being the **focus of attention** all time like those actors.

George: Well, those actors better get on stage soon or their audience is going to leave. Let's **get started**!

C. DIALOGUE USING "REAL SPEAK"

The dialogue below demonstrates how the slang conversation on the previous page would *really* be spoken by native speakers!

— George 'n David 'er 'it the movies —

George: It's a good thing we got tickets early. The movie's a **sellout**!

David: I'm not saprised. The **premiere** w'z a real **red carped event** 'n they' been **plugging** th's movie fer weeks! So, 'ev course it's a **blockbusder**!

George: The cridics must'a been saprised thad it turned out ta be such a **sleeper**!

David: A'll say. They said it w'z gonna be a **bomb** 'n that the performers **couldn' act their way oud 'ev a paper bag**.

George: Well, yesderday I saw a **wride-up** 'n the reviewer said there were a lod 'ev funny **lines** w'th great performances.

David: I can' imagine being **'n the limelide** all the time like those acters.

George: Well, those acters bedder ged on stage soon 'r their audience is gonna leave. Let's **get the show on the road**!

KEY TO "REAL SPEAK"

MUST HAVE = MUSTA

Musta is the most common reduction of "must have." However, don't be surprised if you also hear **must'ev** which is a popular variation.

RULES

Letters in an unstressed word (when the voice lowers in pitch) are often dropped when preceded by a stressed word (when the voice rises in pitch) as can be seen in the following example:

HOW DOES IT WORK?

They must have been plugging this movie for weeks! } The up arrow indicates a stressed word and the down arrow indicates an unstressed word.

They must hav**e** been plugging this movie for weeks!
They must hav been plugging this movie for weeks! } The **e** in "have" is silent.

They must **hav** been plugging this movie for weeks!
They must   **a**   been plugging this movie for weeks! } In the combination "must have," "must" is always stressed and "have" is not. The **h** and **v** in "have" are dropped since they have a weaker (or less stressed) sound than the **a**.

They **musta** been plugging this movie for weeks!

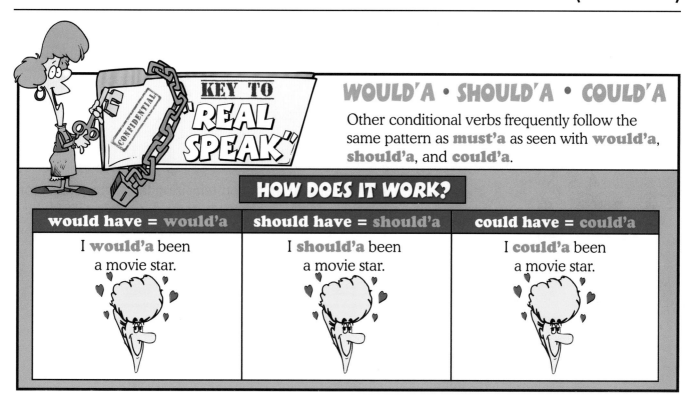

KEY TO "REAL SPEAK"

WOULD'A · SHOULD'A · COULD'A

Other conditional verbs frequently follow the same pattern as **must'a** as seen with **would'a**, **should'a**, and **could'a**.

HOW DOES IT WORK?

would have = would'a	should have = should'a	could have = could'a
I **would'a** been a movie star.	I **should'a** been a movie star.	I **could'a** been a movie star.

LET'S USE "REAL SPEAK!"

WRITING

TRACK 20 SOUNDCLOUD

A. SHOULD'A, COULD'A, WOULD'A, MUST'A

Using the list below, fill in the blanks with the correct word(s). Note that one or more of the words in the list may be used more than once!

(Answers on p. 215)

1. George didn't answer the phone. I'm sure he _____ been in the shower.

2. You _____ been there. The movie was great!

3. Look at all those packages. Lee _____ been shopping for hours!

4. You saw Robert Downey Jr. yesterday? I _____ gotten his autograph!

5. You hiked a mountain for eight hours? I _____ loved to join you but I _____ walked that far with my bad knee.

6. I _____ been so happy if Steve asked me on a date. I guess he just doesn't like me.

7. That's so nice of you, but you _____ bought me a gift. I have nothing for you!

8. I'm convinced Burt _____ been lying or he _____ been so nervous.

could'a	must'a	should'a	would'a
couldn'a	mustn'a	shouldn'a	wouldn'a

LET'S LEARN!

SPEAKING

TRACK 21
SOUNDCLOUD

VOCABULARY

The following words and expressions were used in the previous dialogues. Let's take a closer look at what they mean.

act one's  way out of a paper bag (to be unable to) *exp.* to be a terrible actor.

BOO!
BOO!

> **EXAMPLE:** I saw a terrible movie on television last night. The actors **couldn't act their way out of a paper bag**!
>
> **TRANSLATION:** I saw a terrible movie on television last night. The actors **were horrible**!
>
> **"REAL SPEAK":** I saw a terr'ble movie on TV las' night. The acters **couldn' act their way oud of a paper bag**!
>
> **NOW YOU DO IT. COMPLETE THE PHRASE ALOUD:**
> *...can't act his/her way out of a paper bag.*

blockbuster *n.* a very successful movie.

> **EXAMPLE:** You have to go see the new movie that just opened. It's a real **blockbuster**!
>
> **TRANSLATION:** You have to go see the new movie that just opened. It's a real **success**!
>
> **"REAL SPEAK":** Ya hafta go see the new movie th't just opened. It's a real **blockbuster**!
>
> *Synonym:* **hit** *n.*
>
> **NOW YOU DO IT. COMPLETE THE PHRASE ALOUD:**
> *The movie ...was a blockbuster!*

bomb *n.* a complete failure (said of a movie, play, etc.).

BOOM!

> **EXAMPLE:** Poor Gina. She produced a movie with her own money and it turned out to be a **bomb**.
>
> **TRANSLATION:** Poor Gina. She produced a movie with her own money and it turned out to be a **complete failure**.
>
> **"REAL SPEAK":** Poor Gina. She praduced a movie with 'er own money 'n it turned out ta be a **bomb**.
>
> *Synonym:* **dud** *n.*
>
> *Note:* In the late nineties, teenagers created the expression *the bomb* meaning "fantastic":
>
> **EXAMPLE:** That movie was **the bomb**!
>
> **TRANSLATION:** That movie was **fantastic**!
>
> **"REAL SPEAK":** That movie w'z **the bomb**!
>
> **NOW YOU DO IT. COMPLETE THE PHRASE ALOUD:**
> *The last ...I saw was a bomb.*

get the show on the road (to) *exp.* to begin something right away.

EXAMPLE: I can only stay at this meeting for thirty minutes, so **let's get the show on the road**.

TRANSLATION: I can only stay at this meeting for thirty minutes, so **let's begin right away**.

"REAL SPEAK": I c'n only stay at this meeding fer thirdy minutes, so **let's get the show on the road**.

NOW YOU DO IT. COMPLETE THE PHRASE ALOUD:
Let's get the show on the road! We're late for...

limelight (to be in the) *exp.* to be the focus of everyone's attention.

EXAMPLE: When you're a movie star, you're always **in the limelight**. Say goodbye to privacy!

TRANSLATION: When you're a movie star, you're always **the focus of everyone's attention**. Say goodbye to privacy!

"REAL SPEAK": When y'r a movie star, y'r ahways **'n the limelight**. Say g'bye da privacy!

Synonym: **spotlight (to be in the)** *exp.*

NOW YOU DO IT. COMPLETE THE PHRASE ALOUD:
I was in the limelight when I...

line *n.* a phrase or word that a performer memorizes from a script.

EXAMPLE: When I got hired to act in the movie, I thought it was going to be a very small part. But when I received the script, I discovered that I had pages and pages of **lines**!

TRANSLATION: When I got hired to act in the movie, I thought it was going to be a very small part. But when I received the script, I discovered that I had pages and pages of **phrases to memorize**!

"REAL SPEAK": When I got hired ta act in the movie, I thod it w'z gonna be a very small part. But when I received the script, I discovered th'd I had pages 'n pages of **lines**!

NOW YOU DO IT. COMPLETE THE PHRASE ALOUD:
...are the lines from (famous play or movie).

plug something (to) *v.* to advertise or promote something.

EXAMPLE: When the actor was interviewed on television, he **plugged** his new movie.

TRANSLATION: When the actor was interviewed on television, he **promoted** his new movie.

"REAL SPEAK": When the acter w'z in'erviewed on TV, he **plugged** 'is new movie.

Variation: **give something a plug (to)** *exp.*

NOW YOU DO IT. COMPLETE THE PHRASE ALOUD:
I saw a commercial on TV plugging...

premiere *n.* the opening of a musical, play, dance, movie, etc. (from French, *première représentation* meaning "first showing").

> **EXAMPLE:** My friend is a big movie director and invited me to the **premiere** of his new film!
>
> **TRANSLATION:** My friend is a big movie director and invited me to the **opening** of his new film!
>
> **"REAL SPEAK":** My fren's a big movie director an' invided me da the **premiere** 'ev 'is new film!
>
> *Synonym:* **grand opening** *exp.*
>
> *Also:* **sneak preview** *exp.* an advance showing before being released to the public.

NOW YOU DO IT. COMPLETE THE PHRASE ALOUD:

Last night, I went to a premiere of...

red carpet event *exp.* an important affair where there is typically a red carpet for celebrities, and other dignitaries, to walk down to the entrance of the event.

> **EXAMPLE:** You can't go to a **red carpet event** dressed like that! Go put on a tuxedo!
>
> **TRANSLATION:** You can't go to an **important affair with celebrities and dignitaries** dressed like that! Go put on a tuxedo!
>
> **"REAL SPEAK":** Ya can't go do a **red carped event** dressed like that! Go pud on a tux!
>
> *Variation 1:* **red-carpet treatment (to give someone the)** *exp.* to treat someone like an important dignitary.
>
> *Variation 2:* **red-carpet welcome (to give someone a)** *exp.* to welcome someone and treat him/her like an honored guest.
>
> *Variation 3:* **roll out the red carpet (to)** *exp.* to welcome someone and treat him/her like an honored guest.

NOW YOU DO IT. COMPLETE THE PHRASE ALOUD:

I've always wanted to go to a red carpet event and meet...

sellout *n.*  said of a performance for which all of the tickets have been sold.

> **EXAMPLE:** I couldn't get tickets for the show at the Bijou tonight. It's a **sellout**!
>
> **TRANSLATION:** I couldn't get tickets for the show at the Bijou tonight. **All of the tickets have been sold**!
>
> **"REAL SPEAK":** I couldn't get tickets fer the show at the Bijou danight. It's a **sellout**!

NOW YOU DO IT. COMPLETE THE PHRASE ALOUD:

...was a sellout!

sleeper *n.* a success after starting slowly.

EXAMPLE:	Megan's play was a bomb when it first opened, but it turned out to be a **sleeper**!
TRANSLATION:	Megan's play was a bomb when it first opened, but it turned out to be a **success after starting slowly**!
"REAL SPEAK":	Megan's play w'z a bomb when it first opened, bud it turned out ta be a **sleeper**!

NOW YOU DO IT. COMPLETE THE PHRASE ALOUD:

The movie ...was a sleeper.

write-up *n.* a  written review of a play, show, etc.

EXAMPLE:	Congratulations on your play! I read a great **write-up** about it in the Los Angeles Times!
TRANSLATION:	Congratulations on your play! I read a great **review** about it in the Los Angeles Times!
"REAL SPEAK":	C'ngradjalations on yer play! I read a great **wride-up** aboud id in the L.A. Times!

NOW YOU DO IT. COMPLETE THE PHRASE ALOUD:

I read a good/bad write up on...

LET'S PRACTICE!

A. I KNOW THE ANSWER, BUT WHAT'S THE QUESTION? *(Answers on p. 215)*

Read the answer and place a check next to the corresponding question.

1.

The answer is...

Because he loves being in the limelight.

Questions:
☐ Why doesn't Henry ever go to parties?
☐ Why did Henry volunteer to give a speech in front of all those people?
☐ Why is Henry on a diet? He looks great!

2.

The answer is...

No. It was a sellout.

Questions:
☐ Were you able to find the movie theater?
☐ Were you able to get tickets for the play?
☐ Were you able to make a reservation at the restaurant?

3.

The answer is...

No. We have to get the show on the road.

Questions:
☐ Do we have time to eat something before we leave?
☐ Would you like mustard on your sandwich?
☐ Do you listen to classical music?

4.

The answer is...

Yes. They've been plugging it for weeks.

Questions:
☐ Do you want to go see the new musical?
☐ Did you play drums in the concert last night?
☐ Is your piano brand new?

5.

The answer is...

No. I heard it was a bomb.

Questions:
☐ That movie was a failure, wasn't it?
☐ That movie made a fortune, didn't it?
☐ That movie was very long, wasn't it?

6.

The answer is...

It wasn't. But it turned out to be a sleeper.

Questions:
☐ Look at the long line! I thought you said this movie wasn't popular.
☐ Look at the long line! Do you think they still have tickets left?
☐ Look at the long line! Do you mind waiting to buy a ticket?

B. FIND YOUR PERFECT MATCH *(Answers on p. 215)*

Write the number of the slang term or idiom from Column A next to its matching picture in Column B as well as next to the matching definition in Column C.

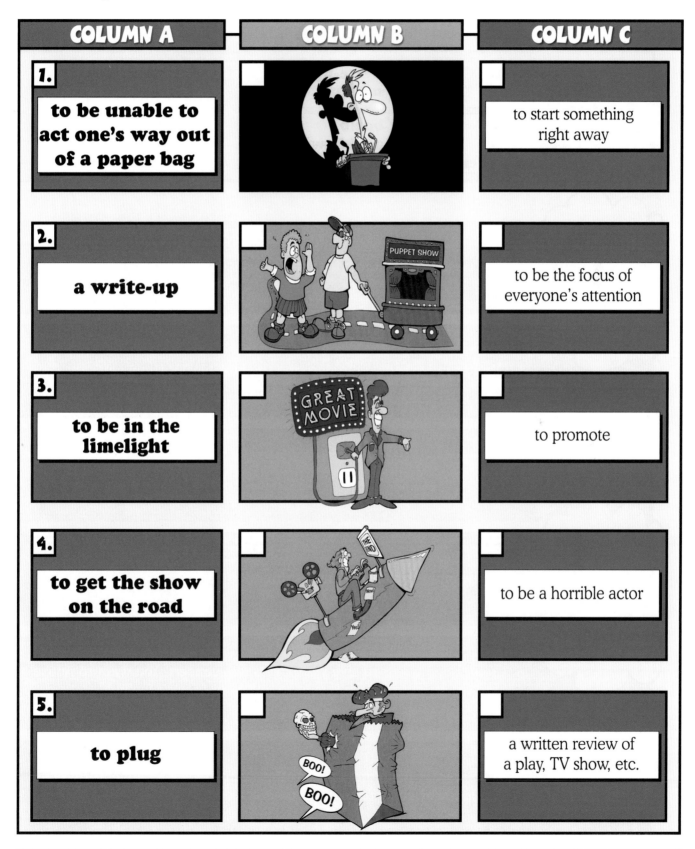

COLUMN A	COLUMN B	COLUMN C
1. to be unable to act one's way out of a paper bag		to start something right away
2. a write-up		to be the focus of everyone's attention
3. to be in the limelight		to promote
4. to get the show on the road		to be a horrible actor
5. to plug		a written review of a play, TV show, etc.

C. IMAGINE THAT... *(Answers on p. 215)*

Someone has presented you with a situation as seen below. Respond to each situation aloud by making a complete sentence using one of the groups of words below. Use each group only once.

✔ blockbuster ✔ sleeper	✔ write-up ✔ sellout	✔ premiere ✔ lines

✔ plug
✔ blockbuster
✔ red carpet event
	✔ bomb
	✔ act his way out
	   of a paper bag
		✔ sellout
		✔ get the show
		   on the road

IMAGINE THAT...

1. You've seen a great movie that you want to tell your friend about.

IMAGINE THAT...

2. Your friend asked you to describe the horrible TV show you saw.

IMAGINE THAT...

3. You are reviewing a fantastic new Broadway play.

IMAGINE THAT...

4. You want to convince your best friend to go with you to the ballet.

IMAGINE THAT...

5. Your friend wants to give you tickets to a concert. You want to refuse the tickets but you don't want to hurt your friend's feelings.

IMAGINE THAT...

6. It's Saturday night and your brother wants to see an adventure movie. Explain why going to see the comedy would be better.

THE SLANGMAN FILES

Popular Idioms, Slang & Jargon
Having to do with:
ENTERTAINMENT

EXERCISES FOR THIS SECTION ARE IN THE WORKBOOK.

"And now for my next number…" *exp.*
1. "And now for my next performance (said by a magician, singer, etc.) • **2.** said in jest after doing something embarrassing (such as a fall, trip, dropping something, etc.).

> EXAMPLE 1: **And now for my next number**, I'd like to sing a song I wrote.

> TRANSLATION: **And now for my next performance**, I'd like to sing a song I wrote.

> "REAL SPEAK": **An' now fer my nex' number**, I'd like ta sing a song I wrote.

> EXAMPLE 2: (After tripping) **And now for my next number**….

> TRANSLATION: (After tripping) **And now for my next performance**….

> "REAL SPEAK": (After tripping) **An' now fer my nex' number**…

"Break a leg!" *exp.* a popular phrase used in the entertainment industry, and elsewhere, meaning "Good luck!"

> EXAMPLE: You have a job interview tomorrow? Great! **Break a leg**!

> TRANSLATION: You have a job interview tomorrow? Great! **Good luck**!

> "REAL SPEAK": Ya godda a job in'erview damorrow? Great! **Break a leg**!

> *Origin:* This expression comes from a theatrical superstition where wishing a dancer good luck is considered bad luck.

concession stand *exp.* a place where customers can purchase snacks or food at a movie theater, amusement park, or any other entertainment venue.

> EXAMPLE: At my theater, you can place your food order online and pay for it, then pick everything up at the **concession stand**!

> TRANSLATION: At my theater, you can place your food order online and pay for it, then pick everything up at the **snack bar**!

> "REAL SPEAK": At my theeder, ya c'n place yer food order online 'n pay fer it, th'n pick ev'rything up at the **concession stand**!

cue *n.* a thing said or done that serves as a signal to an actor, or other performer, to begin their performance.

> EXAMPLE: Your **cue** is when Don says, "When will he arrive?" Then you need to get on stage right away.

> TRANSLATION: Your **signal** is when Don says, "When will he arrive?" Then you need to get on stage right away.

> "REAL SPEAK": Yer **cue** 'ez when Don says, "When will 'e arrive?" Then ya need da ged on stage ride away.

feed an actor his/her lines (to) *exp.* to tell an actor what the next words from the script are in case he forgets.

> **EXAMPLE:** Before we begin rehearsal, who can we find **to feed me my lines**?
>
> **TRANSLATION:** Before we begin rehearsal, who can we find **to tell me what words to say in case I forget**?
>
> **"REAL SPEAK":** B'fore we b'gin rehearsal, who c'n we fin' **da feed me my lines**?
>
> *Synonym:* **prompt (to)** *v.*

flick *n.* movie.

> **EXAMPLE:** Are there any good **flicks** playing tonight?

> **TRANSLATION:** Are there any good **movies** playing tonight?
>
> **"REAL SPEAK":** Are there any good **flicks** playing danight?
>
> *Note:* **chick flick** *exp.* (*chick* is slang for "girl") a movie with emotional moments considered, by some, only appropriate for girls.

green room *exp.* a space in a theater or studio (which historically was painted green) where guest performers can relax when they are not performing.

> **EXAMPLE:** Please relax in our **green room** and I'll call you when it's time for you to go on camera.
>
> **TRANSLATION:** Please relax in our **performers' waiting room** and I'll call you when it's time for you to go on camera.

> **"REAL SPEAK":** Please relax 'n 'ar **green room** an' a'll call ya when it's time fer ya da go on cam'ra.

headliner *n.* a performer or act that is the main attraction on a program.

> **EXAMPLE:** Before the **headliner** comes out on stage, there will be some opening acts first.
>
> **TRANSLATION:** Before the **main attraction** comes out on stage, there will be some opening acts first.
>
> **"REAL SPEAK":** B'fore the **headliner** comes oud on stage, there'll be s'm opening acks first.

moviegoer *n.* a person who goes to see a film in a theater.

> **EXAMPLE:** **Moviegoers** spend more money on food and drinks than they do on the actual movie!
>
> **TRANSLATION:** **People who go to movie theaters** spend more money on food and drinks than they do on the actual movie!
>
> **"REAL SPEAK":** **Moviegoers** spen' more money on food 'n drinks th'n they do on the actual movie!

nosebleed section *exp.* the back seats in a public arena that are farthest from the front row and typically highest in elevation.

> **EXAMPLE:** I could only afford the seats in the **nosebleed section**, so I brought binoculars.
>
> **TRANSLATION:** I could only afford the seats in the **highest section**, so I brought binoculars.
>
> **"REAL SPEAK":** I could only afford the seats 'n the **nosebleed section**, so I brought binoculers.

on demand *exp.* a service where customers can watch any TV show or movie whenever they want.

> **EXAMPLE:** I'm bored tonight. Why don't we watch a good movie **on demand**?
>
> **TRANSLATION:** I'm bored tonight. Why don't we watch a good movie **of our choice on TV**?
>
> **"REAL SPEAK":** I'm bored tanight. Why don' we watch a good movie **on demand**?

one-liner *exp.* a short joke or funny remark.

   EXAMPLE: I thought the movie last night was terrible! It was just **one-liner** after another without any storyline.

   TRANSLATION: I thought the movie last night was terrible! It was just **short joke** after another without any storyline.

   "REAL SPEAK": I thought the movie las' night w'z terr'ble! It w'z jus' **one-liner** after another withoud any storyline.

run the show (to) *exp.* to be in charge.

   EXAMPLE: If you have a complaint about your purchase, you need to speak with the manager. She's the one who **runs the show** here.

   TRANSLATION: If you have a complaint about your purchase, you need to speak with the manager. She's the one who **is in charge** here.

   "REAL SPEAK": If ya have a complain' about cher purchase, ya need da speak w'th the manager. She's the one 'oo **runs the show** here.

show business *exp.* the entertainment industry (which includes theater, movies, television, and pop music).

   EXAMPLE: I love being in **show business**! It's always exciting and you get to meet celebrities!

   TRANSLATION: I love being in **the entertainment industry**! It's always exciting and you get to meet celebrities!

   "REAL SPEAK": I love bein' 'n **show business**! It's ahways exciding an' ya get ta meet celebridies!

   Variation 1: **show biz** *exp.*

   Variation 2: **that business we call 'show'** *exp.*

   Also: **"That's show biz!"** *exp.* said in response to a disappointment:
—My favorite news reporter got replaced yesterday!
—Well, **that's show biz**!

showstopper *n.* an act, song, or performer that gets such long applause, the show is temporarily interrupted.

   EXAMPLE: When Ralph started playing the piano, it was a real **showstopper**!

   TRANSLATION: When Ralph started playing the piano, it was really **an amazing moment that got the longest applause**!

   "REAL SPEAK": When Ralph starded playing the piano, it w'z a real **showstopper**!

shtick *n. (from Yiddish)* a routine, joke or physical comedy often overused.

   EXAMPLE: Every time the actor walked on stage, he fell. It was funny the first few times, then I got tired of the same old **shtick**.

   TRANSLATION: Every time the actor walked on stage, he fell. It was funny the first few times, then I got tired of the same old **comedic routine**.

   "REAL SPEAK": Ev'ry time the acter walked on stage, he fell. It w'z funny the firs' few times, then I got tired 'a the same ol' **shtick**.

sideshow *n.* a small show in addition to the main entertainment (usually at a circus or fair).

   EXAMPLE: During my lecture, Greg was putting on his own **sideshow** trying to get people to buy some books he just wrote.

   TRANSLATION: During my lecture, Greg was putting on his own **small show** trying to get people to buy some books he just wrote.

   "REAL SPEAK": During my lecture, Greg w'z pudding on 'is own **sideshow** tryin' da get people da buy s'm books 'e wrote.

sing a different tune (to) *exp.* to change one's attitude and behavior.

> **EXAMPLE:** Steve sometimes drives when he's drunk and thinks it's funny! Some day he's going to get arrested for it. Then he'll **sing a different tune**.
>
> **TRANSLATION:** Steve sometimes drives when he's drunk and thinks it's funny! Some day he's going to get arrested for it. Then he'll **change his behavior**.
>
> **"REAL SPEAK":** Steve sometimes drives when 'e's drunk an' thinks it's funny! Some day 'e's gonna ged arrested for it. Then 'e'll **sing a diff'rent tune**.

slapstick *adj.* a type of physical acting in which the actors behave in a silly way, such as by throwing things, getting a pie in the face, falling over, etc.

> **EXAMPLE:** Jim Carrey is one of the best **slapstick** comedians of our time!

> **TRANSLATION:** Jim Carrey is one of the best **physically humorous acting** comedians of our time!
>
> **"REAL SPEAK":** Jim Carrey's one 'a the bes' **slapstick** comedians 'ev 'ar time!

slow-mo *exp.* (short for *slow motion*) an effect in film-making where time appears to be slowed down.

> **EXAMPLE:** I love when they use **slow-mo** in car crash scenes! Then you can see every little detail of what's happening!
>
> **TRANSLATION:** I love when they use **the slow motion effect** in car crash scenes! Then you can see every little detail of what's happening!

> **"REAL SPEAK":** I love wh'n they use **slow-mo** 'n car crash scenes! Then ya c'n see ev'ry liddle detail 'ev what's happening!

stand-up comedy *exp.* a comic style where a comedian performs in front of a live audience, speaking directly to them.

> **EXAMPLE:** I love watching **stand-up comedy**, as long as I'm not chosen to go up on stage!
>
> **TRANSLATION:** I love watching **comedians speak directly to the audience**, as long as I'm not chosen to go up on stage!
>
> **"REAL SPEAK":** I love watching **stand-up comedy**, as long `'ez` I'm not chosen da go up on stage!
>
> *Variation:* **stand-up (to do)** *exp.* to perform by speaking directly to an audience.

star-studded event *exp.* a big celebration where there are several celebrities.

> **EXAMPLE:** The Academy Awards is always a **star-studded event**!
>
> **TRANSLATION:** The Academy Awards is always **a celebration with several celebrities**!
>
> **"REAL SPEAK":** The Academy Awards 'ez ahways a **star-studded event**!

steal the show (to) *exp.* to be the best performer in a show.

> **EXAMPLE:** All the performers were fantastic, but no one **stole the show** like Tina!
>
> **TRANSLATION:** All the performers were fantastic, but no one **was as good as** Tina!
>
> **"REAL SPEAK":** All the performers were fantastic, b't no w'n **stole the show** like Tina!

street performer *exp.* a performer who demonstrates his/her talents in public places for tips.

> **EXAMPLE:** I love going to the Third Street Promenade in Santa Monica and watching all the **street performers**!
>
> **TRANSLATION:** I love going to the Third Street Promenade in Santa Monica and watching all the **performers who demonstrate their talents for tips**!

"REAL SPEAK": I love going da the Third Street Promenade 'n San'a Monica 'n watching all the **street performers**!

"The show must go on!" *exp.* a popular phrase in live entertainment meaning that regardless of what happens, the show must continue for the good of the audience.

EXAMPLE: The star of our show broke her leg! But **the show must go on**! I'll play her part instead.

TRANSLATION: The star of our show broke her leg! But **the show must continue**! I'll play her part instead.

"REAL SPEAK": The star 'ev 'are show broke 'er leg! B't **the show mus' go on**! A'll play 'er pard 'nstead.

Note: This phrase is also used outside the entertainment industry: *The bakery forgot to make the cake for Steve's birthday and his party starts in thirty minutes! Well, **the show must go on**! I'll run to the market and get some ice cream.*

tough act to follow (to be a) *exp.* said of a performer, or speaker, who is so impressive, it is not likely that the next person will be as remarkable.

EXAMPLE: What an amazing musician! Ed's going **to be a tough act to follow**! I've never seen anyone play the trumpet like him before!

TRANSLATION: What an amazing musician! **It's going to be difficult for anyone to be as impressive as Ed**! I've never seen anyone play the trumpet like him before!

"REAL SPEAK": Whad 'n amazing musician! Ed's gonna **be a tough ac' ta follow**! I've never seen anyone play the trumpet like him before!

Variation: **hard act to follow (to be a)** *exp.*

Note: This expression is commonly used by a speaker who must talk right after someone who has just made an emotional and powerful speech.

understudy *n. (from the theater)* a person who learns another actor's role in order to be able to act as a replacement with short notice.

EXAMPLE: Ladies and gentlemen… the star of our show is sick, so his role will be played by his **understudy**.

TRANSLATION: Ladies and gentlemen… the star of our show is sick, so his role will be played by his **replacement**.

"REAL SPEAK": Ladies 'n gen'lemen… the star 'ev 'ar show 'ez sick, so 'is role'll be played by 'is **understudy**.

upstage someone (to) *exp. (from the theater)* to unintentionally take people's attention away from someone and redirect it to oneself.

EXAMPLE: Every time Jack and Irene go to a dinner party, Jack **upstages** her because of his big personality.

TRANSLATION: Every time Jack and Irene to a dinner party, Jack **unintentionally takes the attention away from** her because of his big personality.

"REAL SPEAK": Ev'ry time Jack 'n Irene go do a dinner pardy, Jack **upstages** 'er b'cuz of 'is big personalidy.

wait in the wings (to) *exp. (from the theater)* to wait on one of the sides of the stage unseen by the audience.

EXAMPLE: Wait here **in the wings** until you  see the flash of light. At that moment, you guys need to run on stage.

TRANSLATION: Wait here **in the wings** until you see the flash of light. At that moment, you need to run on stage.

"REAL SPEAK": Wait here **'n the wings** until ya see the flash 'ev light. At that moment, ya need da run on stage.

TOP 30 MOVIE QUOTES USED IN CONVERSATIONS

1. **"Bond. James Bond."**
   Dr. No, 1962

2. **"Elementary, my dear Watson."**
   The *Adventures of Sherlock Holmes,* 1929

3. **"Fasten your seatbelts. It's going to be a bumpy night."**
   All About Eve, 1950

4. **"Frankly, my dear, I don't give a damn."**
   Gone With the Wind, 1939

5. **"Go ahead. Make my day."**
   Sudden Impact, 1983

6. **"Hasta la vista, baby."**
   Terminator 2: Judgment Day, 1991

7. **"Hello, gorgeous."**
   Funny Girl, 1968

8. **"Here's looking at you, kid."**
   Casablanca, 1942

9. **"Houston, we have a problem."**
   Apollo 13, 1995

10. **"I'll be back."**
    The Terminator, 1984

11. **"I'll have what she's having."**
    When Harry Met Sally, 1989

12. **"I'm as mad as hell, and I'm not going to take this anymore!"**
    Network, 1976

13. **"I'm going to make him an offer he can't refuse."**
    The Godfather, 1972

14. **"I'm king of the world!"**
    Titanic, 1997

15. **"I'm ready for my close-up, Mr. DeMille."**
    Sunset Boulevard, 1950

16. **"I'm walking here! I'm walking here!"**
    Midnight Cowboy, 1969

17. **"It's alive! It's alive!"**
    Frankenstein, 1931

18. **"Keep your friends close, but your enemies closer."**
    The Godfather II, 1974

19. **"May the Force be with you."**
    Star Wars, 1977

20. **"My precious."**
    The Lord of the Rings: Two Towers, 2002

21. **"Show me the money!"**
    Jerry Maguire, 1996

22. **"Stella! Hey, Stella!"**
    A Streetcar Named Desire, 1951

23. **"There's no place like home."**
    The Wizard of Oz, 1939

24. **"They're here!"**
    Poltergeist, 1982

25. **"Tomorrow is another day!"**
    Gone With the Wind, 1939

26. **"Toto, I've got a feeling we're not in Kansas anymore."**
    The Wizard of Oz, 1939

27. **"What we've got here is failure to communicate."**
    Cool Hand Luke, 1967

28. **"You can't handle the truth!"**
    A Few Good Men, 1992

29. **"You had me at 'hello.'"**
    Jerry Maguire, 1996

30. **"You've got to ask yourself one question: 'Do I feel lucky?' Well, do ya, punk?"**
    Dirty Harry, 1971

slangman
Explains More
idioms & slang for...

—AT THE MOVIES—

SCAN ME!

CHAPTER 3

SCAN THE QR CODE OR GO TO: bit.ly/StreetSpeak1-Chapter3

THIS VIDEO EPISODE CONTAINS...

in'erview
- When the letters **nt** become **n'** in the middle of a word
  - *Ya godda a job **in'erview** tomorrow?*

news
- Typical slang and idioms used in news broadcasts

'ez
- When **'ez** means *as*, **has** or **is**
  - I'll go with you **as** long **as** you let me drive. = *I'll go with you **'ez** long **'ez** you et me drive.*
  - That homework **has** taken me all day to finish! = *That homework **'ez** taken me all day to finish!*
  - Steve **is** my best friend. = *Steve **'ez** my best friend.*

you guys
  - **Y'all** are about to learn the different ways to say "you" (in the plural form) around the U.S.

Idioms & slang used on TV this week plus the latest Teen Slang!
  - Slangman gives you his TOP 5 LIST of the latest idioms and slang from the most popular TV shows in the U.S. plus the newest slang teens are using today!

Newest American slang just entered into the dictionary

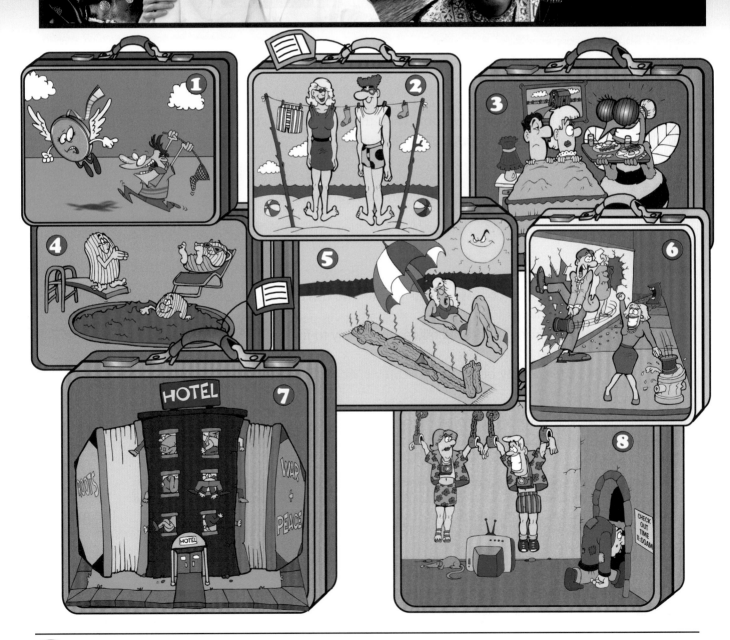

LET'S WARM UP!

MATCH THE PICTURES *(Answers on p. 216)*

As a fun way to get started, see if you can guess the meaning of the idioms and slang words in red by reading each sentence below along with its corresponding numbered illustration.

1. Let's go to dinner tonight then *catch a movie*.
   - ❏ go to the movies
   - ❏ act in a movie

2. After working hard all week, it's nice to go to the beach and *hang out*.
   - ❏ play baseball
   - ❏ relax and do nothing

3. Instead of a hotel, let's stay in a *B and B*.
   - ❏ hotel with bed and breakfast
   - ❏ hotel with bath and beverage

4. Let's go to the pool and *take a dip*.
   - ❏ watch television
   - ❏ go swimming

5. You're so tan! Have you been *soaking up some sun* today?
   - ❏ staying inside
   - ❏ sunbathing

6. Let's *hit the town* and go shopping.
   - ❏ leave town
   - ❏ go into town

7. The hotel didn't have any rooms left. They were *booked solid*.
   - ❏ not yet cleaned
   - ❏ completely filled

8. I hope we can find a hotel *to put us up* for the night.
   - ❏ to lend us money
   - ❏ to accommodate us

9. In New York, you can either take the subway or *grab a cab* anywhere.
   - ❏ jump in front of a taxicab
   - ❏ take a taxicab

10. I'm tired because last night I *stayed up till all hours of the night*.
    - ❏ went to bed early
    - ❏ stayed awake until very late

11. I went *sightseeing* today. What a beautiful city!
    - ❏ visiting some interesting places
    - ❏ exercising

12. I usually get up early, but tomorrow I'm *sleeping in*.
    - ❏ getting up extra early
    - ❏ sleeping later than usual

LET'S TALK!

A. DIALOGUE USING SLANG & IDIOMS

The words introduced on the previous two pages are used in the following dialogue and illustrated in the long picture above. Can you understand the conversation and find the illustration that corresponds to the slang? *Note*: The translation of the words in boldface is on the right-hand page.

— *Chris and Marie are on vacation* —

Chris: It's a good thing this **B and B** was able to **put us up** for the night. All the hotels in town were **booked solid**.

Marie: So, what should we do now? Hey, I have an idea. Tonight, let's **grab a cab** and **hit the town**. Maybe we can go **sightseeing** before dinner!

Chris: And since we're on vacation, we can **stay up till all hours of the night** and **sleep in** tomorrow.

Marie: Great! Then in the afternoon, we can **take a dip** and **hang out** by the pool. It'll be nice to **soak up some sun**.

Chris: And tomorrow night, we could **catch a movie**!

LET'S TALK!

B. DIALOGUE TRANSLATED INTO STANDARD ENGLISH

LET'S SEE HOW MUCH YOU REMEMBER!
Just for fun, bounce around in random order to the words and expressions in boldface below. See if you can remember their slang equivalents without looking at the left-hand page!

— *Chris and Marie are on vacation* —

Chris: It's a good thing this **hotel offering bed and breakfast** was able to **lodge us** for the night. All the hotels in town were **completely filled**.

Marie: So, what should we do now? Hey, I have an idea. Tonight, let's **take a taxicab** and **go into town**. Maybe we can go **visit the interesting places** before dinner!

Chris: And since we're on vacation, we can **stay awake until very late** and **sleep later than usual** tomorrow.

Marie: Great! Then in the afternoon, we can **go swimming** and **relax and do nothing** by the pool. It'll be nice to **sunbathe**.

Chris: And tomorrow night, we could **go to the movies**!

C. DIALOGUE USING "REAL SPEAK"

The dialogue below demonstrates how the slang conversation on the previous page would *really* be spoken by native speakers!

— Chris 'n Marie 'er on vacation —

Chris: It's a good thing th's **B 'n B** w'z able da **pud us up** fer the night. All the hotels 'n town were **booked solid**.

Marie: So, what shu'we do now? Hey, I have 'n idea. Tanight, let's **grab a cab** 'n **hit the town**. Maybe we c'n go **sightseeing** b'fore dinner!

Chris: An' since w'r on vacation, we c'n **stay up till all hours 'a the night** 'n **sleep in** tamorrow.

Marie: Great! Then in the afternoon, we c'n **take a dip** 'n **hang out** by the pool. Id'll be nice ta **soak up s'm sun**.

Chris: An' tamorrow night, we could **catch a movie**!

KEY TO REAL SPEAK

AND • AN • IN = 'N

Since "an," "and," and "in" are all reduced to **'n**, it can get a little confusing. That's why context is so important, as seen below.

RULES

In everyday conversation, when "and" is used to connect two words, it is often pronounced **'n**. To add confusion, "an" and "in" are also reduced to **'n** when followed by another word. So, how do you know when the speaker means "and," "an" or "in" since they are all pronounced the same? It all depends on the context.

HOW DOES IT WORK?

STANDARD ENGLISH	"REAL SPEAK"
and ⟶ **'n** At the zoo, I saw lions **and** tigers **and** bears.	At the zoo, I saw lions **'n** tigers **'n** bears.
and ⟶ **'n** At the zoo, I saw lions **and** tigers **and** bears.	At the zoo, I saw lions **'n** tigers **'n** bears.
in ⟶ **'n** Let's go **in** the house before it starts raining.	Let's go **'n** the house before it starts raining.
Chris **and** Karen bought **an** apartment building **in** France.	Chris **'n** Karen bought **'n** apartment building **'n** France.

BUT!

If there is a pause before **and**, it is commonly reduced to **an'** instead of **'n**. For example:

Today I'm visiting my mother **in** California...**and** tomorrow, I'm visiting my brother in New York!
Today I'm visiting my mother **'n** California...**an'** tomorrow, I'm visiting my brother **'n** New York!

LET'S USE "REAL SPEAK!"

A. PUT THE PAIRS BACK TOGETHER

Below are some common pairs of words that are often connected by **and**. Find the missing piece on the right that completes the pair on the left. Make sure to pronounce **and** in real speak as **'n**.

(Answers on p. 216)

SPEAKING

TRACK 26
SOUNDCLOUD

1.	king and — queen
2.	in and
3.	up and
4.	left and
5.	knife and
6.	salt and
7.	bread and
8.	good and
9.	peanut butter and
10.	black and
11.	top and
12.	hot and
13.	night and
14.	give and
15.	father and
16.	sister and
17.	husband and
18.	shoes and
19.	eyes and
20.	right and
21.	bacon and
22.	cats and

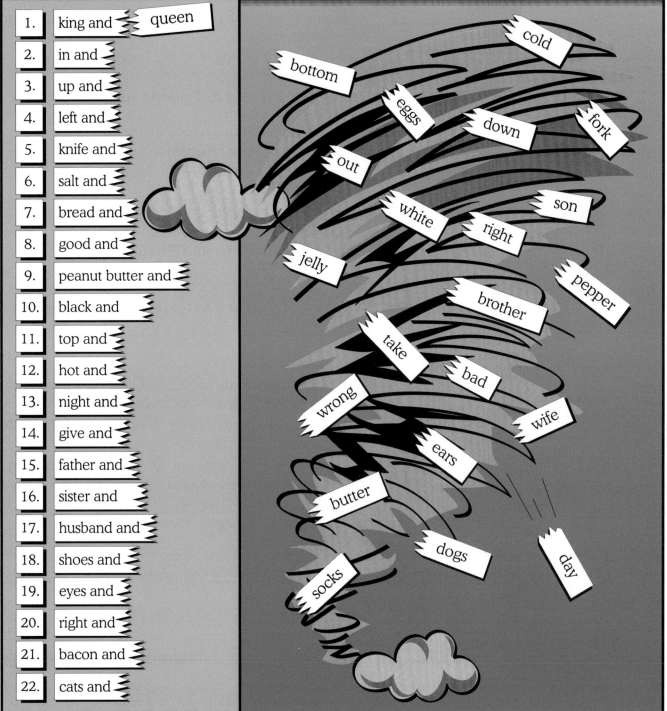

cold
bottom
eggs
down
fork
out
white
right
son
jelly
pepper
brother
take
bad
wrong
wife
ears
butter
dogs
day
socks

LET'S LEARN!

TRACK 27
SOUNDCLOUD

VOCABULARY

The following words and expressions were used in the previous dialogues. Let's take a closer look at what they mean.

B and B *n.* (an abbreviation for "bed and breakfast") generally a home converted into a hotel which offers guests a room for the night including breakfast.

> **EXAMPLE:** We stayed in a charming **B and B** in London last summer.
>
> **TRANSLATION:** We stayed in a charming **bed and breakfast** in London last summer.
>
> **"REAL SPEAK":** We stayed 'n a charming **B 'n B** 'n London las' summer.
>
> **NOW YOU DO IT. COMPLETE THE PHRASE ALOUD:**
> *If I owned a B and B, I would name it...*

booked solid (to be) *exp.* to be completely full, to have no more space available (said of a hotel, cruise ship, airplane, etc. that requires a reservation).

> **EXAMPLE:** I wanted to stay at the famous Ritz Hotel in Paris, but it was **booked solid**.
>
> **TRANSLATION:** I wanted to stay at the famous Ritz Hotel in Paris, but it was **completely full**.
>
> **"REAL SPEAK":** I wan'ed ta stay 'it the famous Ritz Hotel 'n Paris, bud it w'z **booked solid**.
>
> **NOW YOU DO IT. COMPLETE THE PHRASE ALOUD:**
> *I wanted to stay in a hotel in... but it was booked solid.*

catch a movie (to) *exp.* to go to the movies.

> **EXAMPLE:** It's been raining all day long. Well, since we can't do anything outside, do you want to **catch a movie**?
>
> **TRANSLATION:** It's been raining all day long. Well, since we can't do anything outside, do you want to **go to the movies**?
>
> **"REAL SPEAK":** It's been raining all day long. Well, since we can't do anything outside, wanna **catch a movie**?
>
> **NOW YOU DO IT. COMPLETE THE PHRASE ALOUD:**
> *The last time I caught a movie, I saw...*

grab a cab (to) *exp.* to take a taxi.

> **EXAMPLE:** Instead of trying to find parking, let's just **grab a cab** and go out to dinner.
>
> **TRANSLATION:** Instead of trying to find parking, let's just **take a taxi** and go out to dinner.
>
> **"REAL SPEAK":** Instead 'a trying da fin' parking, let's jus' **grab a cab** 'n go out ta dinner.
>
> **NOW YOU DO IT. COMPLETE THE PHRASE ALOUD:**
> *It's best to grab a cab to go from .... to ...*

hang out (to) *phrV.* to relax and do nothing.

EXAMPLE: I'm going to **hang out** by the pool with Debbie today. Do you want to join us?

TRANSLATION: I'm going to **relax and do nothing** by the pool with Debbie today. Do you want to join us?

"REAL SPEAK": I'm gonna **hang out** by the pool with Debbie daday. Wanna join us?

NOW YOU DO IT. COMPLETE THE PHRASE ALOUD:
I usually hang out at...

hit the town (to) *exp.* to go where all the attractions are (usually for a night of fun, dining, dancing, movies, etc.).

EXAMPLE: I'm bored tonight. I have an idea! Let's **hit the town** and go out to dinner and a movie!

TRANSLATION: I'm bored tonight. I have an idea! Let's **go into the main part of town** and go out to dinner and a movie!

"REAL SPEAK": I'm bored tanight. I have 'n idea! Let's **hit the town** 'n go out ta dinner 'n a movie!

NOW YOU DO IT. COMPLETE THE PHRASE ALOUD:
I like to hit the town and...

put up for the night (to) *exp.* to give someone a place to stay for the night.

EXAMPLE: We won't have to pay for a hotel when we go to Los Angeles. I have some friends there who can **put us up for the night**.

TRANSLATION: We won't have to pay for a hotel when we go to Los Angeles. I have some friends there who can **give us a place to stay for the night**.

"REAL SPEAK": We won't hafta pay fer a hotel when we go da L.A. I have s'm frenz there who c'n **pud us up fer the night**.

NOW YOU DO IT. COMPLETE THE PHRASE ALOUD:
When I go to ...'s house, he/she always puts me up for the night.

sightseeing (to go) *exp.* to go look at the attractions and interesting sights.

EXAMPLE: This is my first time in Rome. I can't wait **to go sightseeing**!

TRANSLATION: This is my first time in Rome. I can't wait **to go look at the attractions and interesting sights**!

"REAL SPEAK": This is my firs' time 'n Rome. I can't wait **ta go sightseeing**!

Variation: **sightsee (to)** *v.*

NOW YOU DO IT. COMPLETE THE PHRASE ALOUD:
I like going sightseeing in ...

sleep in (to) *phrV.* to sleep later than usual.

EXAMPLE: Everyday, I wake up at six o'clock in the morning. But next week when I'm on vacation, I'm going to **sleep in**!

TRANSLATION: Everyday, I wake up at six o'clock in the morning. But next week when I'm on vacation, I'm going to **sleep later than usual**!

"REAL SPEAK": Ev'ryday, I wake up 'it six a'clock 'n the morning. B't next week when I'm on vacation, I'm gonna **sleep in**!

NOW YOU DO IT. COMPLETE THE PHRASE ALOUD:
I like to sleep in until...

soak up some sun (to) *exp.* to sunbathe.

EXAMPLE: I'm going to Hawaii tomorrow! I'm not going to do anything but **soak up some sun** and relax!

TRANSLATION: I'm going to Hawaii tomorrow! I'm not going to do anything but **sunbathe** and relax!

"REAL SPEAK": I'm going da Hawaii damorrow! I'm not gonna do anything b't **soak up s'm sun** 'n relax!

Variation: **soak up some rays (to)** *exp.*

Synonym: **catch some rays (to)** *exp.*

NOW YOU DO IT. COMPLETE THE PHRASE ALOUD:
...is a great place to soak up some sun!

stay up till all hours of the night (to) *exp.* to stay up all night long (having a good time, studying, watching television, etc.).

EXAMPLE: The party went on for hours! We **stayed up till all hours of the night** dancing!

TRANSLATION: The party went on for hours! We **stayed up all night** dancing!

"REAL SPEAK": The pardy wen' on fer hours! We **stayed up till all hours 'a the night** dancing!

NOW YOU DO IT. COMPLETE THE PHRASE ALOUD:
I stayed up till all hours of the night doing...

take a dip (to) *exp.* to go swimming.

EXAMPLE: It's such a beautiful warm day today. I think I'll **take a dip**.

TRANSLATION: It's such a beautiful warm day today. I think I'll **go swimming**.

"REAL SPEAK": It's such a beaudif'l warm day daday. I think ah'll **take a dip**.

Synonym: **go for a swim (to)** *exp.*

NOW YOU DO IT. COMPLETE THE PHRASE ALOUD:
Last summer I took a dip when I went to...

LET'S PRACTICE!

TRACK 28
SOUNDCLOUD

A. FIND THE MISSING WORDS *(Answers on p. 216)*

Complete the dialogue by filling in the blanks with the correct word(s) using the list below.

put us up	town	hang out
B&B	sightseeing	soak up
solid	sleep	catch
grab	dip	hours of the night

Tom: This _____ has so much more charm than the hotel we stayed at last night.

Becky: It's a good thing they were able to _____ for the night. It was the only vacancy in the entire city! All the other places were booked _____ .

Tom: We really got lucky. It's so quiet here. It was hard to _____ in at the other hotel because of all the noise. So, what do you want to do tonight?

Becky: Let's go hit the _____!

Tom: Good idea. We could go _____ a movie.

Becky: Actually, I thought it would be fun to go _____ and explore a little. We could _____ a cab and be there in a few minutes.

Tom: After we visit the sights, we could get something to eat at that great restaurant around the corner and then go dancing till all _____.

Becky: That's perfect! Then tomorrow we can relax all day. It would be so nice to wake up late then _____ by the pool and _____ some sun. We could even take a _____ if it's gets too hot!

B. MATCH THE SENTENCES *(Answers on p. 216)*

Match the numbered sentences below with the lettered sentences on the opposite page. Write your answers in the boxes at the bottom of the pages.

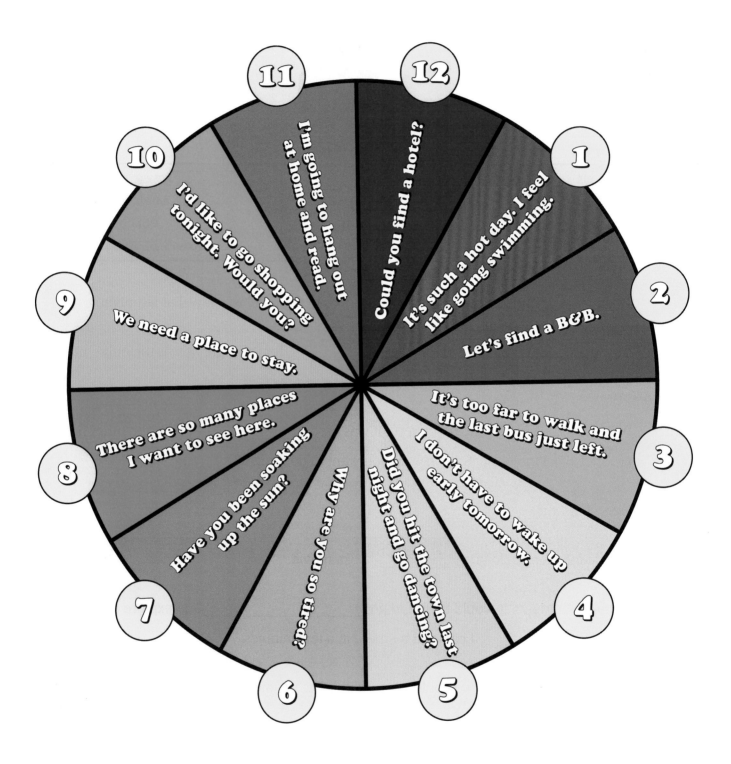

NUMBERS	1	2	3	4	5	6
LETTERS						

B. MATCH THE SENTENCES - *(continued)*

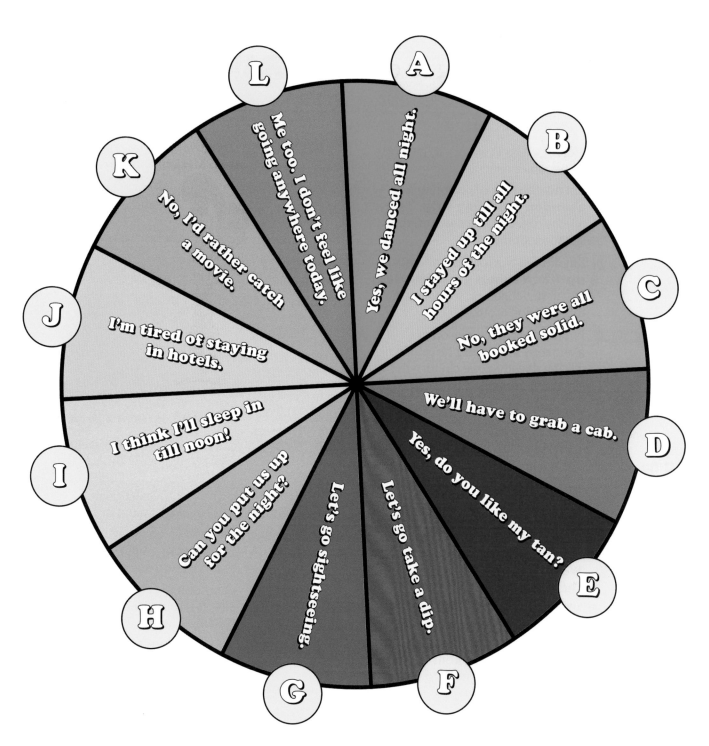

Wheel sentences (clockwise from A):

- **A** — Yes, we danced all night.
- **B** — I stayed up till all hours of the night.
- **C** — No, they were all booked solid.
- **D** — We'll have to grab a cab.
- **E** — Yes, do you like my tan?
- **F** — Let's go take a dip.
- **G** — Let's go sightseeing.
- **H** — Can you put us up for the night?
- **I** — I think I'll sleep in till noon!
- **J** — I'm tired of staying in hotels.
- **K** — No, I'd rather catch a movie.
- **L** — Me too. I don't feel like going anywhere today.

NUMBERS	7	8	9	10	11	12
LETTERS						

THE SLANGMAN FILES

TRACK 30
SOUNDCLOUD

EXERCISES FOR THIS SECTION ARE IN THE WORKBOOK.

Popular Idioms, Slang & Jargon
Having to do with: TRAVEL

abandon a sinking ship (to) *exp.* to give up when something becomes difficult.

> EXAMPLE: I'm not the type of person to **abandon a sinking ship**. If we all stay together, we can turn this situation around!

> TRANSLATION: I'm not the type of person to **give up when things get difficult**. If we all stay together, we can turn this situation around!

> "REAL SPEAK": I'm not the type 'a person ta **abandon a sinking ship**. If we all stay dagether, we c'n turn th's situation around!

> *Synonym 1:* **desert a sinking ship (to)** *exp.*

> *Synonym 2:* **jump ship (to)** *exp.*

all hands on deck (to need) *exp.* to need everyone's help in a particular situation • (lit); a nautical expression meaning for all members of a ship's crew to come to the deck, usually in a time of crisis • *Note:* **hands** is slang for a "ship's crew" or "workers in general."

> EXAMPLE: **We need all hands on deck!** The boss is coming back from vacation in an hour and we need to get this place clean!

> TRANSLATION: **We need everyone's help!** The boss is coming back from vacation in an hour and we need to get this place clean!

> "REAL SPEAK": **We need all hanz on deck!** The boss 'ez coming back fr'm vacation in 'n hour 'n we need da get this place clean!

"Bon voyage!" *exp.* "Have a good trip!" • (lit); a popular French phrase used in the U.S. meaning "Good trip!"

> EXAMPLE: Goodbye! Bring us something back from Mexico! **Bon voyage!**

> TRANSLATION: Goodbye! Bring us something back from Mexico! **Have a good trip!**

> "REAL SPEAK": Goodbye! Bring 'es something back fr'm Mexico! **Bon voyage!**

boondocks *n.* far away in an isolated area • (lit); *(from Filipino/Tagalog)* mountains.

> EXAMPLE: Our hotel is so far away from the city. We're really in the **boondocks!**

> TRANSLATION: Our hotel is so far away from the city. We're really in the **most isolated area!**

> "REAL SPEAK": 'Ar hotel's so far away fr'm the cidy. W'r really 'n the **boondocks!**

> *Variation:* **boonies** *exp. See:* **way out in the boondocks**, p. 93.

carsick (to get) *adj.* to suffer from nausea caused by the motion of a car.

> EXAMPLE: If we're driving far, I need to sit in the front or I'll **get carsick.**

> TRANSLATION: If we're driving far, I need to sit in the front or I'll **get nauseated.**

"REAL SPEAK": If w'r driving far, I need da sit 'n the fron' 'r a'll **get carsick**.

clear sailing ahead (to be) *exp.* said of a situation that no longer has any obstacles.

EXAMPLE: After years of trying to get a permit to rebuild my home, I finally got it! Now **it's clear sailing ahead**!

SS SLANGMAN

TRANSLATION: After years of trying to get a permit to rebuild my home, I finally got it! Now **everything can move forward without any obstacles**!

"REAL SPEAK": After years 'ev trying da ged a permit ta rebuild my home, I fin'lly got it! Now **it's clear sailing ahead**!

"Full steam ahead!" *exp.* "Proceed with as much speed and enthusiasm as possible!" • (lit); a nautical term meaning "Let's use all the steam we have in the engine to move forward!"

EXAMPLE: Now that we have all decided on the best way to get the job done, let's do it! **Full steam ahead**!

TRANSLATION: Now that we have all decided on the best way to get the job done, let's do it! **Let's proceed with as much enthusiasm as possible**!

"REAL SPEAK": Now th't we've all decided on the best way da get the job done, let's do it! **Full steam ahead**!

getaway *n.* vacation.

EXAMPLE: We have a little cabin in the mountains. It's the perfect family **getaway**!

TRANSLATION: We have a little cabin in the mountains. It's the perfect family **vacation**!

"REAL SPEAK": We have a liddle cabin in the mount'ns. It's the perfect fam'ly **gedaway**!

get going (to) *exp.* to leave.

EXAMPLE: We need **to get going** or we're going to be late for the tour bus!

TRANSLATION: We need **to leave** or we're going to be late for the tour bus!

"REAL SPEAK": We need **da get going** 'r w'r gonna be late fer the tour bus!

go down with the ship (to) *exp.* to do everything one can to rectify a bad situation, even at great personal sacrifice • (lit); a maritime tradition that a sea captain holds ultimate responsibility for both his ship and everyone on it, and that in an emergency, he will either save them or die trying.

EXAMPLE: I'm going to do everything I can to make sure my company makes a profit or **go down with the ship** trying!

TRANSLATION: I'm going to do everything I can to make sure my company makes a profit or **die** trying!

"REAL SPEAK": I'm gonna do ev'rything I can da make sher my company makes a profit 'r **go down w'th the ship** trying!

in the same boat (to be) *exp.* to be in the same unfortunate situation as someone else.

EXAMPLE: Don't worry about not passing your driving test the first time. I was **in the same boat**. You just have to keep taking it until you pass!

TRANSLATION: Don't worry about not passing your driving test the first time. I was **in the same unfortunate situation**. You just have to keep taking it until you pass!

"REAL SPEAK": Don't worry about not passing yer driving test the firs' time. I w'z **'n the same boat**. Ya jus' hafta keep taking it 'til ya pass!

island hop (to) *exp.* to go from one island to another.

> **EXAMPLE:** I'm so excited about going to Hawaii! We're going **to island hop** and see every tourist attraction!
>
> **TRANSLATION:** I'm so excited about going to Hawaii! We're going **to go from island to island** and see every tourist attraction!
>
> **"REAL SPEAK":** I'm so excided about going da Hawaii! W'r gonna **island hop** 'n see ev'ry tourist attraction!

learn the ropes (to) *exp.* to learn how to do particular tasks • (lit); a nautical expression meaning "to learn how to use the ropes of the sails in order to control the ship."

> **EXAMPLE:** I know it's your first day at our company, but don't worry. I'll make sure you **learn the ropes**.
>
> **TRANSLATION:** I know it's your first day at our company, but don't worry. I'll make sure you **learn how to do all the important tasks**.
>
> **"REAL SPEAK":** I know it's yer firs' day 'id 'ar company, b't don't worry. A'll make sher ya **learn the ropes**.
>
> *Also:* **teach someone the ropes (to)** *exp.*

like two ships that pass in the night (to be) *exp.* said of people who meet for a brief but intense moment and then part, never to see each other again.

> **EXAMPLE:** I only had one other relationship before I married your father. It only lasted a few weeks. We were **like two ships that pass in the night**.
>
> **TRANSLATION:** I only had one other relationship before I married your father. It only lasted a few weeks. We were **two people who met for a brief but intense moment**.
>
> **"REAL SPEAK":** I only had one other relationship b'fore I married yer father. Id only lasded a few weeks. We were **like two ships th't pass 'n the night**.

live out of a suitcase (to) *exp.* to stay very briefly in several places without having the time to unpack one's suitcase.

> **EXAMPLE:** I'm so glad I'm not traveling for work anymore. I didn't like **living out of a suitcase**.

> **TRANSLATION:** I'm so glad I'm not traveling for work anymore. I didn't like **moving from one place to another without having the time to unpack my belongings**.
>
> **"REAL SPEAK":** I'm so glad I'm not trav'ling fer work anymore. I didn' like **living oudd'ev a suitcase**.

miss the boat (to) *exp.* to lose an opportunity to do something by being too slow to act.

> **EXAMPLE:** Steve just got the job I really wanted! I should have signed up to interview for it. I really **missed the boat**.
>
> **TRANSLATION:** Steve just got the job I really wanted! I should have signed up to interview for it. I really **missed an opportunity**.
>
> **"REAL SPEAK":** Steve jus' got the job I really wan'ed! I should've signed up ta in'erview for it. I really **missed the boat**.

Montezuma's revenge *exp.* diarrhea suffered by travelers, especially visitors to Mexico.

> **EXAMPLE:** If you're not used to it, some of the spicy food in Mexico might give you **Montezuma's revenge**!
>
> **TRANSLATION:** If you're not used to it, some of the spicy food in Mexico might give you **diarrhea**!

"REAL SPEAK": If y'r not used to it, some 'a the spicy food 'n Mexico might give ya **Mon'ezuma's revenge**!

Origin: The name humorously refers to Montezuma II, the ruler of the Aztec civilization who was defeated and killed by Hernán Cortés, the Spanish conquistador. Therefore, it is said that whenever a tourist gets diarrhea while visiting Mexico, it is caused by Montezuma's revenge.

off the beaten track (to be) *exp.* to be located away from the most popular areas of town.

EXAMPLE: Whenever I travel, I prefer staying in hotels that are **off the beaten track**. That way you can meet the locals instead of seeing so many tourists!

TRANSLATION: Whenever I travel, I prefer staying in hotels that are **located away from the most popular areas of town**. That way you can meet the locals instead of seeing so many tourists!

"REAL SPEAK": Whenever I travel, I prafer staying in hotels thad'er **off the beaten track**. That way you c'n meet the locals instead 'a seeing so many terists!

off the rails (to go) *exp.* to go out of control emotionally; insane • (lit); said of a train that derails and is out of control.

EXAMPLE: My mother **went off the rails** when I crashed her new car!

TRANSLATION: My mother **went out of control with anger** when I crashed her new car!

"REAL SPEAK": My mother **wen' off the rails** when I crashed 'er new car!

overboard (to go) *exp.* to do something in an extreme way • (lit); to go over the side of a ship or boat into the water.

EXAMPLE: You bought your new boyfriend a watch that cost $500?! Don't you think you **went overboard**? You don't know if your relationship is even going to last!

TRANSLATION: You bought your new boyfriend a watch that cost $500?! Don't you think you **were extreme**? You don't know if your relationship is even going to last!

"REAL SPEAK": Ya bought cher new boyfriend a watch th't cos' five hundred dollers?! Don'cha think ya **wen' overboard**? Ya don't know if yer relationship's even gonna last!

paid vacation *exp.* time away from work (for holiday, illness, etc.) during which your company pays you your normal salary.

EXAMPLE: I've been at this company for such a long time that I'm entitled to three months of **paid vacation**!

TRANSLATION: I've been at this company for such a long time that I'm entitled to three months of **time away from work and still get paid** !

"REAL SPEAK": I' been 'it th's company fer such a long time th'd I'm entidled da three munts've **paid vacation**!

Variation 1: **paid holiday** *exp.*

Variation 2: **vacation pay** *exp*

Synonym: **paid leave** *exp.*

Note: In British English, the word *holiday* is used in place of *vacation*.

rearrange the deckchairs on the Titanic (to) *exp.* to do something completely useless (because the entire situation is going to face a certain death anyway).

EXAMPLE: Why are you trying to fix your old car? It's like **rearranging the deckchairs on the Titanic**. You keep spending so much money on it and you know it's going to die soon!

TRANSLATION: Why are you trying to fix your old car? It's **completely useless**. You keep spending so much money on it and you know it's going to die soon!

"REAL SPEAK": Why'er ya try'n'a fix yer ol' car? It's like **rearranging the deckchairs on the Titanic**. Ya keep spending so much money on it an' ya know it's gonna die soon!

rock the boat (to) *exp.* to say or do something to disturb a situation that is currently stable.

EXAMPLE: Since you're asking for a raise tomorrow, don't criticize the boss about anything. You certainly don't want **to rock the boat** at this point!

TRANSLATION: Since you're asking for a raise tomorrow, don't criticize the boss about anything. You certainly don't want **to disturb a situation that's currently stable** at this point!

"REAL SPEAK": Since y'r asking fer a raise tamorrow, don' criticize the boss aboud anything. Ya certainly don't wanna **rock the boad** 'it this point!

run a tight ship (to) *exp.* to be very strict in managing an organization or operation.

EXAMPLE: My boss **runs a really tight ship**. If you're late coming back from lunch by even a minute, you'll get reprimanded!

TRANSLATION: My boss **is very strict**. If you're late coming back from lunch by even a minute, you'll get reprimanded!

"REAL SPEAK": My boss **runs a really tight ship**. If y'r late coming back fr'm lunch by even a minute, you'll get reprimanded!

sail through something (to) *exp.* to succeed very easily at something.

EXAMPLE: Usually the lines going through airport security take over an hour. Today I just **sailed through**!

TRANSLATION: Usually the lines going through airport security take over an hour. Today I just **went through very easily**!

"REAL SPEAK": Ujally the lines going through airport securidy take over 'n hour. Taday I jus' **sailed through**!

seasick (to be) *adj.* to suffer from nausea caused by the motion of a ship at sea.

EXAMPLE: If you feel **seasick** on the boat, just sip on a soft drink. It'll calm your stomach.

TRANSLATION: If you feel **seasick** on the boat, just sip on a carbonated beverage. It'll calm your stomach.

"REAL SPEAK": If ya feel **nauseaded** on the boat, jus' sip on a sof'drink. Id'll calm yer stomach.

Note: The term "soft drink" is used primarily in the west of the U.S. and is considered a regionalism which is a term or expression specific to a particular region and not part of the standard language of the country.

shipshape (to be) *adj.* to be very neat and have everything in its correct place.

EXAMPLE: The gardeners cleaned up right after they trimmed the trees. I was impressed they left everything **shipshape**!

TRANSLATION: The gardeners cleaned up right after they trimmed the trees. I was impressed they left everything **very neat and orderly**!

"REAL SPEAK": The gardeners cleaned up ride after they trimm' the trees. I w'z impressed they left ev'rything **shipshape**!

staycation (to take a) *exp.* (a combination of "stay" and "vacation") a vacation where one stays close to home.

EXAMPLE: Instead of the hassle and expense of traveling far away, could we just **take a staycation** and do some relaxing gardening?

TRANSLATION: Instead of the hassle and expense of traveling far away, could we just **take a vacation at home** and do some relaxing gardening?

"REAL SPEAK": Instead 'a the hassle 'n expense 'ev trav'ling far away, cu'we jus' **take a staycation** 'n do s'm relaxing gardening?

"That ship has sailed!" *exp.* used in reference to an opportunity that has passed or a situation that can no longer be changed.

EXAMPLE: You want to ask Heather out on a date? But you broke up with her a few months ago! I don't think she'd ever go out with you again. **That ship has sailed!**

TRANSLATION: You want to ask Heather out on a date? But you broke up with her a few months ago! I don't think she'd ever go out with you again. **That opportunity has passed!**

"REAL SPEAK": Ya wanna ask Heather oud on a date? B't ya broke up w'th 'er a few munts ago! I don' think she'd ever go out w'th you again. **That ship 'ez sailed!**

thumb a ride (to) *exp.* to hitchhike.

EXAMPLE: When I was younger, I went across the U.S. by **thumbing a ride!**

TRANSLATION: When I was younger, I went across the U.S. by **hitchhiking!**

"REAL SPEAK": Wh'n I w'z younger, I wen' across the U.S. by **thumbing a ride!**

time off *exp.* time away from work through vacation, illness, personal time, etc.

EXAMPLE: I'm taking **time off** from work next week to visit my family in Paris.

TRANSLATION: I'm taking **time away** from work for a week to visit my family in Paris.

"REAL SPEAK": I'm takin' **time off** fr'm work fer a week ta visit my fam'ly 'n Paris.

train of thought (to lose one's) *exp.* to forget what one was talking about.

EXAMPLE: Harold interrupts all the time. He makes me **lose my train of thought!**

TRANSLATION: Harold interrupts all the time. He makes me **forget what I was saying!**

"REAL SPEAK": Harold interrup's all the time. He makes me **lose my train 'ev thought!**

"Whatever floats your boat!" *exp.* "Do whatever makes you happy!"

EXAMPLE: You like jogging in the snow?! Well, **whatever floats your boat!**

TRANSLATION: You like jogging in the snow?! Well, **do whatever makes you happy!**

"REAL SPEAK": Ya like jogging 'n the snow?! Well, **whadever floats yer boat!**

"When in Rome!" *exp.* a shortened version of "When in Rome, do as the Romans do!" meaning "When visiting any foreign country, follow the customs of those who live in it."

EXAMPLE: This is my first time in Paris, so I want to try their national delicacy of snails in garlic and butter. **When in Rome!**

TRANSLATION: This is my first time in Paris, so I want to try their national delicacy of snails in garlic and butter. **When visiting a foreign country follow the customs of those who live in it!**

"REAL SPEAK": This 'ez my firs' time 'n Paris, so I wanna try their national delicacy 'ev snails 'n garlic 'n budder. **When 'n Rome!**

IDIOMS & SLANG FOR "RELAX"

chill (to) *v.* to relax and do nothing.

> **EXAMPLE:** I'm taking a trip to the mountains on Saturday. I can't wait to just **chill** for an entire week!
>
> **TRANSLATION:** I'm taking a trip to the mountains on Saturday. I can't wait to just **relax and do nothing** for an entire week!
>
> **"REAL SPEAK":** I'm taking a trip ta the mount'ns on Sadurday. I can't wait ta jus' **chill** fer 'n entire week!
>
> *Variation 1:* **chill out (to)** *phrV.*
>
> *Variation 2:* **chillax (to)** *v.* (teen slang) a combination of *chill* and *relax*.
>
> *Variation 3:* **take a chill pill (to)** *exp.*

de-stress (to) *v.* to relax by getting rid of one's stress.

> **EXAMPLE:** Taking the kids with us on a weekend trip is not the way to **de-stress**. I'll have my mother babysit!
>
> **TRANSLATION:** Taking the kids with us on a weekend trip is not the way to **relax**. I'll have my mother babysit!
>
> **"REAL SPEAK":** Takin' the kids with us on a weeken' trip isn't the way da **de-stress**. A'll have my mother babysit!

goof off (to) *phrV.* to play; to spend one's time doing nothing of importance.

> **EXAMPLE:** While we're on vacation, I don't want to think about work. I just want to **goof off**!
>
> **TRANSLATION:** While we're on vacation, I don't want to think about work. I just want to **play**!
>
> **"REAL SPEAK":** While w'r on vacation, I don't wanna think about work! I jus' wanna **goof off**!

hang out (to) *phrV.* to relax and do nothing in particular.

> **EXAMPLE:** Do you want to **hang out** at my house tonight? We can watch TV and eat popcorn!
>
> **TRANSLATION:** Do you want to **relax** at my house tonight? We can watch TV and eat popcorn!
>
> **"REAL SPEAK":** Ya wanna **hang out** 'it my house tanight? We c'n watch TV 'n eat popcorn!

kick back (to) *phrV.* to sit back and relax (by kicking one's feet up and putting them on something).

> **EXAMPLE:** Let's **kick back** and watch a movie tonight.
>
> **TRANSLATION:** Let's **sit back, relax,** and watch a movie tonight.
>
> **"REAL SPEAK":** Let's **kick back** 'n watch a movie danight.
>
> *Variation:* **kick it (to)** *phrV.*

loaf around (to) *phrV.* to do nothing of importance, to relax.

> **EXAMPLE:** I can't wait to **loaf around** after work!
>
> **TRANSLATION:** I can't wait to **relax and do nothing** after work!
>
> **"REAL SPEAK":** I can't wait ta **loaf around** afder work!

mellow out (to) *phrV.* to slow one's pace and relax.

> **EXAMPLE:** What a stressful day! I need to go home and **mellow out**.
>
> **TRANSLATION:** What a stressful day! I need to go home and **slow down and relax**.
>
> **"REAL SPEAK":** Whad a stressful day! I need da go home 'n **mellow out**.

put one's brain on hold (to) *exp.* to stop thinking about anything stressful and relax.

> **EXAMPLE:** It's not going to do you any good to sit and worry. You need to force yourself to **put your brain on hold**.

TRANSLATION: It's not going to do you any good to sit and worry. You need to force yourself to **stop thinking about anything stressful and relax**.

"REAL SPEAK": It's not gonna do ya any good da sit 'n worry. Ya need da force yerself ta **put cher brain on hold**.

Note: This expression is in reference to pressing the "hold" button on a phone. When a person is "on hold," the conversation stops until the button is pressed again.

Variation: **put one's brain on pause (to)** *exp.* This expression is in reference to the "pause" button on a recording device. When pressed, the device stops until the button is pressed again.

put one's feet up (to) *exp.* to sit down and relax by reclining with one's feet raised and supported.

EXAMPLE: After our long hike, I just want to go home and **put my feet up**!

TRANSLATION: After our long hike, I just want to go home and **sit down with my feet raised**!

"REAL SPEAK": After 'ar long hike, I jus' wanna go home 'n **put my feed up**!

take it down a notch (to) *exp.* to calm down a little by bringing down one's level of agitation (much like you would turn down the volume on a virtual "dial" of a TV one notch at a time).

EXAMPLE: Stop yelling at me! **Take it down a notch**! This is nothing to get so upset about!

TRANSLATION: Stop yelling at me! **Calm down a little**! This is nothing to get so upset about!

"REAL SPEAK": Stop yelling 'it me! **Take it down a notch**! This 'ez nothing da get so upsed about!

take it easy (to) *exp.* to relax with no obligations.

EXAMPLE: This was the most stressful week I've ever had! I'm just going to **take it easy** all weekend.

TRANSLATION: This was the most stressful week I've ever had! I'm just going to **relax with no obligations** all weekend.

"REAL SPEAK": This w'z the mos' stressful week I've ever had! I'm just gonna **take id easy** all weekend.

Also: **"Take it easy!"** *exp.* "Don't get so upset! Calm down!"

unwind (to) *v.* (pronounced *un-wine'd*) to relax from being tense (like a wind-up toy that slows down).

EXAMPLE: You need to learn how to **unwind**. You're always so tense!

TRANSLATION: You need to learn how to **slow down and relax**. You're always so tense!

"REAL SPEAK": Ya need da learn how da **unwind**. Y'r ahways so tense!

veg out (to) *phrV.* to relax in a lazy and inattentive way.

EXAMPLE: After looking for a job all week, I just want to **veg out** this weekend.

TRANSLATION: After looking for a job all week, I just want to **relax and do nothing** this weekend.

"REAL SPEAK": After looking fer a job all week, I jus' wanna **veg out** th's weekend.

Variation: **veg (to)** *v.*

Note: This expression comes from the lack of mental activity in a patient who is in a vegetative state. The patient is referred to as "a vegetable" in extremely informal slang.

IDIOMS & SLANG FOR "TENSE"

basket case (to be a) *exp.* to be extremely tense to the point of being helpless.

> **EXAMPLE:** I was so worried about losing my job, I was a **basket case** all day!
>
> **TRANSLATION:** I was so worried about losing my job, I was **overwhelmed with tension all day!**
>
> **"REAL SPEAK":** I w'z so worried about losing my job, I w'z a **basket case** all day!

beside oneself (to be) *exp.* to be tense with anger or worry.

> **EXAMPLE:** My wife is over two hours late! I'm **beside myself!** I hope she's ok!

> **TRANSLATION:** My wife is over two hours late! I'm **so worried!** I hope she's ok!
>
> **"REAL SPEAK":** My wife's over two hours late! I'm **beside myself!** I hope she's ok!

bundle of nerves (to be a) *exp.* to be filled with worry and tension.

> **EXAMPLE:** I'm supposed to find out whether or not I'm getting hired for a new job. I hope they call me soon. I'm **a bundle of nerves!**
>
> **TRANSLATION:** I'm supposed to find out whether or not I'm getting hired for a new job. I hope they call me soon. I'm **so tense!**
>
> **"REAL SPEAK":** I'm sappos'ta find out whether 'r nod I'm gedding hired fer a new job. I hope they call me soon. I'm **a bundle 'a nerves!**

climbing the walls (to be) *exp.* to be feeling frustrated, helpless, and tense.

> **EXAMPLE:** I hope I receive my passport before my trip overseas! I'm **climbing the walls** waiting for it!
>
> **TRANSLATION:** I hope I receive my passport before my trip overseas! I'm **so tense** waiting for it!
>
> **"REAL SPEAK":** I hope I receive my passport b'fore my trip overseas! I'm **climbing the walls** waiding for it!

drive someone up the wall (to) *exp.* to make someone tense and upset.

> **EXAMPLE:** Stop bothering me! I'm trying to get some work done. You're **driving me up the wall!**

> **TRANSLATION:** Stop bothering me! I'm trying to get some work done. You're **making me feel tense and upset!**
>
> **"REAL SPEAK":** Stop bothering me! I'm trying da get s'm work done. Y'r **driving me up the wall!**
>
> *Also:* See: **drive someone up the wall (to)**, *p. 144.*

edgy (to be) *adj.* to be irritable, tense, nervous.

> **EXAMPLE:** Why are you so **edgy** today? You've been screaming at everyone!

TRANSLATION: Why are you so **irritable** today? You've been screaming at everyone!

"REAL SPEAK": Why'er ya so **edgy** today? Ya been screaming 'id ev'ryone!

feel it in one's bones (to) *exp.* to have an intuition that something bad is happening.

EXAMPLE: I know Jennifer is in trouble. I just **feel it in my bones**.

TRANSLATION: I know Jennifer is in trouble. I just **have a feeling that something bad has happened**.

"REAL SPEAK": I know Jennifer's 'n trouble. I jus' **feel id 'n my bones**.

Note: This expression can also be used when something good is about to happen. For example: *I just know that when Henry walks in that door, he's going to announce he got the promotion! I can* **feel it in my bones***!*

fidgety (to be) *adj.* to be tense and restless.

EXAMPLE: You've been sitting there jiggling your leg for an hour. Why are you so **fidgety**?

TRANSLATION: You've been sitting there jiggling your leg for an hour. Why are you so **tense and restless**?

"REAL SPEAK": Ya been sidding there jiggling yer leg fer 'n hour. Why're ya so **fidgedy**?

flipping out (to be) *adj.* to be extremely tense.

EXAMPLE: My mechanic promised he'd have my car ready for my trip two hours ago! When I called him, I got his voicemail. I'm **flipping out**!

TRANSLATION: My mechanic promised he'd have my car ready for my trip two hours ago! When I called him, I got his voicemail. I'm **so tense**!

"REAL SPEAK": My mechanic promised 'e'd have my car ready fer my trip two hours ago! When I called 'im, I god his voicemail. I'm **flippin' out**!

Also: **flip out (to)** *phrV.* to be tense with anger from surprise or shock.

freaking out (to be) *adj.* to be extremely tense.

EXAMPLE: What's wrong with you today? Every little thing is totally **freaking you out**?

TRANSLATION: What's wrong with you today? Every little thing is totally **making you super tense**?

"REAL SPEAK": What's wrong w'th ya taday? Ev'ry liddle thing 'ez totally **freakin' ya out**?

high-strung (to be) *adj.* to be so tense that the slightest sound or touch can cause a person to overreact.

EXAMPLE: I said hello to Deb today and she started yelling at me! That girl is **high-strung**. She needs to take a long vacation!

TRANSLATION: I said hello to Deb today and she started yelling at me! That girl is **super tense**. She needs to take a long vacation!

"REAL SPEAK": I said hello da Deb taday 'n she starded yelling 'it me! That girl 'ez **high-strung**. She needs da take a long vacation!

hyper about something (to get) *exp.* • **1.** to get very agitated and upset about something • **2.** to become very energetic.

EXAMPLE 1: Why are you getting so **hyper**?! I told you I'd clean the kitchen before our friends come over!

TRANSLATION: Why are you getting so **agitated and upset**?! I told you I'd clean the kitchen before our friends come over!

"REAL SPEAK": Why'er ya gedding so **hyper**?! I told 'ja I'd clean the kitchen b'fore 'ar friends come over!

EXAMPLE 2: After just one cup of coffee, I get so **hyper** that I can clean the entire house in only 20 minutes!

TRANSLATION: After just one cup of coffee, I get so **energetic** that I can clean the entire house in only 20 minutes!

"REAL SPEAK": Afder just one cup 'a coffee, I get so **hyper** th'd I c'n clean the entire house 'n only twen'y minutes!

jumpy (to be) *adj.* to be so tense to the point of jumping at the slightest sound or touch.

EXAMPLE: I snuck up behind Greg to give him a hug and he almost punched me! I forgot how **jumpy** he is!

TRANSLATION: I snuck up behind Greg to give him a hug and he almost punched me! I forgot how **tense** he is!

"REAL SPEAK": I snuck up b'hin' Greg da give 'im a hug an' he ahmost punched me! I fergot how **tense** 'e is!

keyed up (to be) *exp.* to be tense with nervousness or excitement.

EXAMPLE: I had such a stressful day yesterday, I couldn't sleep. I was **keyed up** all night!

TRANSLATION: I had such a stressful day yesterday, I couldn't sleep. I was **tense** all night!

"REAL SPEAK": I had such a stressful day yesderday, I couldn' sleep. I w'z **keyed up** all night!

losing it (to be) *exp.* to be extremely stressed to the point of yelling in anger.

EXAMPLE: I don't know what's wrong with me. I've been **losing it** all day! It's not like me to scream at people like this!

TRANSLATION: I don't know what's wrong with me. I've been **yelling in anger** all day! It's not like me to scream at people like this!

"REAL SPEAK": I dunno what's wrong w'th me. I been **losing id** all day! It's not like me da scream 'it people like this!

nerve-(w)racking (to be) *exp.* to be extremely stressful.

EXAMPLE: My wife is going to give birth any moment! All this waiting around is **nerve-(w)racking**!

TRANSLATION: My wife is going to give birth any moment! All this waiting around is **extremely stressful**!

"REAL SPEAK": My wife's gonna give birth any moment! All this waiding around 'ez **nerve-(w)racking**!

nervous wreck (to be a) *exp.* to be overwhelmed with tension.

EXAMPLE: Sandra was a **nervous wreck** before her wedding. But once her mother arrived, she calmed down.

TRANSLATION: Sandra was **overwhelmed with tension** before her wedding. But once her mother arrived, she calmed down.

"REAL SPEAK": Sandra w'z a **nervous wreck** b'fore 'er wedding. B't once 'er mother arrived, she calm' down.

nuts (to go) *exp.* to be going crazy (with tension).

EXAMPLE: I've been **going nuts** all day waiting to hear from my sister after her surgery!

TRANSLATION: I've been **going crazy with tension** all day waiting to hear from my sister after her surgery!

"REAL SPEAK": I been **going nuts** all day waiding da hear fr'm my sister afder 'er surgery!

on the edge (to be) *exp.* to be close to feeling overwhelmed with tension.

EXAMPLE: I've been **on the edge** all day. I just feel like something bad is about to happen.

TRANSLATION: I've been **tense** all day. I just feel like something bad is about to happen.

"REAL SPEAK": I been **on the edge** all day. I jus' feel like something bad 'ez about ta happen.

out of one's mind (to go) *exp.* to go crazy with tension from anger or helplessness.

EXAMPLE: If we don't get to the airport in fifteen minutes, we're going to miss our flight! This traffic is making me **go out of my mind**!

TRANSLATION: If we don't get to the airport in fifteen minutes, we're going to miss our flight! This traffic is making me **crazy with stress**!

"REAL SPEAK": If we don' get ta the airpord in fifteen minutes, w'r gonna miss 'ar flight! This traffic 'ez making me **go oudda my mind**!

stressed out (to be) *exp.* to be extremely tense.

EXAMPLE: Planning this surprise party has me so **stressed out**! I just want to make sure I didn't forget anything!

TRANSLATION: Planning this surprise party has me so **tense**! I just want to make sure I didn't forget anything!

"REAL SPEAK": Planning this saprise pardy has me so **stressed out**! I jus' wanna make sher I didn' ferged anything!

Note: Although **stressed** and **stressed out** are identical in meaning, **stressed out** is used more frequently.

sweat something (to) *exp.* to worry about something.

EXAMPLE: Don't **sweat the traffic**! We have plenty of time before our flight leaves.

TRANSLATION: Don't **worry about the traffic**! We have plenty of time before our flight leaves.

"REAL SPEAK": Don't **sweat the traffic**! We 'ave plen'y 'a time b'fore 'ar flight leaves.

Variation: **sweat it out (to)** *exp.* to worry a lot • *I was really **sweating it out** until the professor gave us our grades. I passed!*

Also: **"No sweat!"** *exp.* "No problem!" • *I'm happy to pick you up at the airport. **No sweat!***

tizzy (to get in a) *exp.* to be very upset.

EXAMPLE: I don't know why you're **getting in a tizzy** because Karen is a little late. Relax. I'm sure she'll be here any minute.

TRANSLATION: I don't know why you're **very upset** because Karen is a little late. Relax. I'm sure she'll be here any minute.

"REAL SPEAK": I dunno why y'r **gedding 'n a tizzy** b'cuz Karen's a liddle late. Relax. I'm sher she'll be here any minute.

"What's eating you?" *exp.* "What's making you so tense and upset?"

EXAMPLE: You're not your usual fun, upbeat self! **What's eating you** today?

TRANSLATION: You're not your usual fun, upbeat self! **What's bothering you** today?

"REAL SPEAK": Y'r not cher usual fun, upbeat self! **What's eading you** taday?

wig out (to) *phrV.* to lose control of one's emotions.

> **EXAMPLE:** Matt **wigs out** over the slightest problem. He really needs to *take a chill pill!*

> **TRANSLATION:** Matt **loses control of his emotions** over the slightest problem. He really needs to *relax!*

> **"REAL SPEAK":** Matt **wigs oud** over the slightest problem. He really needs da *take a chill pill!*

work one's last good nerve (to) *exp.* to annoy someone up to the point of losing emotional control.

> **EXAMPLE:** I was so relaxed after my vacation, but the moment I came back, my boss started **working my last good nerve!**

> **TRANSLATION:** I was so relaxed after my vacation, but the moment I came back, my boss started **annoying me up to the point of losing emotional control!**

> **"REAL SPEAK":** I w'z so relaxed after my vacation, b't the momen' I came back, my boss starded **working my las' good nerve!**

worked up (to get) *exp.* to get very upset and stressed.

> **EXAMPLE:** See? There was no reason for you to **get so worked up**. I told you we'd arrive in plenty of time!

> **TRANSLATION:** See? There was no reason for you to **get upset**. I told you we'd arrive in plenty of time!

> **"REAL SPEAK":** See? There w'z no reason for ya da **get so worked up**. I tol'ja we'd arrive 'n plen'y 'a time!

worried sick (to be) *exp.* to worry to the point of feeling ill.

> **EXAMPLE:** Where have you been?! I called and called you but you never picked up! I was **worried sick** something terrible happened to you!

> **TRANSLATION:** Where have you been?! I called and called you but you never picked up! I was **making myself sick with worry** something terrible happened to you!

> **"REAL SPEAK":** Where'ev ya been?! I called 'n called 'ju b't ya never picked up! I w'z **worried sick** something terr'ble happen' ta you!

wound up too tight (to be) *exp.* to be constantly tense.

> **EXAMPLE:** Anything you say to Beth will make her start yelling at you. She's always been **wound up too tight**.

> **TRANSLATION:** Anything you say to Beth will make her start yelling at you. She's always been **constantly tense**.

> **"REAL SPEAK":** Anything ya say da Beth'll make 'er start yelling at cha. She's ahways been **wound up too tight**.

SLANGMAN TV

Slangman Explains More idioms & Slang for...

~ON VACATION~

SCAN ME!

CHAPTER 4

SCAN THE QR CODE OR GO TO: bit.ly/StreetSpeak1-Chapter4

THIS VIDEO EPISODE CONTAINS...

"Real Speak"
- When to use **'n** for "and," "an" or "in"

soft drink
- The many ways to say "carbonated beverage" around the U.S.

regionalism
- Common words and expressions that are used in a specific region of the U.S. and not in others

Idioms & slang used on TV this week plus the latest Teen Slang!
- Slangman gives you his TOP 5 LIST of the latest idioms and slang from the most popular TV shows in the U.S. plus the newest slang teens are using today!

Newest American slang just entered into the dictionary

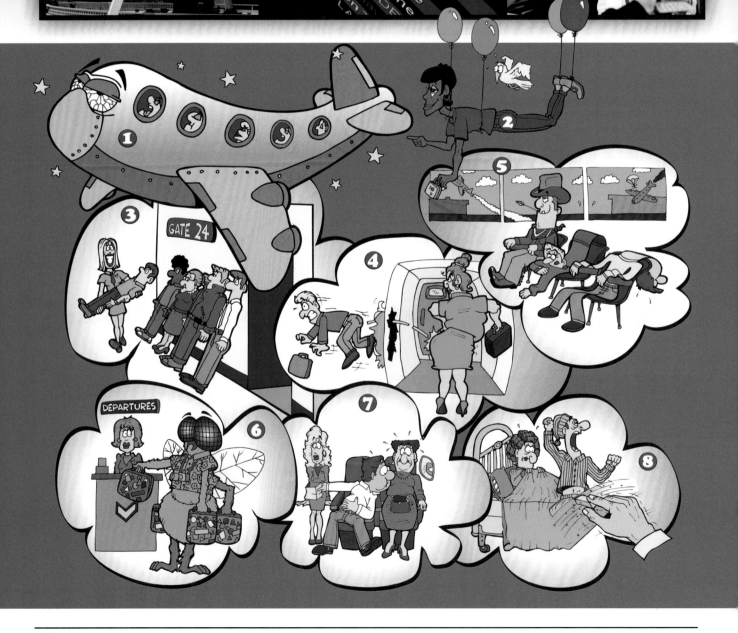

LET'S WARM UP!

MATCH THE PICTURES *(Answers on p. 217)*

As a fun way to get started, see if you can guess the meaning of the idioms and slang words in red by reading each sentence below along with its corresponding numbered illustration.

1. I hate taking the **red eye**. I always arrive so tired.
2. I don't take a lot of clothes with me when I go on business trips. I prefer to **travel light**.
3. Since I didn't have a reservation, I was put on **standby**.
4. I **got bumped** because I was late to the airport.
5. I'm sorry I'm late. We had a three-hour **layover** in Texas.
6. As a **frequent flyer**, I was given a free ticket!
7. I got sick during the flight and needed a **barf bag**.
8. After not sleeping all night, I'm **wiped out**.
9. When I arrived in Paris, I was **wired** because I was so excited!
10. When you fly from L.A. to New York, do you get **jet lag**?
11. Lois lives **way out in the boonies**. I got lost five times on the way to her house!
12. It's easier to travel with only a **carry-on**.

A. stop

B. tired from crossing time zones

C. a passenger waiting list

D. bag used for airsickness

E. in a distant and remote location

F. person who travels often

G. small suitcase that can be carried on the plane

H. exhausted

I. overnight flight

J. lost my seat in the airplane

K. travel with few items

L. full of energy

LET'S TALK!

A. DIALOGUE USING SLANG & IDIOMS

The words introduced on the previous two pages are used in the following dialogue and illustrated in the long picture above. Can you understand the conversation and find the illustration that corresponds to the slang? *Note*: The translation of the words in boldface is on the right-hand page.

— Karen is at the airport waiting for Steve to arrive —

Steve: I'm sorry we're so late. We had an unexpected two-hour **layover** some place **way out in the boonies**. You know, I almost missed the flight entirely because of all the traffic! So I arrived late and **got bumped**. Luckily, they agreed to put me on **standby**. All I had was a **carry-on**, so it was easy.

Karen: It's a good thing you **travel light**. Well, with the **jet lag**, I imagine you're pretty **wiped out**.

Steve: Actually, I'm pretty **wired** after all that traveling. At least I got a free ticket for being a **frequent flyer**!

Karen: So, how was it traveling on the **red eye**?

Steve: It got a little bumpy for a while. Luckily, I never had to use the **barf bag**!

LET'S TALK!

B. DIALOGUE TRANSLATED INTO STANDARD ENGLISH

LET'S SEE HOW MUCH YOU REMEMBER!
Just for fun, bounce around in random order to the words and
expressions in boldface below. See if you can remember their
slang equivalents without looking at the left-hand page!

— Karen is at the airport waiting for Steve to arrive —

Steve: I'm sorry we're so late. We had an unexpected two-hour **stop** some place **far away and remote**. You know, I almost missed the flight entirely because of all the traffic! So I arrived late and **my seat was given away**. Luckily, they agreed to put me on **a waiting list**. All I had was a **bag small enough to take on the airplane**, so it was easy.

Karen: It's a good thing you **travel with little luggage**. Well, with the **fatigue due to the time difference**, I imagine you're pretty **exhausted**.

Steve: Actually, I'm pretty **tense with excitement** after all that traveling. At least I got a free ticket for being a **regular airline traveler**!

Karen: So, how was it traveling on the **overnight flight**?

Steve: It got a little bumpy for a while. Luckily, I never had to use the **airsickness bag**!

C. DIALOGUE USING "REAL SPEAK"

The dialogue below demonstrates how the slang conversation
on the previous page would *really* be spoken by native speakers!

— *Karen's at the airport waiding fer Steve ta arrive* —

Steve: I'm sorry w'r so late. We had 'n unexpected two-hour **layover** some place **way out 'n the boonies**. Ya know, I almost missed the flide entirely 'cuz of all the traffic! So I arrived late 'n **got bumped**. Luckily, they agreed da put me on **stan'by**. All I had w'z a **carry-on**, so it w'z easy.

Karen: It's a good thing ya **travel light**. Well, with the **jet lag**, I imagine yer preddy **wiped out**.

Steve: Akshelly, I'm preddy **wired** after all that trav'ling. At least I godda free ticket fer being a **frequent flyer**!

Karen: So, how w'z it trav'ling on the **red eye**?

Steve: It god a liddle bumpy fer a while. Luckily, I never had ta use the **barf bag**!

KEY TO REAL SPEAK

TO = TA OR DA

As seen in the "Real Speak" dialogue above, the reduction of **to** to **ta** and **da** is used by everyone!

RULES

Often in everyday conversation, **to** is pronounced *ta* when following an unvoiced consonant (*meaning a sound such as* **sh**, **k**, **b**, **g**, **t**, **ss**, *etc., which does not involve your vocal chords*).

However, when following either a voiced consonant (*meaning a sound which causes your vocal chords to vibrate*), a vowel, or the letter **d**, **to** is often pronounced *da*.

HOW DOES IT WORK?

TO = TA (when **to** follows an unvoiced sound)	**TO = DA** (when **to** follows a voiced consonant, a vowel, or the letter **d**)
*How much will it cost **ta** ride the bus **ta** work?*	*I try **da** do a good job at work.*
*I'd like **ta** take a trip **ta** Tokyo this summer.*	*Do you know the way **da** Hollywood from here?*
*He went **ta** Paris **ta** study this year.*	*Don't ask me **da** do that again!*
*We walked **ta** the park **ta** feed the pigeons.*	*Do you know how **da** fix the toaster?*
*We stopped **ta** have something **ta** eat.*	*Brush your teeth before you go **da** the dentist.*
*Nancy wants **ta** invite Carol **ta** the party.*	*You ran all the way **da** John's house? That's far!*
*Betsy skipped **ta** school.*	*I need **da** go **da** my aunt's house.*

LET'S USE "REAL SPEAK!"

A. "ACROSS" WORD PUZZLE *(Answers on p. 217)*

The following sentences are written in "Real Speak." Rewrite the entire sentence in standard English using one letter per box.

> *Will ya go da the market ta get me something da eat?*

1

> *I have ta try da find a present ta give ta my wife.*

2

> *Ya need da know how da drive 'n order da buy a car.*

3

> *If I need ya da help me move tamorrow, A'll ask.*

4

> *It's really too cold da go da the beach th's morning.*

5

Is it or isn't it?

B. "TA BE" OR NOT "TA BE..." *(Answers on p. 217)*

Say the following sentences in real speak deciding when to use "ta" and when to use "da."

1. I went **to** the market **to** *pick up* some bread.

2. Can you tell me how **to** get **to** the post office from here?

3. Steve wanted **to** go **to** the park but I wanted **to** go shopping instead.

4. I'd love **to** join you but I have work **to** do.

5. On the way **to** the airport, I had **to** stop **to** get gas.

6. We need **to** close the windows before it starts **to** rain.

7. I don't like **to** go **to** the dentist.

8. Jennifer's two friends were too tired **to** go **to** the movies.

LET'S LEARN!

SPEAKING

TRACK 34
SOUNDCLOUD

VOCABULARY

The following words and expressions were used in the previous dialogues. Let's take a closer look at what they mean.

barf bag *exp.* a bag used for air sickness (usually in the back pocket of the seat in front of the passenger).

EXAMPLE: I sat next to a man who was airsick during the entire flight. He never stopped using the **barf bag**.

TRANSLATION: I sat next to a man who was airsick during the entire flight. He never stopped using the **airsickness bag**.

"REAL SPEAK": I sat next to a man who w'z airsick during the entire flight. He never stopped using the **barf bag**.

NOW YOU DO IT. COMPLETE THE PHRASE ALOUD:
An unusual use for a barf bag is...

boonies (way out in the) *exp.* *(from Tagalog/Filipino)* in a place that is far away and remote.

EXAMPLE: My grandmother lives **way out in the boonies**. It takes us hours to get to her house.

TRANSLATION: My grandmother lives **in a far away and remote place**. It takes us hours to get to her house.

"REAL SPEAK": My gramma lives **way oud 'n the boonies**. It takes us hours da get to 'er house.

Synonym: **boondocks (way out in the)** *exp.*

NOW YOU DO IT. COMPLETE THE PHRASE ALOUD:
My friend ...lives way out in the boonies.

bumped (to get) *exp.* to lose one's seat in an airplane, train, etc.

EXAMPLE: I **got bumped** for being five minutes late! Now I have to take a later flight.

TRANSLATION: I **lost my seat** for being five minutes late! Now I have to take a later flight.

"REAL SPEAK": I **got bumped** fer being five minutes late! Now I hafta take a lader flight.

Also: **bumped up (to get)** *exp.* to get upgraded to a higher class of travel.

NOW YOU DO IT. COMPLETE THE PHRASE ALOUD:
When I was traveling to ...I got bumped.

carry-on *n.* a small bag that one can easily "carry on" and place in the airplane.

EXAMPLE: When you go to Paris for the week, just take a **carry-on**. That way you can avoid the long line at baggage claim.

TRANSLATION: When you go to Paris for the week, just take a **small bag which you can easily carry with you on the airplane**. That way you can avoid the long line at baggage claim.

"REAL SPEAK": When ya go da Paris fer the week, jus' take a **carry-on**. That way you c'n avoid the long line 'it baggage claim.

NOW YOU DO IT. COMPLETE THE PHRASE ALOUD:
In my carry-on, I always pack my...

frequent flyer *exp.* a person who travels often by air and is part of a special program offering free flights for those who travel frequently.

EXAMPLE: As a **frequent flyer**, I can get a free ticket to anywhere in the world after I've traveled 100,000 miles!

TRANSLATION: As a **member of the airline's special program offering free flights for those who travel often**, I can get a free ticket to anywhere in the world after I've traveled 100,000 miles!

"REAL SPEAK": As a **frequent flyer**, I c'n ged a free ticket ta anywhere 'n the world after I've traveled a hundred thousan' miles!

NOW YOU DO IT. COMPLETE THE PHRASE ALOUD:
As a frequent flyer, I got a free trip to...

jet lag *exp.* fatigue due to the time change between one's point of departure and one's destination.

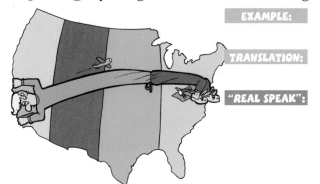

EXAMPLE: I never get **jet lag** when I travel to Europe. But when I travel back home, I'm exhausted!

TRANSLATION: I never get **tired from the time change** when I travel to Europe. But when I travel back home, I'm exhausted!

"REAL SPEAK": I never get **jet lag** when I travel da Europe. B't when I travel back home, I'm exhausted!

NOW YOU DO IT. COMPLETE THE PHRASE ALOUD:
The worst jet lag I had was when I traveled to...

layover *n.* a stop in one or more cities when traveling by air.

EXAMPLE: On our way to Paris, we had a three-hour **layover** in Amsterdam.

TRANSLATION: On our way to Paris, we had a three-hour **stop** in Amsterdam.

"REAL SPEAK": On 'ar way da Paris, we had a three-hour **layover** 'n Amsterdam.

Synonym: **stopover** *n.*

NOW YOU DO IT. COMPLETE THE PHRASE ALOUD:
The longest layover I ever had was...

red-eye *n.* a flight that occurs overnight and whose passengers arrive at their destination with "red eyes" from staying awake.

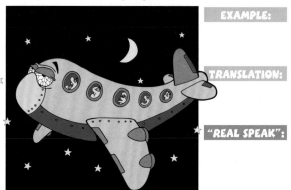

EXAMPLE: I'm taking the **red eye** to New York instead of taking a flight during the daytime because I can save a lot of money.

TRANSLATION: I'm taking the **overnight flight** to New York instead of taking a flight during the daytime because I can save a lot of money.

"REAL SPEAK": I'm taking the **red eye** ta New York instead of taking a flight during the daytime 'cuz I c'n save a lod 'a money.

NOW YOU DO IT. COMPLETE THE PHRASE ALOUD:
The last time I took a red eye was...

standby (to be on) *exp.* to be on a passenger waiting list for an available seat.

EXAMPLE:	Since I didn't have a reservation, the airline put me on **standby**.
TRANSLATION:	Since I didn't have a reservation, the airline put me on **a passenger waiting list for an available seat**.
"REAL SPEAK":	Since I didn't have a reservation, the airline put me on **stan'by**.

NOW YOU DO IT. COMPLETE THE PHRASE ALOUD:
I would fly standby if...

travel light (to) *exp.* to travel with few pieces of luggage (usually only a small piece of luggage).

EXAMPLE:	I always **travel light**, even when I go overseas. Then I can buy lots of souvenirs!
TRANSLATION:	I always **travel with a small light piece of luggage**, even when I go overseas. Then I can buy lots of souvenirs!
"REAL SPEAK":	I always **travel light**, even when I go overseas. Then I c'n buy lots 'a souvenirs!

NOW YOU DO IT. COMPLETE THE PHRASE ALOUD:
When I travel light, I never pack my...

wiped out (to be) *exp.* to be exhausted.

EXAMPLE:	After traveling for two days, I'm **wiped out**. All I want to do is go to bed!
TRANSLATION:	After traveling for two days, I'm **exhausted**. All I want to do is go to bed!
"REAL SPEAK":	After trav'ling fer two days, I'm **wiped out**. All I wanna do is go da bed!

NOW YOU DO IT. COMPLETE THE PHRASE ALOUD:
I'm wiped out because...

wired (to be) *adj.* to be tense with excitement.

EXAMPLE:	After all of this excitement today, I don't know how I'm going to sleep tonight. I'm so **wired**!
TRANSLATION:	After all of this excitement today, I don't know how I'm going to sleep tonight. I'm so **tense with excitement**!
"REAL SPEAK":	After all 'a this excitement taday, I dunno how I'm gonna sleep tanight. I'm so **wired**!

Synonym: **buzzed (to be)** *adj.* • **1.** to be extremely energetic • **2.** to be slightly intoxicated.

NOW YOU DO IT. COMPLETE THE PHRASE ALOUD:
I'm wired because...

LET'S PRACTICE!

A. COMPLETE THE FAIRY TALE *(Answers on p. 217)*

Fill in the blanks by choosing the correct word from the list below. Note that two extra words are on the list from the previous lesson!

TRACK 35
SOUNDCLOUD

Once upon a time, there was a young girl named Cinderella who lived way out in the _____ and wanted something fun to do. So one day, she decided to use her frequent _____ miles and get a free ticket to somewhere exciting. She made an appointment to sell her script to a big producer in Hollywood. She always thought that her life story would make a good movie or even a musical!

Later that day, taking only a _____-on, she left for the airport. She always believed in _____ light. Unfortunately, when she arrived at the airport, she got _____ because she was late. So, she was put on _____ for the next available flight. Finally, several hours later and completely wiped _____, she was put on the _____ eye for Hollywood, California!

The flight was so bumpy she started to feel airsick and feared that she might have to use the _____ bag. Fortunately, just then the plane made a landing in Denver. After a two-hour _____, she was once again on her way to Hollywood, the land of fame and fortune.

By the time she arrived, she was so _____ that she couldn't sleep and stayed up till all _____ of the night. Unfortunately, the combination of no sleep and jet _____ caused her to _____ in late and miss her appointment with the producer!

She was so disappointed that she decided to take the next flight back home. However, as fate would have it, she found herself sitting in the airplane next to Howard, a very handsome young man, formerly known as Prince.

Cinderella and Howard, formerly known as Prince, fell in love and moved to Chicago where they lived happily ever after in a double-wide mobile home.

wired	layover	standby	sleep
boonies	traveling	lag	barf
flyer	bumped	out	
carry	hours	red	

B. CONTEXT EXERCISE

Look at the phrase in the left column, then find the best match in the right column. Write the appropriate letter in the box.
(Answers on p. 218)

TRACK 36
SOUNDCLOUD

1. Why are you so tired?

2. Why don't you visit Nancy more often?

3. I thought you left for Los Angeles today. What happened?

4. I hope you'll visit me when you come through London.

5. It was hard traveling with so many suitcases.

6. There was so much turbulence on the plane that I got airsick.

7. You're only taking that little suitcase on your trip?

8. It's midnight but I'm not tired. It's three hours earlier than where I arrived from. But I know I'll be tired when I wake up tomorrow morning.

9. I haven't slept in two days because I've been traveling. I'm looking forward to going to bed.

10. It didn't cost me anything to fly here!

11. I wasn't able to buy a ticket for this flight.

12. I shouldn't have had so much coffee on the plane.

A. I just arrived on the **red eye** this morning from New York. And the night before, I was up with the baby all night!

B. I'm using a special **frequent flyer** ticket.

C. I'm afraid I'll only be there for a ten-minute **layover**.

D. Yes. I believe in **traveling light**.

E. I got to the airport late and got **bumped**!

F. I'm so **wiped out**.

G. Next time, I'm only bringing a **carry-on**.

H. Now I'm **wired**!

I. I hope this **jet lag** doesn't last long!

J. It was the first time I ever needed a **barf bag**.

K. She lives **way out in the boonies**!

L. Fortunately, they agreed to put me on **standby**.

C. COMPLETE THE PHRASE *(Answers on p. 218)*

Complete the opening dialogue using the list below. Try not to look at the dialogue at the beginning of the lesson until you're done!

BARF	LIGHT	BOONIES	WIRED
LAYOVER	LAG	BUMPED	WIPED
EYE	FLYER	CARRY-ON	STANDBY

— *Karen is at the airport waiting for Steve to arrive* —

Steve: I'm sorry we're so late. We had an unexpected two-hour _____ some place

way out in the _____. You know, I almost missed the flight entirely because

of all the traffic! So I arrived late and **got** _____. Luckily, they agreed to put

me on _____. All I had was a _____, so it was easy.

Karen: It's a good thing you **travel** _____. Well, with the **jet** _____, I imagine

you're pretty _____ **out**.

Steve: Actually, I'm pretty _____ after all that traveling. At least I got a free ticket for

being a **frequent** _____!

Karen: So, how was it traveling on the **red** _____?

Steve: It got a little bumpy for a while. Luckily, I never had to use the _____ **bag**!

Popular Idioms, Slang & Jargon
Having to do with: FLYING

EXERCISES FOR THIS SECTION ARE IN THE WORKBOOK.

arrive in the nick of time (to) *exp.* to arrive at the right moment.

EXAMPLE: Because of all the traffic, I was late to the airport. Luckily I arrived at the gate **in the nick of time**. They were about to give away my seat!

TRANSLATION: Because of all the traffic, I was late to the airport. Luckily I arrived at the gate **at the right moment**. They were about to give away my seat!

"REAL SPEAK": B'cuz 'ev all the traffic, I w'z late ta the airport. Luckily I arrived 'it the gate **'n the nick 'a time**. They were about ta give away my seat!

Variation: **to get somewhere in the nick of time** *exp.* • *We got to the airport in the nick of time!*

baggage claim *exp.* the area in an airport where passengers get their luggage after arriving at their destination.

EXAMPLE: It will be easy to find my luggage in **baggage claim**. I have three bright orange suitcases.

BAGGAGE CLAIM

TRANSLATION: It will be easy to find my luggage in **the area where passengers get their luggage after the flight**. I have three bright orange suitcases.

"REAL SPEAK": Id'll be easy da fin' my luggage 'n **baggage claim**. I 'ave three bride orange suitcases.

cockpit *n.* the small closed space where the pilot sits in an aircraft.

EXAMPLE: Years ago, the airline allowed passengers to visit the **cockpit**. The view out of the window was amazing!

TRANSLATION: Years ago, the airline allowed passengers to visit the **small closed space where the pilot sits in the aircraft**. The view out of the window was amazing!

"REAL SPEAK": Years ago, the airline allowed passengers ta visit the **cockpit**. The view oudda the window w'z amazing!

control tower *exp.* a building at an airport where air traffic is monitored and directed.

EXAMPLE: Last night, the computers in the **control tower** at the airport malfunctioned. So airplanes couldn't land for more than two hours!

TRANSLATION: Last night, the computers in the **building that directs air traffic** at the airport malfunctioned. So airplanes couldn't land for more than two hours!

"REAL SPEAK": Las' night, the c'mpuder 'n the **c'ntrol tower** 'it the airport malfunctioned. So airplanes couldn' land fer more th'n two hours!

cool one's jets (to) *exp.* to calm down.

EXAMPLE: There's nothing to get so upset about! You really need to step outside and **cool your jets**!

TRANSLATION: There's nothing to get so upset about! You really need to step outside and **calm down**!

"REAL SPEAK": There's nothing da get so upsed about! Ya really need da step outside 'n **cool yer jets**!

flight attendant *exp.* an airline employee who serves meals, and attends to passengers' comfort and safety.

EXAMPLE: When the airplane started bouncing, the **flight attendants** explained exactly what was happening. That made all the passengers calm down.

TRANSLATION: When the airplane started bouncing, the **in-flight airline employees** explained exactly what was happening. That made all the passengers calm down.

"REAL SPEAK": When the airplane starded bouncing, the **flide attendants** explained exac'ly what w'z happ'ning. That made all the passengers calm down.

Synonym: **cabin crew** *exp.* Note that **cabin** is airline jargon for "the interior of the aircraft" and **crew** is airline (and nautical) jargon for "employees."

fly by the seat of one's pants (to) *exp.* to do something by instinct rather than logic or knowledge; to improvise.

EXAMPLE: You're going to try and repair your car yourself?! But you don't know the first thing about cars! You can't just **fly by the seat of your pants**! You need a real mechanic.

TRANSLATION: You're going to try and repair your car yourself?! But you don't know the first thing about cars! You can't just **improvise**! You need a real mechanic.

"REAL SPEAK": Y'r gonna try 'n r'pair yer car yerself?! But cha don't know the firs' thing about cars! Ya can't jus' **fly by the seat 'a yer pants**! Ya need a real mechanic.

gate *n.* an area where passengers go to or leave their plane • (lit); an opening in a fence.

EXAMPLE: We only have five minutes to get to our **gate** or we'll miss our flight! Run!

TRANSLATION: We only have five minutes to get to our **entrance to the plane** or we'll miss our flight! Run!

"REAL SPEAK": We only ave five minutes ta get ta 'ar **gade** 'r we'll miss 'ar flight! Run!

MORE ON... TV SLANGMAN

hangar *n.* a large building that stores airplanes.

EXAMPLE: My dad is a pilot and took me on a tour of some of the **hangars** at the airport. I got to see the planes up close!

TRANSLATION: My dad is a pilot and took me on a tour of some of the **buildings that store airplanes** at the airport. I got to see the planes up close!

"REAL SPEAK": My dad's a pilot 'n took me on a tour 'ev some 'a the **hangers** 'it the airport. I got ta see the planes up close!

headwind *n.* a wind blowing in the opposite direction of the airplane, causing it to slow.

EXAMPLE: We were supposed to arrive in Los Angeles at noon, but because of the strong **headwind**, we arrived an hour late!

TRANSLATION: We were supposed to arrive in Los Angeles at noon, but because of the strong **opposing wind causing the airplane to slow**, we arrived an hour late!

"REAL SPEAK": We were sapos'ta arrive 'n LA 'it noon, but b'cuz 'a the strong **headwind**, we arrived 'n hour late!

Antonym: **tailwind** - *See p. 104*

hijack (to) *v.* to take control of an aircraft by forcing the pilot to divert the aircraft to a different destination.

EXAMPLE: On our way to Denver, our plane was **hijacked**! We ended up in a country I never even heard of! It was so scary!

TRANSLATION: On our way to Denver, our plane was **diverted to a different destination**! We ended up in a country I never even heard of! It was so scary!

"REAL SPEAK": On 'ar way da Denver, 'ar plane w'z **hijacked**! We ended up 'n a country I never even heard of! It w'z so scary!

hub *n.* a transfer point to get passengers to their final destination.

EXAMPLE: The last time I went to New York, we made a stop at a major **hub** in Atlanta. It was so crowded, I had to wait in line for three hours to board my next plane!

TRANSLATION: The last time I went to New York, we made a stop at a major **transfer point** in Atlanta. It was so crowded, I had to wait in line for three hours to board my next plane!

"REAL SPEAK": The las' time I went ta New York, we made a stop 'id a major **hub** 'n Atlan'a. It w'z so crowded, I had da wait 'n line fer three hours ta board my nex' plane!

jetway *n.* a portable bridge placed against an aircraft door to allow passengers to embark or disembark.

EXAMPLE: Ladies and gentlemen, please remain in your seats until the **jetway** is in place and the exit door has been opened.

TRANSLATION: Ladies and gentlemen, please remain in your seats until the **portable bridge** is in place and the exit door has been opened.

"REAL SPEAK": Ladies 'n gen'lemen, please remain 'n yer seats until the **jetway** 'ez 'n place an' the exit door 'ez been opened.

kill time (to) *exp.* to do something that keeps you busy while you are waiting for something else to happen.

EXAMPLE: We have three hours before our flight. Why don't we **kill time** and get something to eat?

TRANSLATION: We have three hours before our flight. Why don't we **keep ourselves busy** and get something to eat?

"REAL SPEAK": We 'ave three hours b'fore 'ar flight. Why don' we **kill time** 'n get somethin' da eat?

landing *n.* the act of an airplane returning to the ground.

> **EXAMPLE:** Are we already in Dallas? That was such a smooth **landing**, I didn't **even realize we arrived!**
>
> **TRANSLATION:** Are we already in Dallas? That was such a smooth **return to the ground**, I didn't even realize we arrived!
>
> **"REAL SPEAK":** Are we ahready 'n Dallas? That w'z such a smooth **landing**, I didn' even re'lize we arrived!
>
> *Antonym:* **takeoff** - *See p. 104*

make a mad dash for something (to) *exp.* to rush.

> **EXAMPLE:** I had to **make a mad dash for** the airport because I overslept! I made it in time by one minute!

> **TRANSLATION:** I had to **rush to** the airport because I overslept! I made it in time by one minute!
>
> **"REAL SPEAK":** I had da **make a mad dash fer** the airport b'cuz I overslept! I made it 'n time by one minute!
>
> *Synonym 1:* **rush like crazy (to)** *exp.*
>
> *Synonym 2:* **scramble (to)** *v.*

make good time (to) *exp.* to complete a trip quickly.

> **EXAMPLE:** Even with the traffic, we **made good time** to the airport. It usually takes an hour to get there. This time it only took forty minutes!
>
> **TRANSLATION:** Even with the traffic, we **completed our trip quickly** to the airport. It usually takes an hour to get there. This time it only took forty minutes!

> **"REAL SPEAK":** Even w'th the traffic, we **made good time** ta the airport. It ujally takes 'n hour da get there. This time id only took fordy minutes!

make it with time to spare (to) *exp.* to arrive ahead of schedule.

> **EXAMPLE:** There was no traffic on the freeway today! In fact, I **made it to my appointment with time to spare!**
>
> **TRANSLATION:** There was no traffic on the freeway today! In fact, I **arrived ahead of schedule!**
>
> **"REAL SPEAK":** There w'z no traffic on the freeway daday! In fact, I **made it to my appointment w'th time da spare!**
>
> *Note:* In this expression, the expression **to make it** was used as a slang synonym of "to arrive." Other slang synonyms could be used in its place such as:
>
> • **breeze in (to)** *phrV.*
>
> • **get there (to)** *exp.*
>
> • **pull in (to)** *phrV.* used in reference to the parking space at your destination
>
> • **show up (to)** *phrV.*

make up for lost time (to) *exp.* to do something very fast to compensate for a slow start.

> **EXAMPLE:** I can't believe how late our taxi is! As soon as we arrive at the airport, we need to run! We need to **make up for lost time**, if we don't want to miss our flight!
>
> **TRANSLATION:** I can't believe how late our taxi is! As soon as we arrive at the airport, we need to run! We need to **compensate for our slow start**, if we don't want to miss our flight!
>
> **"REAL SPEAK":** I can't b'lieve how lade 'ar taxi is! As soon 'ez we arrive 'it the airport, we need da run! We need da **make up fer los' time**, if we don' wanna miss 'ar flight!

nosedive (to take a) *exp.* said of an aircraft that makes a sudden and fast fall to the ground with the front, or **nose**, pointing down.

EXAMPLE:	The airplane lost altitude in an instant! I actually thought we were about to **take a nosedive**!
TRANSLATION:	The airplane lost altitude in an instant! I actually thought we were about **to make a sudden fall to the ground front first**!
"REAL SPEAK":	The airplane lost altitude 'n 'n instant! I aksh'lly thought we were about ta **take a nosedive**!

on the fly (to do something) *exp.* to do something quickly but not perfectly.

EXAMPLE:	One of the wheels came off my old suitcase, so I fixed it **on the fly**. I'm going to buy some new luggage as soon as I get home!
TRANSLATION:	One of the wheels came off my old suitcase, so I fixed it **quickly but not perfectly**. I'm going to buy some new luggage as soon as I get home!
"REAL SPEAK":	One 'a the wheels came off my ol' suitcase, so I fixed id **on the fly**. I'm gonna buy s'm new luggage 'ez soon 'ez I get home!

onboard with something (to get) *exp.* to support and work together on something such as a strategy.

EXAMPLE:	We all need to **get onboard with** this strategy or it's never going to work. I'm going to need everyone's help!
TRANSLATION:	We all need to **support and work together on** this strategy or it's never going to work. I'm going to need everyone's help!
"REAL SPEAK":	We all need da **ged onboard w'th** th's stradegy or it's never gonna work. I'm gonna need ev'ryone's help!

round-trip ticket *exp.* a ticket that allows a passenger to go to, and from, a destination.

EXAMPLE:	It's less expensive if you buy a **round-trip ticket** for your vacation than buying two one-way tickets!
TRANSLATION:	It's less expensive if you buy a **ticket which is good for your destination and return flight home** for your vacation than buying two one-way tickets!

"REAL SPEAK":	It's less expensive if ya buy a **roun'-trip ticket** fer yer vacation th'n buying two one-way tickets!

runway *n.* a strip of smooth ground where airplanes take off and land.

EXAMPLE:	We circled over the airport for an hour because there was so much traffic on the **runway**! This is the last time I travel during a holiday!

TRANSLATION:	We circled over the airport for an hour because there was so much traffic on the **strip of smooth ground used for landings and take offs**! This is the last time I travel during a holiday!
"REAL SPEAK":	We circled over the airport fer 'n hour b'cuz there w'z so much traffic on the **runway**! This 'ez the las' time I travel during a holiday!

Synonym: **tarmac** *n.*

skycap *n.* an airline employee who assists passengers with their luggage.

EXAMPLE:	We have too much luggage to carry ourselves. Let's get a **skycap** to help us.
TRANSLATION:	We have too much luggage to carry ourselves. Let's get an **airline employee who assists with luggage** to help us.
"REAL SPEAK":	We 'ave too much luggage ta carry 'arselves. Let's ged a **skycap** ta help us.

Synonym: **porter** *n.*

"Sparks are going to fly!" *exp.* "A big verbal fight is about to happen!"

> **EXAMPLE:** **Sparks are going to fly** when your dad finds out you crashed his car!
>
> **TRANSLATION:** **There's going to be a big verbal fight** when your dad finds out you crashed his car!
>
> **"REAL SPEAK":** **Sparks 'er gonna fly** when yer dad fin's out ya crashed 'is car!

tailwind *exp.* a wind blowing in the same direction as the airplane, causing it to accelerate.

> **EXAMPLE:** We arrived early in Dallas because we had a **tailwind** the entire flight.
>
> **TRANSLATION:** We arrived early in Dallas because we had a **wind blowing in the same direction as the plane** the entire flight.
>
> **"REAL SPEAK":** We arrived early 'n Dallas b'cuz we had a **tailwin'** the entire flight.
>
> *Antonym:* **headwind** - *See p. 100*

takeoff *n.* the act of an airplane leaving the ground.

> **EXAMPLE:** I love **takeoffs**! You can really feel the power of the airplane as it lifts into the air!
>
> **TRANSLATION:** I love **when the airplane leaves the ground**! You can really feel the power of the airplane as it lifts into the air!
>
> **"REAL SPEAK":** I love **takeoffs**! Ya c'n really feel the power 'a the airplane as it lif's inta the air!
>
> *Antonym:* **landing** - *See p. 102*

terminal *n.* the building where passengers of an aircraft (or train, bus, ship, etc.) arrive or depart.

> **EXAMPLE:** Oh, no! We're in the wrong **terminal**! We want the one for international flights!
>
> **TRANSLATION:** Oh, no! We're in the wrong **building for arrivals and departures**! We want the one for international flights!
>
> **"REAL SPEAK":** Oh, no! W'r in the wrong **termin'l**! We want the one fer in'ernational flights!

"That's not going to fly!" *exp.* "That is not going to be acceptable!"

> **EXAMPLE:** Steve is going to ask for a raise after being here for only a week?! I can promise you right now...**that's not going to fly** with the boss!
>
> **TRANSLATION:** Steve is going to ask for a raise after being here for only a week?! I can promise you right now...**that's not going to be acceptable** with the boss!
>
> **"REAL SPEAK":** Steve's gonna ask fer a raise afder being here fer only a week?! I c'n promise ya right now...**that's not gonna fly** w'th the boss!
>
> *Synonym:* **"That's not going to go over well!"** *exp.*

"When pigs fly!" *exp.* a humorous way to say, "Never!"

> **EXAMPLE:** My mother is scared of air travel. You'll see her in an airplane **when pigs fly**!

> **TRANSLATION:** My mother is scared of air travel. You'll **never** see her in an **airplane**!
>
> **"REAL SPEAK":** My mother's scared 'ev air travel. You'll see 'er in 'n airplane **when pigs fly**!
>
> *Synonym:* **"The day after NEVER!"** *exp.*

IDIOMS & SLANG FOR "SLEEP"

catch some Z's (to) *exp.* to get some sleep (since "ZZzzzzzzzz" is often used in comic strips over a sleeping person's head to indicate the sound of snoring).

> **EXAMPLE:** I didn't sleep last night. I'm going to try and **catch some Z's** now.
>
> **TRANSLATION:** I didn't sleep last night. I'm going to try and **get some sleep** now.
>
> **"REAL SPEAK":** I didn' sleep 'id all las' night. I'm gonna try 'n **catch s'm Z's** now.
>
> *Note:* **to catch some** is popular slang for "to get some." For example: *I'm going* **to catch some** *sun.*

catnap *n.* a short, light sleep.

> **EXAMPLE:** I'm going to take a **catnap**, so I'm rested when we arrive.
>
> **TRANSLATION:** I'm going to take a **short, light sleep**, so I'm rested when we arrive.
>
> **"REAL SPEAK":** I'm gonna take a liddle **catnap**, so I'm rested wh'n we arrive.

conk out (to) *phrV.* to fall deeply asleep quickly • (lit); to stop functioning: *My car* **conked out** *on the highway!*

> **EXAMPLE:** I was so tired that the moment I lied down, I **conked out**!
>
> **TRANSLATION:** I was so tired that the moment I lied down, I **fell into a deep sleep**!
>
> **"REAL SPEAK":** I w'z so tired th't the momen' I lied down, I **conked out**!

doze off (to) *phrV.* to fall asleep for a short period of time.

> **EXAMPLE:** I was watching a movie and **dozed off** for an hour.
>
> **TRANSLATION:** I was watching a movie **fell asleep** for an hour.
>
> **"REAL SPEAK":** I w'z watching a movie an' **dozed off** fer 'n hour.
>
> *Note:* **doze (to)** *v.* to sleep lightly.

drift off to sleep (to) *exp.* to fall asleep gradually.

> **EXAMPLE:** I was reading my book and after ten minutes, I **drifted off to sleep**.
>
> **TRANSLATION:** I was reading my book and after ten minutes, I **gradually fell asleep**.
>
> **"REAL SPEAK":** I w'z reading my book an' afder ten minutes, I **drifded off ta sleep**.

hit the hay (to) *exp.* to go to bed.

> **EXAMPLE:** It's 10pm already? Time to **hit the hay**! I have an early day tomorrow.
>
> **TRANSLATION:** It's 10pm already? Time to **go to bed**! I have an early day tomorrow.
>
> **"REAL SPEAK":** It's 10pm already? Time da **hit the hay**! I have 'n early day damarrow.

lie-down (to have a) *exp.* to rest.

> **EXAMPLE:** After that long flight, I need to **have a lie-down** before we explore the city.
>
> **TRANSLATION:** After that long flight, I need to **lie down and rest** before we explore the city.
>
> **"REAL SPEAK":** After that long flight, I need da **have a lie-down** b'fore we explore the cidy.

lights out *exp.* time to go to sleep • (lit); bedtime in a school dormitory, military barracks, or other institution, when lights should be turned off.

> **EXAMPLE:** Ok. **Lights out**! I'm going to try and get some rest before we arrive.
>
> **TRANSLATION:** Ok. **Time to go to sleep**! I'm going to try and get some rest before we arrive.
>
> **"REAL SPEAK":** Ok. **Lights out**! I'm gonna try 'n get s'm res' b'fore we arrive.
>
> *Note:* **out like a light (to be)** *exp.* to fall asleep in an instant (like turning off a light).

lull to sleep (to) *exp.* to put to sleep by something relaxing like soft music, being rocked, listening to the sound of waves, etc.

> EXAMPLE: In Hawaii, we had a room right on the ocean. The sound of the waves **lulled me to sleep** every night!

> TRANSLATION: In Hawaii, we had a room right on the ocean. The sound of the waves **relaxed me into sleep** every night!

> "REAL SPEAK": In Hawaii, we had a room ride on the ocean. The sound 'a the waves **lulled me da sleep** ev'ry night!

micro nap (to take a) *exp.* to take a short nap.

> EXAMPLE: I didn't sleep well on the plane. I was only able to **take a micro nap** which is better than nothing.

> TRANSLATION: I didn't sleep well on the plane. I was only able to **take a short nap** which is better than nothing.

> "REAL SPEAK": I did' sleep well on the plane. I w'z only able da **take a micro nap** which 'ez bedder th'n nothing.

> *Note:* **micro sleep (to take a)** *exp.*

nod off (to) *phrV.* to fall asleep, usually unintentionally and for a short period of time, as one's head falls or "nods" forward.

> EXAMPLE: I **nodded off** for a few minutes, as I was watching a movie.

> TRANSLATION: I **fell asleep** for a few minutes, as I was watching a movie.

> "REAL SPEAK": I **nodded off** fer a few minutes, 'ez I w'z watching a movie.

out cold (to be) *exp.* to fall asleep instantly and deeply.

> EXAMPLE: I had only one drink on the airplane and was **out cold** the entire flight!

> TRANSLATION: I had only one drink on the airplane and was **in a deep sleep** the entire flight!

> "REAL SPEAK": I had only one drink on the airplane 'n w'z **out cold** the entire flight!

sack out (to) *phrV.* to fall asleep.

> EXAMPLE: I **sacked out** right after we took off and didn't wake up until we landed!

> TRANSLATION: I **fell asleep** right after we took off and didn't wake up until we landed!

> "REAL SPEAK": I **sacked out** ride after we took off 'n did' wake up 'till we landed!

> *Note:* This expression comes from the term "sleep sack" which is specially designed for newborns and provides a snug, secure feeling. Today, *sack* is slang for "bed" and it's common to hear, *It's time to **hit the sack**!; It's time to **go to bed**!*

saw wood (to) *exp.* to snore.

> EXAMPLE: You must feel really rested! You were **sawing wood** for the past several hours!

> TRANSLATION: You must feel really rested! You were **snoring** for the past several hours!

> "REAL SPEAK": Ya mus' feel really rested! You were **sawing wood** fer the pas' sev'ral hours!

shuteye (to get some) *exp.* to get some sleep.

> EXAMPLE: I need to **get some shuteye** or I'm going to be exhausted when we arrive.

> TRANSLATION: I need to **get some sleep** or I'm going to be exhausted when we arrive.

> "REAL SPEAK": I need da **get s'm shuteye** 'r I'm gonna be exhausted wh'n we arrive.

siesta (to take a) *exp.* *(from Spanish)* to take a nap.

> EXAMPLE: I always like **taking a siesta** right after lunch. It wakes me up for the rest of the day!

TRANSLATION: I always like **taking a nap** right after lunch. It wakes me up for the rest of the day!

"REAL SPEAK": I ahways like **taking a siesta** ride afder lunch. It wakes me up fer the rest 'a the day!

sleep a wink (not to) *exp.* to be unable to sleep at all.

EXAMPLE: I **didn't sleep a wink** during the entire sixteen-hour flight! I don't know how I'm going to function our first day here!

TRANSLATION: I **didn't sleep at all** during the entire sixteen-hour flight! I don't know how I'm going to function our first day here!

"REAL SPEAK": I **did' sleep a wink** during the entire sixteen-hour flight! I dunno how I'm gonna function 'ar firs' day here!

sleep like a baby (to) *exp.* to sleep soundly.

EXAMPLE: I was so tired when we got home from our long trip, I **slept like a baby** all night.

TRANSLATION: I was so tired when we got home from our long trip, I **slept soundly** all night.

"REAL SPEAK": I w'z so tired wh'n we got home fr'm 'ar long trip, I **slep' like a baby** all night.

Synonym 1: **sleep like a log (to)** *exp.*

Synonym 2: **sleep like a rock (to)** *exp.*

"Sleep tight!" *exp.* "Sleep well!" (a common wish you say to someone who is about to go to sleep).

EXAMPLE: Have a good night! **Sleep tight!**

TRANSLATION: Have a good night! **Sleep well!**

"REAL SPEAK": Have a good night! **Sleep tight!**

Origin: Some believe that this expression comes from the days of Shakespeare when mattresses were placed on a series of overlapping ropes that needed to be tightened before lying down.

sleep with one eye open (to) *exp.* to sleep very lightly, aware of everything that is happening.

EXAMPLE: I can't totally relax during a flight. I always **sleep with one eye open**.

TRANSLATION: I can't totally relax during a flight. I always **sleep very lightly and am aware of everything**.

"REAL SPEAK": I can't todally relax during a flight. I ahways **sleep w'th one eye open**.

slumberland (to be off to) *exp.* to go to sleep • (lit) to go to the place where sleep, or slumber, happens.

EXAMPLE: I'm **off to slumberland**. Wake me when we get there.

TRANSLATION: I'm **going to sleep**. Wake me when we get there.

"REAL SPEAK": I'm **off ta slumberland**. Wake me when we get there.

sound asleep (to be) *exp.* to be in a deep sleep.

EXAMPLE: There was a thunderstorm last night? I didn't hear a thing! I must have been **sound asleep**!

TRANSLATION: There was a thunderstorm last night? I didn't hear a thing! I must have been **in a deep sleep**!

"REAL SPEAK": There w'z a thunderstorm las' night? I did' hear a thing! I must'a been **sound asleep**!

snooze (to take a) *exp.* to take a nap.

EXAMPLE: I'm going to **take a snooze**, so I'm refreshed when we arrive.

TRANSLATION: I'm going to **take a nap**, so I'm refreshed when we arrive.

"REAL SPEAK": I'm gonna **take a snooze**, so I'm refreshed wh'n we arrive.

wide awake (to be) *exp.* to be fully awake.

EXAMPLE: Timmy was **wide awake** during the entire flight!

TRANSLATION: Timmy was **completely awake** during the entire flight!

"REAL SPEAK": Timmy w'z **wide awake** during the entire flight!

SLANGMAN TV

Slangman Explains More Idioms & Slang for...

—AT THE AIRPORT—

SCAN ME!

CHAPTER 5

SCAN THE QR CODE OR GO TO: bit.ly/StreetSpeak1-Chapter5

THIS VIDEO EPISODE CONTAINS...

late
- TOP 5 LIST of expressions meaning "late"

orange
- How people from the east and west coast pronounce the word "orange" plus many other regional accents around the U.S.

'ave
- When the **h** and **wh** sound disappears
  - I **have** an idea. = *I 'ave an idea.*
  - Look **who** just walked in! = *Look 'oo just walked in!*

Idioms & slang used on TV this week plus the latest Teen Slang!
- Slangman gives you his TOP 5 LIST of the latest idioms and slang from the most popular TV shows in the U.S. plus the newest slang teens are using today!

Newest American slang just entered into the dictionary

LESSON 6 AT A RESTAURANT

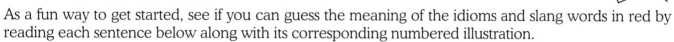

LET'S WARM UP!

MATCH THE PICTURES *(Answers on p. 218)*

As a fun way to get started, see if you can guess the meaning of the idioms and slang words in red by reading each sentence below along with its corresponding numbered illustration.

1. I eat too much. I need to ***cut down***.
   - ❏ eat less
   - ❏ eat more

2. Let's order hamburgers and ***a side of*** fries.
   - ❏ a small amount of
   - ❏ an additional order of

3. I'm going to ***skip*** the salad. I've eaten enough vegetables today.
   - ❏ omit
   - ❏ add

4. Let's split an order of ***sliders***. You get eight of them, so that should be plenty for each!
   - ❏ small hamburgers
   - ❏ small beverages

5. I love desserts. I have a ***sweet tooth***.
   - ❏ dislike for sweets
   - ❏ passion for sweets

6. You think you can eat all that?! ***Your eyes are bigger than your stomach***!
   - ❏ You always finish everything on your plate
   - ❏ You believe you can eat more than you can

7. I'll finish this sandwich tomorrow. I can eat the ***leftovers*** for lunch.
   - ❏ remaining food
   - ❏ freshly prepared food

8. Leave your money at home. Lunch ***is on me***.
   - ❏ is my treat
   - ❏ spilled all over me

9. I'm hungry. Let's ***grab a bite*** before the movie.
   - ❏ visit the dentist
   - ❏ get something to eat

10. Irene ate a box of chocolates today. She's a real ***chocaholic***!
    - ❏ chocolate hater
    - ❏ chocolate lover

11. What a meal! I really ***pigged out***!
    - ❏ ate lightly
    - ❏ ate in excess

12. I can't eat any more. I need a ***doggie bag***.
    - ❏ bag to carry food home
    - ❏ bag of donuts

LET'S TALK!

A. DIALOGUE USING SLANG & IDIOMS

The words introduced on the previous two pages are used in the following dialogue and illustrated in the long picture above. Can you understand the conversation and find the illustration that corresponds to the slang? *Note*: The translation of the words in boldface is on the right-hand page.

SPEAKING

TRACK 39
SOUNDCLOUD

— *Cecily and Jim are **grabbing a bite** —*

Cecily:	Since today is your birthday, lunch **is on me**!
Jim:	Well, I was planning on **cutting down**, but if you're paying, I'm going to **pig out**!
Cecily:	Good! It's your birthday! Have whatever you want. I feel like having a big juicy hamburger and **a side of** fries. How about you?
Jim:	I think I'll get an order of **sliders**… and some onion rings, potato salad, baked beans, cole slaw, and some biscuits. And to satisfy my **sweet tooth**, I'll get a slice of chocolate pie. You know what a **chocaholic** I am!
Cecily:	Jim, **your eyes are bigger than your stomach**.
Jim:	Maybe you're right. Okay. **Skip** the salad.
Cecily:	I have a feeling you're going to need a **doggie bag** for all the **leftovers**. And I'm going to need to get a second job to pay for this lunch!

LET'S TALK!

B. DIALOGUE TRANSLATED INTO STANDARD ENGLISH

LET'S SEE HOW MUCH YOU REMEMBER!
Just for fun, bounce around in random order to the words and
expressions in boldface below. See if you can remember their
slang equivalents without looking at the left-hand page!

— *Cecily and Jim are* **getting something to eat** —

Cecily: Since today is your birthday, lunch **is my treat**!

Jim: Well, I was planning on **dieting**, but if you're paying, I'm going to **eat in excess**!

Cecily: Good! It's your birthday! Have whatever you want. I feel like having a big juicy hamburger and **an extra order of** fries. How about you?

Jim: I think I'll get some **mini hamburgers**… an order of onion rings, potato salad, baked beans, cole slaw, and some biscuits. And to satisfy my **passion for sweets**, I'll get a slice of chocolate pie. You know what a **chocolate lover** I am!

Cecily: Jim, **you believe you can eat more than you actually can**.

Jim: Maybe you're right. Okay. **Omit** the salad.

Cecily: I have a feeling you're going to need a **bag used to carry food home** for all the **excess food**. And I'm going to need to get a second job to pay for this lunch!

C. DIALOGUE USING "REAL SPEAK"

The dialogue below demonstrates how the slang conversation on the previous page would *really* be spoken by native speakers!

— *Cecily 'n Jim 'er **grabbing a bite*** —

Cecily: Since taday's yer birthday, lunch **'ez on me**!

Jim: Well, I w'z planning on **cudding down**, b'd if y'r payin', I'm gonna **pig out**!

Cecily: Good! It's yer birthday! Have whadever ya want. I feel like having a big juicy burger 'n **a side 'a** fries. How 'bout you?

Jim: I think A'll ged 'n order 'ev **sliders**... an' s'm onion rings, patato salad, baked beans, cole slaw, an' s'm biscuits. An' da sadisfy my **sweet tooth**, A'll ged a slice 'a choc'lit pie. Ya know whad a **chocaholic** I am!

Cecily: Jim, **yer eyes 'er bigger th'n yer stomach**.

Jim: Maybe y'r right. Okay. **Skip** the salad.

Cecily: I have a feeling y'r gonna need a **doggie bag** fer all the **leftovers**. An' I'm gonna need da ged a secon' job da pay fer th's lunch!

GOING TO = GONNA

This is one of the most common reductions in American English and is sure to be heard when talking with just about any native speaker!

RULES

When **going to** is used to show future, it is often shortened (or *reduced*) to *gonna*.

HOW DOES IT WORK?

We're **going to** grab a bite. We're **goingxto** grab a bite.	In the phrase **going to**, the hard sounds of **g** at the end of a word and **t** at the beginning of a word, disappear in everyday speech.
We're **goin o** grab a bite. We're **guhn uh** grab a bite.	Many vowel combinations (such as the **oi** in **going**) and unstressed vowels (such as the **o** in **to**) are commonly pronounced **uh**.
We're **gonna** grab a bite.	This shortened version of **going to** is so common in everyday speech that it is often seen written in magazines and newspapers to indicate spoken language.

BUT!

Going to is *never* shortened to *gonna* when it indicates going from one place to another!

INCORRECT	CORRECT
Are you **gonna** the meeting?	Are you *going to* the meeting?
I'm **gonna** the office tonight.	I'm *going to* the office tonight.
Everyone was **gonna** the restaurant.	Everyone was *going to* the restaurant.
Are you **gonna** the movies?	Are you *going to* the movies?
Why aren't they **gonna** the party with us?	Why aren't they *going to* the party with us?
She's **gonna** Paris today!	She's *going to* Paris today!

LET'S USE "REAL SPEAK!"

A. NOW YOU'RE GONNA DO A "GONNA" EXERCISE

Repeat the sentences replacing "going to" with "gonna."
(Answers p. 218)

TRACK 40
SOUNDCLOUD

1. I'm so hungry! I'm going to **pig out** tonight!

2. This restaurant serves such big portions. I'm going to need a **doggie bag**.

3. I'm starting to get fat. I'm going to have to **cut down** on desserts.

4. I'd like a hamburger but I'm going to **skip** the fries.

5. I'm going to have lunch with Irene today. No one has a **sweet tooth** like her!

6. If David is anything like his mother, he's going to be a **chocaholic** when he grows up.

7. We have a lot of extra food from the party. Steve is going to take home the **leftovers**.

8. I'm hungry. I'm going to go **grab a bite**.

B. IS IT "GONNA" OR "GOING TO"? *(Answers on p. 219)*

Read the following paragraph and underline all the instances where "going to" can be reduced to "gonna." But be careful! There are two places where "going to" cannot change!

TRACK 41
SOUNDCLOUD

Janet and I are **going to** a great French restaurant tonight and we're **going to** pig out! I'm probably **going to** need a doggie bag because they serve so much food. After dinner, we're **going to** my mother's house and I'm **going to** bring her the leftovers. In fact, I'm **going to** order an extra chocolate dessert that I'm **going to** surprise her with. I know that's **going to** make her happy because she's a bigger chocaholic than I am!

LET'S LEARN!

VOCABULARY

The following words and expressions were used in the previous dialogues. Let's take a closer look at what they mean.

chocaholic *n.* one who loves chocolate.

EXAMPLE:	My father is a **chocaholic**. He'll eat anything with chocolate on it!
TRANSLATION:	My father is a **lover of chocolate**. He'll eat anything with chocolate on it!
"REAL SPEAK":	My father's a **chocaholic**. He'll ead anything w'th choc'lit on it!
Note:	This is a play-on-words on the term *alcoholic*, meaning "a person addicted to alcohol." The suffix *-aholic* can be added to many words to suggest that the subject is addicted to something. For example: *food-aholic, shop-aholic, gym-aholic, etc.*

NOW YOU DO IT. COMPLETE THE PHRASE ALOUD:
I think Kim is a chocaholic because...

cut down on something (to) *exp.* to do a particular activity less such as eating or drinking.

EXAMPLE:	I love desserts, but I'm trying **to cut down** because I've started to put on weight!
TRANSLATION:	I love desserts, but I'm trying **to eat less of them** because I've started to put on weight!
"REAL SPEAK":	I love desserts, bud I'm trying **ta cut down** 'cuz I've starded da pud on weight!
Variation:	**cut back on something (to)** *exp.*
Also:	**cut out something (to)** *exp.* to eliminate something completely.

NOW YOU DO IT. COMPLETE THE PHRASE ALOUD:
I'm trying to cut down on...

doggie bag *exp.* a bag used to carry leftover food home from a restaurant.

EXAMPLE:	I can't finish all this food. I'm going to ask our waiter for a **doggie bag**.
TRANSLATION:	I can't finish all this food. I'm going to ask our waiter for a **bag to take this food home**.
"REAL SPEAK":	I can't finish all this food. I'm gonna ask 'ar waider fer a **doggie bag**.
Note:	This term was originally used to refer to a bag that people could use to take bones home from a restaurant to their dog or "*doggie*" (a child's term for "dog").

NOW YOU DO IT. COMPLETE THE PHRASE ALOUD:
I need a doggie bag to take home this...

eyes that are bigger than one's stomach (to have) *exp.* to think one can eat more than one actually can.

EXAMPLE:	You're going to eat all that food? I have a feeling **your eyes are bigger than your stomach**.
TRANSLATION:	You're going to eat all that food? I have a feeling **you think you can eat more than you can**.
"REAL SPEAK":	Yer gonna ead all that food? I have a feeling **yer eyes 'er bigger th'n yer stomach**.

NOW YOU DO IT. COMPLETE THE PHRASE ALOUD:
My mom said my eyes are bigger than my stomach because...

grab a bite (to) *exp.* to get something to eat.

EXAMPLE:	I'm starting to get hungry. Do you want to **grab a bite** somewhere?
TRANSLATION:	I'm starting to get hungry. Do you want to **get something to eat** somewhere?
"REAL SPEAK":	I'm starding da get hungry. Ya wanna **grab a bite** somewhere?
Variation:	**grab a bite to eat (to)** *exp.*

NOW YOU DO IT. COMPLETE THE PHRASE ALOUD:
Yesterday I grabbed a bite at...

leftovers *n.pl.* remaining food that couldn't be finished.

EXAMPLE:	Do you want to come to my house for dinner? We have a lot of **leftovers** from the party last night.
TRANSLATION:	Do you want to come to my house for dinner? We have a lot of **remaining food** from the party last night.
"REAL SPEAK":	Ya wanna come ta my house fer dinner? We have a lod 'a **leftovers** fr'm the pardy las' night.

NOW YOU DO IT. COMPLETE THE PHRASE ALOUD:
My favorite leftovers are...

on someone  **(to be)** *exp.* to be paid for by someone else.

EXAMPLE:	Since you did such a big favor for me yesterday, **dinner is on me**.
TRANSLATION:	Since you did such a big favor for me yesterday, **I'm paying for dinner**.
"REAL SPEAK":	Since ya did such a big faver fer me yesderday, **dinner's on me**.

NOW YOU DO IT. COMPLETE THE PHRASE ALOUD:
In honor of your... lunch is on me.

pig out (to) *phrV.* to eat in excess, to overeat, to eat like a pig.

EXAMPLE: I don't think I'm going to eat dinner tonight. I **pigged out** during lunch and I'm still full!

TRANSLATION: I don't think I'm going to eat dinner tonight. I **overate** during lunch and I'm still full!

"REAL SPEAK": I don' think I'm gonna eat dinner tanight. I **pigged out** during lunch 'n I'm still full!

Synonym: **pork out (to)** *phrV.*

NOW YOU DO IT. COMPLETE THE PHRASE ALOUD:

The last time I pigged out was...

side of something (a) *exp.* (used when ordering food) an extra order of something.

EXAMPLE: Since my hamburger doesn't come with anything extra, I'm going to get **a side of** cole slaw.

TRANSLATION: Since my hamburger doesn't come with anything extra, I'm going to get **an extra order of** cole slaw.

"REAL SPEAK": Since my burger doesn't come with anything extra, I'm gonna ged **a side 'a** cole slaw.

Note: *Cole slaw* (or *slaw*) is a popular salad made of shredded cabbage and mayonnaise.

NOW YOU DO IT. COMPLETE THE PHRASE ALOUD:

I'm so hungry that I'm going to order a side of...

skip something (to) *v.* to omit something from one's food order.

EXAMPLE: I'm going to **skip** the salad today and just have a sandwich and a drink.

TRANSLATION: I'm going to **decide against ordering** the salad today and just have a sandwich and a drink.

"REAL SPEAK": I'm gonna **skip** the salad taday 'n just have a san'wich 'n a drink.

NOW YOU DO IT. COMPLETE THE PHRASE ALOUD:

I'm going to skip dessert because last night I...

slider *n.* a mini hamburger served on a little bun and usually served three or more per order.

EXAMPLE: Let's order the **sliders**! They serve six on a plate and each one has a different topping!

TRANSLATION: Let's order the **mini hamburgers on little buns**! They serve six on a plate and each one has a different topping!

"REAL SPEAK": Let's order the **sliders**! They serve six on a plate an' each one has a diff'rent topping!

sweet tooth (to have a) *exp.* to have a passion for sweets.

> **EXAMPLE:** Did you see all the candy Liz ate? She must really have a **sweet tooth**!
>
> **TRANSLATION:** Did you see all the candy Liz ate? She must really have a **passion for sweets**!
>
> **"REAL SPEAK":** Did'ja see all the candy Liz ate? She must really have a **sweet tooth**!
>
> **NOW YOU DO IT. COMPLETE THE PHRASE ALOUD:**
>
> *I think... has a sweet tooth because yesterday I saw him/her eat a...*

LET'S PRACTICE!

TRACK 43
SOUNDCLOUD

A. CHOOSE THE RIGHT WORD

Underline the appropriate word that best completes the phrase.
(Answers on p. 219)

1. I want a hamburger, but nothing too big. I think I'll order a few (**gliders**, **sliders**, **slippers**).

2. I can't finish all this food. I think I'm going to need a (**kitty**, **birdie**, **doggie**) bag.

3. I'm starting to get fat! I'd better start to cut (**down**, **up**, **out**).

4. I'm hungry. Let's go grab a (**chew**, **bite**, **swallow**) before the movie.

5. I'm going to (**jump**, **hop**, **skip**) dessert. I'm trying to lose weight.

6. Did you see all the dessert Cecily ate? She must really have a sweet (**tooth**, **mouth**, **ear**).

7. Since today is your birthday, dinner is (**on**, **off**, **over**) me.

8. I'm starving! I'm really going to (**cow**, **giraffe**, **pig**) out during dinner!

9. Why did you order so much food? I think your (**ears**, **eyes**, **elbows**) are bigger than your stomach!

10. I'm going to order a (**top**, **bottom**, **side**) of French fries to go with my hamburger.

11. I think we bought too much food for the party. Look at all these left(**uppers**, **overs**, **downers**)!

12. No one loves (**chalk**, **chocolate**, **choking**) as much as my mother. She's such a chocaholic!

B. CROSSWORD PUZZLE

Fill in the crossword puzzle by choosing the correct word from the list below.

(Answers on p. 219)

cutting	chocaholic	sweet
stomach	side	leftovers
on	slider	pig
skip	bag	bite

ACROSS

1. You want to order two hamburgers, French fries, salad, and dessert?! I think your eyes are bigger than your ____ !

18. I'm hungry. We have a little extra time before the show starts. Let's grab a ____ at that new restaurant that just opened yesterday.

19. Since today is your birthday, lunch is ____ me.

23. I have to start ____ down or I'm going to get fat!

27. Why don't we order a ____ of spaghetti that we can share with our meal?

32. I'm going to ____ dessert today. I couldn't eat another thing.

38. I couldn't possibly eat another bite. I'm going to ask the waiter for a doggie ____ .

DOWN

1. For dessert I ate a big piece of chocolate cake, a slice of lemon pie, six chocolate chip cookies, and a brownie. I've always had a ____ tooth!

6. Tessa could easily eat an entire chocolate cake all by herself. Everyone knows she's a real ____.

17. I think I bought too much food for the party. We'll never be able to eat all this food. I suppose we can always eat the ____ tomorrow.

33. Yesterday for dinner, I went to an all-you-can-eat restaurant. You should have seem me ____ out!

C. MATCH THE COLUMN

Match the words in boldface with the definition in the right column. Write the letter of the definition in the box.

(Answers on p. 219)

1. I love candy, cakes, pies, and anything with chocolate! I guess you could say I have a ***sweet tooth***.

2. Let's go ***grab a bite*** before the movie starts. I know a great restaurant just around the corner.

3. Why don't we order some ***sliders***? That way we can get a taste of a variety of different flavors!

4. If you don't start ***cutting down***, you're going to gain weight.

5. I couldn't possibly eat another bite. I'm so full! I'd better ask the waiter for a ***doggie bag***.

6. Look at that beautiful buffet. I've never seen so much food! Let's go ***pig out***.

7. Thank you for treating me to lunch yesterday. Let's go out to dinner today. ***It's on me***.

8. I'm going to ***skip*** the salad tonight since I just had one during lunch.

9. If you're still hungry, you could always order ***a side of*** bread rolls or a salad.

10. That was such a delicious meal, but there's so much food we didn't even touch. Well, I guess we can always have ***leftovers*** tomorrow.

11. Why did you take such a huge piece of pie? You'll never be able to finish that. I think ***your eyes are bigger than your stomach***.

12. I think Joe is a ***chocaholic***. He just ate an entire chocolate cake and two chocolate ice cream cones!

A. eating less

B. passion for sweets

C. omit

D. eat in excess

E. chocolate lover

F. get something to eat

G. the remaining food that couldn't be finished

H. I'll treat

I. mini hamburgers

J. bag used to carry remaining food home from a restaurant

K. an extra order of

L. you believe you can eat more than you actually can

LET'S REVIEW!

THE GOOD, THE BAD, AND THE... *(Answers on p. 219)*

There were several slang terms and idioms in the first three lessons that were used to describe something either very good or very bad. Write the number of the slang term or idiom in **Column A** next to its matching picture in **Column B** as well as next to the matching definition in **Column C**.

COLUMN A	COLUMN B	COLUMN C
1. to be a blast		to be overpriced
2. to die for		to be very successful
3. to be a bomb		to be a lot of fun
4. to be a rip-off	BOOM!	to be fantastic
5. to be a blockbuster		to be a total failure

TRACK 46
SOUNDCLOUD

Popular Idioms, Slang & Jargon
Having to do with:
RESTAURANT

EXERCISES FOR THIS SECTION ARE IN THE WORKBOOK.

à la carte *exp.* (from French – pronounced *ah lah kart*) food that is ordered from the menu as a separate item • (lit); according to the menu.

MORE ON... SLANGMAN

> **EXAMPLE:** Vegetables aren't included with your dinner. If you want spinach and broccoli, you need to order them **à la carte**.

> **TRANSLATION:** Vegetables aren't included with your dinner. If you want spinach and broccoli, you need to order them **separately**.

> **"REAL SPEAK":** *Veggies* aren' included w'th yer dinner. If ya want spinach 'n broccoli, ya need da order th'm **ah lah kart**.

à la mode *exp.* (from French – pronounced *ah lah moh'd*) served with ice cream • (lit); according to the latest fashion.

> **EXAMPLE:** I'd like to order the apple pie. Does it come **à la mode**?

> **TRANSLATION:** I'd like to order the apple pie. Does it come **with ice cream**?

> **"REAL SPEAK":** I'd like ta order the apple pie. Does it come **ah lah moh'd**?

aftertaste *exp.* a taste, typically an unpleasant one, remaining in the mouth after eating or drinking something.

> **EXAMPLE:** The chocolate cake was good, but it left a bitter **aftertaste**! Maybe they used a sugar substitute or something.

> **TRANSLATION:** The chocolate cake was good, but it left a bitter **taste after I finished eating it**! Maybe they used a sugar substitute or something.

> **"REAL SPEAK":** The chocolate cake w'z good, b'd it left a bidder **afdertaste**! Maybe they used a sugar substitute 'r something.

al dente *exp.* (from Italian – pronounced *ahl dentay*) a description of pasta that is cooked but firm to the bite • (lit); to the tooth.

> **EXAMPLE:** I don't like pasta this soft. I prefer it **al dente**.

> **TRANSLATION:** I don't like pasta this soft. I prefer it **firm to the bite**.

> **"REAL SPEAK":** I don' like pasta th's soft. I prafer id **ahl dentay**.

apéritif *n.* an alcoholic drink served before the meal to stimulate one's appetite • (lit); (from French – pronounced *ah-pay-ree-teef)* an "opener" as in "to open the appetite."

> **EXAMPLE:** Let's start dinner with an **apéritif**, then we can order a little later.

> **TRANSLATION:** Let's start dinner with an **alcoholic beverage to simulate our appetites**, then we can order a little later.

> **"REAL SPEAK":** Let's start dinner w'th 'n **ah-pay-ree-teef**, then we c'n order a liddle lader.

au jus *exp.* describing meat that is served with its own juices as a gravy • (lit); (from French – prounounced *oh-joo*) with juice.

> **EXAMPLE:** I'm going to order the roast beef **au jus**. I love all that natural gravy!
>
> **TRANSLATION:** I'm going to order the roast beef **served in its own juices**. I love all that natural gravy!
>
> **"REAL SPEAK":** I'm gonna order the roas' beef **oh joo**. I love all that nach'ral gravy!

booze *n.* alcohol in general.

> **EXAMPLE:** I hope they serve **booze** in this restaurant. I could really use a drink!
>
> **TRANSLATION:** I hope they serve **alcohol** in this restaurant. I could really use a drink!
>
> **"REAL SPEAK":** I hope they serve **booze** 'n th's rest'rant. I could really use a drink!

brunch *n.* a meal, usually served on Sundays, eaten in place of **br**eakfast and **l**u**nch** = **brunch**.

> **EXAMPLE:** **Brunch** is my favorite meal. That's when restaurants usually offer buffets where you can eat all you want!
>
> **TRANSLATION:** **The meal where breakfast and lunch is combined** is my favorite meal. That's when restaurants usually offer buffets where you can eat all you want!
>
> **"REAL SPEAK":** **Brunch** 'ez my fav'rit meal. That's wh'n rest'rants ujally offer buffets where ya c'n ead all ya want!

MORE ON... TV SLANGMAN

cover *n.* (short for **cover charge**) an amount added to the bill at a restaurant or nightclub for entertainment or service.

> **EXAMPLE:** Is there a **cover** to eat in this restaurant? That's going to be an expensive meal!
>
> **TRANSLATION:** Is there an **additional charge for entertainment or service** to eat in this restaurant? That's going to be an expensive meal!
>
> **"REAL SPEAK":** Is there a **cover** da eat 'n th's rest'rant? That's gonna be 'n expensive meal!

cover someone (to) *exp.* to pay for someone.

> **EXAMPLE:** Don't worry about forgetting your wallet. I'll **cover you**.
>
> **TRANSLATION:** Don't worry about forgetting your wallet. I'll **pay for you**.
>
> **"REAL SPEAK":** Don't worry about fergedding yer wallet. A'll **cover ya**.
>
> *Variation:* **have someone covered (to)** *exp.* *Don't worry. I got you covered; Don't worry. I'll pay for you.*

dine in (to) *phrV.* to eat at the restaurant rather than taking the food home to eat.

> **EXAMPLE:** Let's **dine in**, so we can sit and gossip! I can't wait to tell you what happened today!

> **TRANSLATION:** Let's **eat here in the restaurant**, so we can sit and gossip! I can't wait to tell you what happened today!
>
> **"REAL SPEAK":** Let's **dine in**, so we c'n sit 'n gossip! I can't wait ta tell ya what happen' today!

earlybird special *exp.* a discounted dinner served earlier than traditional dinner hours.

> **EXAMPLE:** If we arrive at the restaurant before five o'clock, we can get the **earlybird special** and save $10 each!
>
> **TRANSLATION:** If we arrive at the restaurant before five o'clock, we can get the **early discounted dinner** and save $10 each!
>
> **"REAL SPEAK":** If we arrive 'it the rest'rant b'fore five a'clock, we c'n get the **earlybird special** 'n save ten dollers each!

eat out (to) *phrV.* to eat at a restaurant "out" of one's home.

> EXAMPLE: Let's **eat out** tonight. I don't feel like cooking.
>
> TRANSLATION: Let's **eat at a restaurant** tonight. I don't feel like cooking.
>
> "REAL SPEAK": Let's **ead out** tanight. I don' feel like cooking.

eats *n.pl.* food in general.

> EXAMPLE: I'm hungry. Where can we find some good **eats** in this city?
>
> TRANSLATION: I'm hungry. Where can we find some good **food** in this city?
>
> "REAL SPEAK": I'm hungry. Where c'n we fin' s'm good **eats** 'n th's cidy?

entrée *n.* (from French – pronounced *ahn-tray*) the main course of a meal in the U.S.

> EXAMPLE: I think I'll have the fish as my **entrée**. I want something light, so I have room for dessert!

> TRANSLATION: I think I'll have the fish as my **main course**. I want something light, so I have room for dessert!
>
> "REAL SPEAK": I think a'll have the fish 'ez my **ahn-tray**. I want something light, so I have room fer dessert!

filet mignon *n.* (from French – pronounced *fee-lay meen-yohn*) a very high-quality, tender, and expensive piece of beef • (lit); cute filet.

> EXAMPLE: As a special treat for your birthday dinner, I've ordered you the **filet mignon**!
>
> TRANSLATION: As a special treat for your birthday dinner, I've ordered you the **most tender and expensive piece of beef**!

> "REAL SPEAK": As a special treat fer yer birthday dinner, I ordered ya the **fee-lay meen-yohn**!

grub *n.* food in general.

> EXAMPLE: Yuck! The **grub** in this restaurant is horrible!
>
> TRANSLATION: Yuck! The **food** in this restaurant is horrible!
>
> "REAL SPEAK": Yuck! The **grub** 'n th's rest'rant 'ez horrible!

MORE ON... TV SLANGMAN

happy hour *exp.* a period of the day just before dinner when drinks and food are sold at reduced prices in a bar or restaurant.

> EXAMPLE: Let's leave work a little early and go to **happy hour**!
>
> TRANSLATION: Let's leave work a little early and go to **a restaurant where they serve drinks and food at a reduced price before dinner**!
>
> "REAL SPEAK": Let's leave work a liddle early 'n go da **happy hour**!

hors d'oeuvre *n.* (from French – pronounced *or derv*) a small portion of a tasty food served as an appetizer at the beginning of a meal.

> EXAMPLE: I'm so hungry! While we're waiting for our dinner, let's order an **hors d'oeuvre**.
>
> TRANSLATION: I'm so hungry! While we're waiting for our dinner, let's order an **appetizer**.
>
> "REAL SPEAK": I'm so hungry! While w'r wading fer 'ar dinner, let's order 'n **or derv**.
>
> *Synonym:* **amuse-bouche** *n.* (from French – pronounced *ahmuz-boosh*) • (lit); mouth amuser.

lay off something (to) *exp.* to stop eating a particular food usually due to allergies or high calories.

> EXAMPLE: I need to **lay off** desserts for a while until I lose some weight.
>
> TRANSLATION: I need to **stop eating** desserts for a while until I lose some weight.
>
> "REAL SPEAK": I need da **lay off** desserts fer a while 'til I lose s'm weight.

lite *adj.* relating to low-calorie by using low-fat or low-sugar ingredients.

> **EXAMPLE:** I love this restaurant. They have a **lite** dessert menu, so I never feel guilty ordering!

> **TRANSLATION:** I love this restaurant. They have a **low calorie** dessert menu, so I never feel guilty ordering!

> **"REAL SPEAK":** I love th's rest'rant. They 'ave a **lite** dessert menu, so I never feel guilty ordering!

low-cal *adj.* a very common shortened version of "low calorie."

> **EXAMPLE:** Is this soft drink **low-cal**? I'm on a strict diet and can't have anything with sugar.

> **TRANSLATION:** Is this soft drink **low-calorie**? I'm on a strict diet and can't have anything with sugar.

> **"REAL SPEAK":** Is th's soft drink **low-cal**? I'm on a stric' diet and can't have anything w'th sugar.

maître d' *n.* (from French – pronounced *may-der dee* by Americans) the head person in a restaurant who is in charge of the servers and typically takes reservations.

> **EXAMPLE:** Oh, look! There's a table by that window! Let's ask the **maître d'** if he can move us.

> **TRANSLATION:** Oh, look! There's a table by that window! Let's ask the **head of the restaurant** if he can move us.

> **"REAL SPEAK":** Oh, look! There's a table by that window! Let's ask the **may-der dee** 'ef 'e c'n move us.

pancake *n.* a flat hot cake made of batter, usually fried and turned in a pan and served with butter and syrup.

> **EXAMPLE:** Every Sunday morning, my family used to go out to our favorite local restaurant and eat **pancakes** with lots of syrup and butter!

> **TRANSLATION:** Every Sunday morning, my family used to go out to our favorite local restaurant and eat **flat hot cakes** with lots of syrup and butter!

> **"REAL SPEAK":** Ev'ry Sunday morning, my fam'ly usta go out to 'ar fav'rit local rest'rant 'n eat **pancakes** w'th lots 'ev syrup 'n budder!

> *Synonym 1:* **flapjack** *n.*
>
> *Synonym 2:* **griddle cake** *exp.*
>
> *Synonym 3:* **hotcake** *n.*

short stack *exp.* an order of pancakes that contains 2-3 pancakes.

> **EXAMPLE:** Pancakes are so filling! I think I'll just order a **short stack**.

> **TRANSLATION:** Pancakes are so filling! I think I'll just order a **small stack of 2 or 3 pancakes**.

> **"REAL SPEAK":** Pancakes 'er so filling! I think a'll just order a **short stack**.

snack on something (to) *exp.* to eat something light.

> **EXAMPLE:** If you're hungry, why don't you just **snack on something**? Breakfast will be ready in an hour.

TRANSLATION: If you're hungry, why don't you just **have a little snack**? Breakfast will be ready in an hour.

"REAL SPEAK": If y'r hungry, why doncha jus' **snack on something**? Breakfast'll be ready in 'n hour.

starter *n.* appetizer.

EXAMPLE: I haven't eaten all day! Why don't we order a few **starters** and share them?

TRANSLATION: I haven't eaten all day! Why don't we order a few **appetizers** and share them?

"REAL SPEAK": I haven' eaten all day! Why don' we order a few **starders** 'n share 'em?

stiff a server (to) *exp.* to leave a restaurant without giving the server a gratuity.

EXAMPLE: I served twelve people at that table all night and they **stiffed me**!

TRANSLATION: I served twelve people at that table all night and they **left without giving me a gratuity**!

"REAL SPEAK": I serve' twelve people 'it that table all night an' they **stiffed me**!

takeout *n.* food ordered from a restaurant that is packaged to bring home or "take out" of the restaurant.

EXAMPLE: I'm too tired to cook. Let's order some **takeout** tonight.

TRANSLATION: I'm too tired to cook. Let's order some **food we can take home** tonight.

"REAL SPEAK": I'm too tired da cook. Let's order s'm **takeout** tanight.

tip *n.* a gratuity a customer can add to the final restaurant bill, typically 15-20%.

EXAMPLE: Our server was really great. I'm going to give him an extra big **tip**.

TRANSLATION: Our server was really great. I'm going to give him an extra big **gratuity**.

"REAL SPEAK": 'Ar server w'z really great. I'm gonna give 'im 'n extra big **tip**.

Origin: The term **tip** is a shortened version of the acronym TIPS meaning "**T**o **I**nsure **P**rompt **S**ervice."

to-go (to order something) *exp.* to order something from a restaurant that is taken to eat somewhere else.

EXAMPLE: Before we pay the bill, I need to order some **soup to-go** for my sister. She's sick at home.

TRANSLATION: Before we pay the bill, I need to order some **soup to take home** for my sister. She's sick at home.

"REAL SPEAK": B'fore we pay the bill, I need da order s'm **soup ta-go** fer my sister. She's sick 'it home.

Also: **To-Go Menu** *n.* a menu with items that can be ordered to be packed and taken out of the restaurant.

wine and dine someone (to) *exp.* to treat someone to a restaurant which serves expensive food and drinks.

EXAMPLE: I'm going to **wine and dine my boss** and then ask her for a raise.

TRANSLATION: I'm going to **take my boss to an expensive dinner with fine food and drinks** and then ask her for a raise.

"REAL SPEAK": I'm gonna **wine 'n dine my boss** 'n then ask 'er fer a raise.

wolf down one's food (to) *exp.* to eat quickly without hardly chewing.

EXAMPLE: Don't **wolf down your lunch** or you'll get a stomach ache!

TRANSLATION: Don't **eat your lunch so fast** or you'll get a stomach ache!

"REAL SPEAK": Don't **wolf down yer lunch** 'r you'll ged a stomach ache!

SLANGMAN
Explains More idioms & Slang for...

—AT A RESTAURANT—

SCAN ME!

CHAPTER 6

SCAN THE QR CODE OR GO TO: bit.ly/StreetSpeak1-Chapter6

THIS VIDEO EPISODE CONTAINS...

à la carte
- Foreign words that Americans use every day without even realizing it!

Yuck!
- Grunts and groans used in everyday conversations

eat
- Popular expressions and idioms using "eat"

Idioms & slang used on TV this week plus the latest Teen Slang!
- Slangman gives you his TOP 5 LIST of the latest idioms and slang from the most popular TV shows in the U.S. plus the newest slang teens are using today!

Newest American slang just entered into the dictionary

LET'S WARM UP!

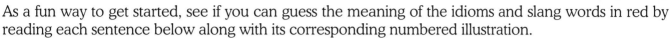

MATCH THE PICTURES *(Answers on p. 220)*

As a fun way to get started, see if you can guess the meaning of the idioms and slang words in red by reading each sentence below along with its corresponding numbered illustration.

1. I drove my car over a nail and got a **blowout**.
   - ❏ flat tire
   - ❏ scratch on my car

2. My car was **totaled** in an accident. Now I have to buy a new one.
   - ❏ destroyed
   - ❏ damaged slightly

3. Yesterday a driver **ran a light** and almost hit me!
   - ❏ crashed into a light post
   - ❏ drove through a red light

4. Would you like to go for a **spin** in my new car?
   - ❏ short drive
   - ❏ walk

5. I'm going to be late for work! I'd better **punch it**!
   - ❏ accelerate suddenly
   - ❏ stop suddenly

6. I was in a **fender-bender** today. The car repairs shouldn't cost very much.
   - ❏ minor car accident
   - ❏ major car accident

7. Yesterday, it took me an hour to drive home during **rush hour**, and I only live a mile away!
   - ❏ the time when everyone is driving on the road
   - ❏ the time when no one is driving on the road

8. I'll be glad to drive you to the market. **Hop in**!
   - ❏ start jumping
   - ❏ get in

9. Bob got **hauled in** for speeding! He may have to spend the night in jail!
   - ❏ an award
   - ❏ arrested

10. The **bumper-to-bumper traffic** made me late!
    - ❏ light traffic
    - ❏ heavy traffic

11. The **cop** just arrested that man for bank robbery!
    - ❏ fire fighter
    - ❏ police officer

12. I just bought my car yesterday and it already stopped working! What a **lemon**!
    - ❏ wonderful car
    - ❏ defective car

13. Jason is so excited about his new **wheels**!
    - ❏ tires
    - ❏ car

14. I don't drive with Dan because he has a **lead foot**!
    - ❏ broken foot
    - ❏ tendency to drive very fast

LET'S TALK!

A. DIALOGUE USING SLANG & IDIOMS

The words introduced on the previous two pages are used in the following dialogue and illustrated in the long picture above. Can you understand the conversation and find the illustration that corresponds to the slang? *Note:* The translation of the words in boldface is on the right-hand page.

— John is showing Mark his new car —

Mark: Wow, John! Nice **wheels**!

John: Thanks! I just bought it. Hopefully it's better than that **lemon** I bought last year. **Hop in** and I'll take you for a **spin**!

Mark: Just be careful. I know about that **lead foot** of yours. You don't want to get into a **fender-bender**! And you definitely don't want to get **hauled in** for speeding or **running a light**.

John: Don't worry. I promise I'm not going to **total my car** or get stopped by a **cop** my first day having a new car! Besides, it's **rush hour** and we're not going to be able to go very fast with all the **bumper-to-bumper traffic**. But once it clears up, I'm going to **punch it**!

Mark: Ok, cool! Oh, you may want to avoid Ventura Boulevard. They haven't fixed some of the big cracks yet and you sure don't want to get a **blowout**!

LET'S TALK!

B. DIALOGUE TRANSLATED INTO STANDARD ENGLISH

LET'S SEE HOW MUCH YOU REMEMBER!
Just for fun, bounce around in random order to the words and
expressions in boldface below. See if you can remember their
slang equivalents without looking at the left-hand page!

— *John is showing Mark his new car* —

Mark: Wow, John! Nice **wheels**!

John: Thanks! I just bought it. Hopefully it's better than that **defective car** I bought last year. **Get in** and I'll take you for a **short drive**!

Mark: Just be careful. I know about your **tendency to drive fast**. You don't want to get into a **car accident**! And you definitely don't want to get **arrested** for speeding or **driving through a red light**.

John: Don't worry. I promise I'm not going to **destroy my car** or get stopped by a **cop** my first day having a new car. Besides, it's **the time when most of the cars are on the road** and we're not going to be able to go very fast with all the **heavy traffic**. But once it clears up, I'm going to **accelerate quickly**!

Mark: Ok, cool! Oh, you may want to avoid Ventura Boulevard. They haven't fixed some of the big cracks yet and you sure don't want to get a **flat tire**!

C. DIALOGUE USING "REAL SPEAK"

The dialogue below demonstrates how the slang conversation on the previous page would *really* be spoken by native speakers!

— *John's showing Mark 'is new car* —

Mark: Wow, John! Nice **wheels**!

John: Thanks! I jus' bod it. Hopefully it's bedder th'n that **lemon** I bought last year. **Hop in** 'n a'll take ya fer a **spin**!

Mark: Jus' be careful. I know about that **lead food** 'a yers. Ya don't wannna ged indo a **fender-bender**! And ya def'nitely don't wannna get **hauled in** fer speeding 'r **running a light**.

John: Don't worry. I promise I'm not gonna **todal my car** 'r get stopped by a **cop** my firs' day having a new car! B'sides, it's **rush hour** 'n we're not gonna be able da go very fast w'th all the **bumper-da-bumper traffic**. B't once it clears up, I'm gonna **punch it**!

Mark: Ok, cool! Oh, you may wannew avoid Ventura Boulevard. They haven' fix' some 'a the big cracks yet an' ya sher don't wanna ged a **blowout**!

WANT TO = WANNA

In the above dialogue using "Real Speak," **want to** became **wanna**. This is a very informal style of speech and can certainly be used in business as well.

RULES

In everyday conversation, **want to** is commonly reduced to **wanna**, and "wants to" is commonly reduced to **wansta**. Personal pronouns *I, you, we* and *they* use **wanna**; *he* and *she* use **wansta**, as demonstrated on the opposite page.

HOW DOES IT WORK?

I **want to** go for a spin. I **wan̶t̶t̶o** go for a spin.	In the phrase **want to**, the sound of both *t's* disappears in everyday speech.
I **wan o** go for a spin. I **wan uh** go for a spin.	All unstressed vowels (such as the **o** in **to** of **want to**) are commonly pronounced **uh**.
I **wanna** go for a spin.	This shortened version of **want to** is so common in everyday speech that it is often seen written in magazines and newspapers to indicate spoken language.

WANNA / WANSTA CHART

I	I **want to** go for a *spin*.	→	I **wanna** go for a *spin*.
you	Do you **want to** *hop in* and go?	→	Do you **wanna** *hop in* and go?
we	We **want to** miss *rush hour*.	→	We **wanna** miss *rush hour*.
they	They **want to** buy some new *wheels*.	→	They **wanna** some new *wheels*.
he	He **wants to** avoid buying a *lemon*.	→	He **wansta** avoid buying a *lemon*.
she	She **wants to** *grab a cab*.	→	She **wansta** *grab a cab*.

LET'S USE "REAL SPEAK!"

A. WANNA OR WANSTA

Answer the question in Column A aloud using the words in Column B. Make sure to use "wanna" or "wansta" in your answers.

(Answers on p. 220)

SPEAKING

TRACK 48
SOUNDCLOUD

COLUMN A	COLUMN B
1. Do you want to catch a movie tonight?	[Yes] [see] [comedy]
2. What does your brother want to do tonight?	[He] [pig out] [pizza]
3. What do your friends want to order for dinner?	[Everybody] [hamburgers] [side of fries]
4. Does Steve want to take home the leftovers?	[Yes] [he] [doggie bag]
5. Do you want to take a drive in my new car?	[Yes] [spin] [beach]
6. Where does your mother want to go for dinner?	[She] [eat] [French restaurant]
7. Does anybody want to play cards tonight?	[Nobody] [play cards] [watch TV]
8. Does the cat want to go outside?	[No] [sleep] [sofa]

LET'S LEARN!

SPEAKING
TRACK 49
SOUNDCLOUD

VOCABULARY

The following words and expressions were used in the previous dialogues. Let's take a closer look at what they mean.

blowout *n.* (said because the air "blows out" of the tire) a punctured tire.

EXAMPLE:	I was late to work because I got a **blowout** on the highway this morning.
TRANSLATION:	I was late to work because I got a **punctured tire** on the highway this morning.
"REAL SPEAK":	I w'z late ta work 'cuz I god a **blowoud** on the highway th's morning.
Synonym:	**flat** *n.* (short for: *flat tire*).

NOW YOU DO IT. COMPLETE THE PHRASE ALOUD:

My car got a blowout on my way to...

bumper-to-bumper traffic *exp.* traffic that is so heavy that there is no room between cars.

EXAMPLE:	It took me two hours to get home because of all the **bumper-to-bumper traffic** and I only live a few miles from work!
TRANSLATION:	It took me two hours to get home because of all the **heavy traffic** and I only live a few miles from work!
"REAL SPEAK":	It took me two hours ta get home b'cu 'ev of all the **bumper-da-bumper traffic** an' I only live a few miles fr'm work!

NOW YOU DO IT. COMPLETE THE PHRASE ALOUD:

The road to ...is known for having a lot of bumper-to-bumper traffic.

cop *n.* police officer (originally called a *copper*).

EXAMPLE:	Be careful not to speed on this street. I just saw a **cop**.
TRANSLATION:	Be careful not to speed on this street. I just saw a **police officer**.
"REAL SPEAK":	Be careful not ta speed on th's street. I jus' saw a **cop**.
Note:	This popular term (used even among police officers) came from the days of gangsters when police officers were known for wearing a copper badge.

NOW YOU DO IT. COMPLETE THE PHRASE ALOUD:

The job of a cop is to...

fender-bender *n.* a minor car accident.

> **EXAMPLE:** I got into a car accident this morning, but don't worry. It was just a **fender-bender**.
>
> **TRANSLATION:** I got into a car accident this morning, but don't worry. It was just a **minor accident**.
>
> **"REAL SPEAK":** I god into a car accident th's morning, b' don't worry. I'w'z just a **fender-bender**.

NOW YOU DO IT. COMPLETE THE PHRASE ALOUD:
The last time I saw a fender-bender was...

hauled in (to get) *exp.* to get taken to the police station; to be arrested.

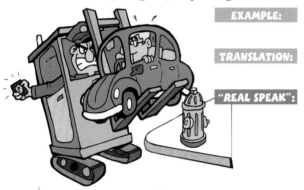

> **EXAMPLE:** Did you hear the news? Jim got **hauled in** for drunk driving!
>
> **TRANSLATION:** Did you hear the news? Jim got **taken to the police station** for drunk driving!
>
> **"REAL SPEAK":** Did'ja hear the news? Jim got **hauled in** fer drunk driving!

NOW YOU DO IT. COMPLETE THE PHRASE ALOUD:
I've never been hauled in for...

hop in (to) *phrV.* to get into a car.

> **EXAMPLE:** I'd be happy to drive you to the grocery store this morning. **Hop in**!
>
> **TRANSLATION:** I'd be happy to drive you to the grocery store this morning. **Get in the car**!
>
> **"REAL SPEAK":** I'd be happy da drive ya da the groc'ry store th's morning. **Hop in**!

NOW YOU DO IT. COMPLETE THE PHRASE ALOUD:
Hop in! I'd be glad to drive you to...

lead foot (to have a) *exp.* said of a driver who has a tendency to drive faster than the speed limit (as if his/her foot were made of lead, causing the car's gas pedal to be pressed too far down).

> **EXAMPLE:** My brother got his third speeding ticket in two weeks! My father is always yelling at him about his **lead foot**.
>
> **TRANSLATION:** My brother got his third speeding ticket in two weeks! My father is always yelling at him about his **tendency to drive too fast**.
>
> **"REAL SPEAK":** My brother god 'is third speeding ticket 'n two weeks! My dad's ahways yelling ad 'im aboud 'is **lead foot**.

NOW YOU DO IT. COMPLETE THE PHRASE ALOUD:
My (family member or friend) has a lead foot!

lemon *n.* a machine, typically a car, that is defective.

EXAMPLE: Right after I bought my car, it died! The car dealership replaced it because it was clearly a **lemon**.

TRANSLATION: Right after I bought my car, it died! The car dealership replaced it because it was clearly a **defective car**.

"REAL SPEAK": Ride afder I bought my car, it died! The car dealership r'placed it b'cuz it w'z clearly a **lemon**.

Synonym: **piece of junk** *n.*

NOW YOU DO IT. COMPLETE THE PHRASE ALOUD:
The... I bought was a total lemon!

punch it (to) *exp.* to press the accelerator pedal down suddenly.

EXAMPLE: **Punch it**! We only have five minutes before the movie starts!

TRANSLATION: **Accelerate immediately**! We only have five minutes before the movie starts!

"REAL SPEAK": **Punch it**! We only 'ave five minutes b'fore the movie starts!

NOW YOU DO IT. COMPLETE THE PHRASE ALOUD:
We're late for.... Punch it!

run a light (to) *exp.* to go through a traffic signal during a red light.

EXAMPLE: Did you see that?! That guy **ran the light** and almost hit us!

TRANSLATION: Did you see that?! That guy **went through the traffic signal during a red light** and almost hit us!

"REAL SPEAK": Did'ja see that?! That guy **ran the light** 'n almost hid us!

NOW YOU DO IT. COMPLETE THE PHRASE ALOUD:
The danger in running a red light is...

rush hour *exp.* the time when most drivers are on the road at the same time (usually at the opening or close of business).

EXAMPLE: Let's meet for dinner tonight, but let's make it around seven o'clock. I don't want to drive during **rush hour**.

TRANSLATION: Let's meet for dinner tonight, but let's make it around seven o'clock. I don't want to drive during **the time when most drivers are on the road at the same time**.

"REAL SPEAK": Let's meet fer dinner danight, b't let's make id aroun' seven a'clock. I don't wanna drive during **rush hour**.

Note: This term is still commonly used although it's no longer accurate, since in most big cities **rush hour** actually lasts for *several* hours!

NOW YOU DO IT. COMPLETE THE PHRASE ALOUD:
During rush hour, it takes me ...hours to get to...

spin (to take a) *exp.* to take a short drive with no particular destination.

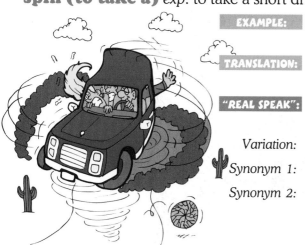

> **EXAMPLE:** It's such a beautiful day! Why don't we **take a spin** in my new car?
>
> **TRANSLATION:** It's such a beautiful day! Why don't we **take a relaxing drive** in my new car?
>
> **"REAL SPEAK":** It's such a beaudif'l day! Why don' we **take a spin** 'n my new car?
>
> *Variation:* **spin (to go for a)** *exp.*
>
> *Synonym 1:* **jaunt (to take a)** *exp.*
>
> *Synonym 2:* **ride (to take a)** *exp.*
>
> **NOW YOU DO IT. COMPLETE THE PHRASE ALOUD:**
> *Do you like my new car? Let's take a spin to... so we can show it to...*

total a car (to) *exp.* to completely destroy a car in an accident.

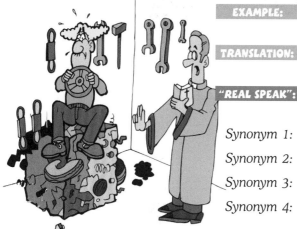

> **EXAMPLE:** Did you hear the news? Pat **totaled his car** in an accident last night! Luckily, no one was hurt.
>
> **TRANSLATION:** Did you hear the news? Pat **destroyed his car** in an accident last night! Luckily, no one was hurt.
>
> **"REAL SPEAK":** Did'ja hear the news? Pat **todaled 'is car** in 'n accident las' night! Luckily, no one w'z hurt.
>
> *Synonym 1:* **bash up a car (to)** *exp.*
>
> *Synonym 2:* **smash up a car (to)** *exp.*
>
> *Synonym 3:* **wrack up a car (to)** *exp.*
>
> *Synonym 4:* **wreck a car (to)** *exp.*
>
> **NOW YOU DO IT. COMPLETE THE PHRASE ALOUD:**
> *If I total my father's new car, he will...*

wheels *n.pl.* car.

> **EXAMPLE:** I love your new **wheels**! Is that the new electric car everyone has been talking about?
>
> **TRANSLATION:** I love your new **car**! Is that the new electric car everyone has been talking about?
>
> **"REAL SPEAK":** I love yer new **wheels**! Izat the new electric car ev'ryone's b'n talking about?
>
> *Variation:* **set of wheels** *exp.*
>
> **NOW YOU DO IT. COMPLETE THE PHRASE ALOUD:**
> *The first wheels I ever drove...*

LET'S PRACTICE!

TRACK 50
SOUNDCLOUD

A. CORRECT OR INCORRECT

Decide whether the words in boldface have been used correctly or incorrectly by checking the appropriate box.

(Answers on p. 220)

1. George just bought some brand new **wheels**. Now he'll be able to walk everywhere!
   ❏ CORRECT   ❏ INCORRECT

2. You're driving too fast! **Punch it**!
   ❏ CORRECT   ❏ INCORRECT

3. Becky always drives too fast. She has a real **lead foot**.
   ❏ CORRECT   ❏ INCORRECT

4. I made it home easily because there was **bumper-to-bumper traffic** the entire way.
   ❏ CORRECT   ❏ INCORRECT

5. I just bought a fantastic car! It's such a **lemon**!
   ❏ CORRECT   ❏ INCORRECT

6. Do you need a ride to the market? **Hop in**!
   ❏ CORRECT   ❏ INCORRECT

7. I feel like taking a walk today. Let's go for a **spin**.
   ❏ CORRECT   ❏ INCORRECT

8. Let's try to drive out of the city around **rush hour**. That's when there won't be many cars on the road.
   ❏ CORRECT   ❏ INCORRECT

9. On the way to my mother's house, I drove over a nail and got a **blowout**.
   ❏ CORRECT   ❏ INCORRECT

10. I heard you got into an accident yesterday and **totaled** your car! Were you hurt? Is your car really ruined?
    ❏ CORRECT   ❏ INCORRECT

11. That driver almost **ran the light** and hit me!
    ❏ CORRECT   ❏ INCORRECT

12. My sister wants to be a **cop** because she loves fighting fires.
    ❏ CORRECT   ❏ INCORRECT

B. BLANK-BLANK *(Answers on p. 220)*

Fill in the blank with the correct word(s) from Column B.

TRACK 51
SOUNDCLOUD

	COLUMN A	COLUMN B
1.	It took me an hour to drive home because of all the _____.	**cop**
2.	It's such a beautiful day. Let's put the top down and _____ in my new sports car.	**go for a spin**
3.	That was really close! That driver didn't stop! He _____ and almost hit us!	**totaled**
4.	You drive too fast! You're just like your father. You have a _____!	**punch it**
5.	We have to drive to the hospital fast. The contractions are coming every minute! _____!!	**wheels**
6.	The car wasn't damaged too badly in the accident. It was just a little _____.	**ran a light**
7.	I'm going to the market, too. _____. I'd be happy to give you a ride there.	**hauled in**
8.	It looks like I'm going to have to buy a new car after the accident. My poor car was _____.	**fender-bender**
9.	I need to replace my new car. Unfortunately, it's a _____.	**lemon**
10.	I had to buy a new tire this morning because I got a _____ on the way to work.	**blowout**
11.	My sister is a _____. Last week, she arrested two robbers!	**bumper-to-bumper traffic**
12.	Look at all the cars on the road! I hate driving during _____!	**rush hour**
13.	My father used to drive my mother everywhere. But yesterday she got her own _____.	**hop in**
14.	Did you hear the news? Rob got _____ for drunk driving!!	**lead foot**

C. TRUE OR FALSE

Decide whether or not the definition of the word in boldface is true or false by checking an "X" in the correct box.

(Answers on p. 220)

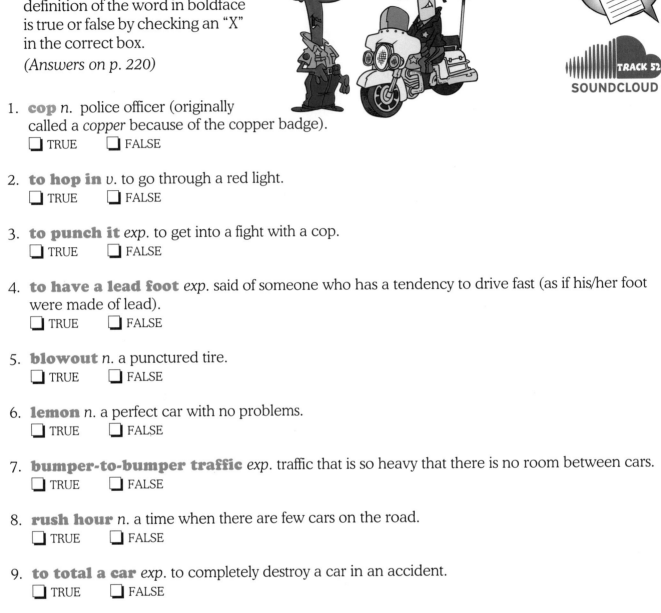

READING

TRACK 52
SOUNDCLOUD

1. **cop** *n.* police officer (originally called a *copper* because of the copper badge).
   ☐ TRUE   ☐ FALSE

2. **to hop in** *v.* to go through a red light.
   ☐ TRUE   ☐ FALSE

3. **to punch it** *exp.* to get into a fight with a cop.
   ☐ TRUE   ☐ FALSE

4. **to have a lead foot** *exp.* said of someone who has a tendency to drive fast (as if his/her foot were made of lead).
   ☐ TRUE   ☐ FALSE

5. **blowout** *n.* a punctured tire.
   ☐ TRUE   ☐ FALSE

6. **lemon** *n.* a perfect car with no problems.
   ☐ TRUE   ☐ FALSE

7. **bumper-to-bumper traffic** *exp.* traffic that is so heavy that there is no room between cars.
   ☐ TRUE   ☐ FALSE

8. **rush hour** *n.* a time when there are few cars on the road.
   ☐ TRUE   ☐ FALSE

9. **to total a car** *exp.* to completely destroy a car in an accident.
   ☐ TRUE   ☐ FALSE

10. **wheels** *n.pl.* car.
    ☐ TRUE   ☐ FALSE

11. **to run a light** *exp.* to drive with the headlights on.
    ☐ TRUE   ☐ FALSE

12. **to take a spin** *exp.* to take a short drive with no particular destination.
    ☐ TRUE   ☐ FALSE

13. **to get hauled in** *exp.* to be taken to the police station; to be arrested.
    ☐ TRUE   ☐ FALSE

14. **fender-bender** *n.* a quick ride in the car.
    ☐ TRUE   ☐ FALSE

LET'S REVIEW!

IN OTHER WORDS... SYNONYMS! *(Answers on p. 220)*

In the vocabulary section of previous lessons, you may have noticed that there were synonyms offered for many of the slang terms and idioms you have learned. Write the number of the picture from Column A next to its matching synonym in Column B.

COLUMN A

1. blowout

2. mess with someone

3. rock bottom

4. blockbuster

5. bomb

6. premiere

7. lemon

8. get a grip

9. wired

10. spin

11. pig out

12. pick up

COLUMN B

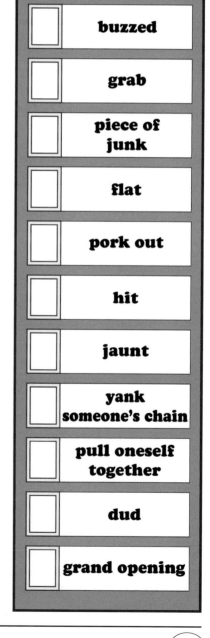

- [ ] dirt cheap
- [ ] buzzed
- [ ] grab
- [ ] piece of junk
- [ ] flat
- [ ] pork out
- [ ] hit
- [ ] jaunt
- [ ] yank someone's chain
- [ ] pull oneself together
- [ ] dud
- [ ] grand opening

EXERCISES FOR THIS SECTION ARE IN THE WORKBOOK.

Popular Idioms, Slang & Jargon
Having to do with: THE ROAD

backseat driver *exp.* a passenger in a car who gives the driver unwanted advice.

EXAMPLE: I don't mean to be a **backseat driver** but you're taking the long way to the airport. Why don't you take the surface streets and avoid the traffic? We need to get there ASAP!

TRANSLATION: I don't mean to be a **passenger who gives the driver unwanted advice** but you're taking the long way to the airport. Why don't you take the surface streets and avoid the traffic? We need to get there as soon as possible!

"REAL SPEAK": I don' mean da be a **backseat driver** b't cher takin' the long way da the airport. Why doncha take the surface streets 'n avoid the traffic? We need da get there ASAP !

beat the traffic (to) *exp.* to leave earlier than most people in order to avoid driving when the roads are crowded and slow.

EXAMPLE: We need to leave early for the airport in order to **beat the traffic**.

TRANSLATION: We need to leave early for the airport in order to **leave before the traffic gets bad on the roads**.

"REAL SPEAK": We need da leave early fer the airpord 'n order da **beat the traffic**.

burn one's bridges (to) *exp.* to destroy one's reputation and future opportunities • (lit); to destroy a bridge or path behind oneself so others cannot follow.

EXAMPLE: Arnold treated everyone terribly when he was president of his company. Now that he's looking for a job, no one will hire him. He **burned all his bridges**!

TRANSLATION: Arnold treated everyone terribly when he was president of his company. Now that he's looking for a job, no one will hire him. He **destroyed all his future opportunities by having a terrible reputation**!

"REAL SPEAK": Arnold treaded ev'ryone terr'bly when 'e w'z president of 'is company. Now thad 'e's looking fer a job, no one'll hire 'im. He **burned all 'is bridges**!

crossroads (to be at a) *exp.* to make a very important decision that can be life changing • (lit); to be at an intersection of two or more roads.

EXAMPLE: David is **at a crossroads** in his life. He retired last year and now needs to either move to a city where the cost of living is a lot lower or go back to work.

TRANSLATION: David is **at a point where he needs to make a big decision** in his life. He retired last year and now needs to either move to a city where the cost of living is a lot lower or go back to work.

"REAL SPEAK": David's **ad a crossroads** in 'is life. He retired last year 'n now needs ta either move to a cidy where the cost 'a living's a lot lower 'r go back ta work.

drive a hard bargain (to) *exp.* to be inflexible when negotiating a deal.

EXAMPLE: I negotiated with the owner of the used car for over an hour. He **drives a hard bargain**. He finally agreed to lower the price by only $50.

TRANSLATION: I negotiated with the owner of the used car for over an hour. He **is very inflexible when negotiating**. He finally agreed to lower the price by only $50.

"REAL SPEAK": I negoshiaded w'th the owner 'ev the used car fer over 'n hour. He **drives a hard bargain**. He fin'lly agreed da lower the price by only fifdy dollers.

drive someone crazy (to) *exp.* to irritate someone a lot.

EXAMPLE: Greg was **driving me crazy** all through dinner. He kept complaining about all the food!

TRANSLATION: Greg was **really irritating me** all through dinner. He kept complaining about all the food!

"REAL SPEAK": Greg w'z **driving me crazy** all through dinner. He kep' complaining aboud all the food!

drive someone up the wall (to) *exp.* to annoy someone greatly.

EXAMPLE: Your questions are **driving me up the wall**! If you want to learn how to use your new computer program, read the manual yourself!

TRANSLATION: Your questions are **really annoying me**! If you want to learn how to use your new computer program, read the manual yourself!

"REAL SPEAK": Yer questions 'er **driving me up the wall**! If ya wanna learn how da use yer new c'mpuder program, read the manual yerself!

Also: See: **drive someone up the wall (to)**, *p. 81.*

fall asleep at the wheel (to) *exp.* to fail to accomplish one's responsibilities • (lit); said of a driver who falls asleep at the **wheel**, which is short for "steering wheel."

EXAMPLE: Steve knew the boss was coming to the office to do an inspection but forgot to tell us! He really **fell asleep at the wheel**!

TRANSLATION: Steve knew the boss was coming to the office to do an inspection but forgot to tell us! He really **failed at accomplishing his responsibilities**!

"REAL SPEAK": Steve knew the boss w'z coming ta the office ta do 'n inspection b't fergot ta tell us! He really **fell asleep 'it the wheel**!

fall off the back of a truck (to) *exp.* said of merchandise that was acquired through suspicious means.

EXAMPLE: When I asked Vivian how she could afford such a big new TV, she said it **fell off the back of a truck**. She never gave me a direct answer!

TRANSLATION: When I asked Vivian how she could afford such a big new TV, she said **she found it in the street**. She never gave me a direct answer!

"REAL SPEAK": When I ast Vivian how she could afford such a big new TV, she said it **fell off the back 'ev a truck**. She never gay'me a direct answer!

fall off the wagon (to) *exp.* to go back to drinking alcohol after a period of stopping.

EXAMPLE: Eric told me he gave up alcohol forever. Today I found out he **fell off the wagon** and drinks several bottles of beer every night!

TRANSLATION: Eric told me he gave up alcohol forever. Today I found out he **is back to drinking alcohol again** and drinks several bottles of beer every night!

"REAL SPEAK": Eric tol' me he gave up alcohol ferever. Today I found oud 'e **fell off the wagon** 'n drinks sev'ral boddles 'a beer ev'ry night!

fifth wheel (to feel like a) *exp.* to feel in the way, as unnecessary and unwanted as a fifth wheel of a vehicle.

EXAMPLE: Thank you for inviting me to go with you and your girlfriend to the movies, but I'd **feel like a fifth wheel**.

TRANSLATION: Thank you for inviting me to go with you and your girlfriend to the movies, but I'd **feel like I'm in the way**.

"REAL SPEAK": Thanks fer inviding me da go w'th you 'n yer girlfrien' ta the movies, b'd I'd **feel like a fifth wheel**.

Variation: **third wheel (to feel like a)** *exp.*

fork in the road (to be at a) *exp.* to be in a situation where two or more important choices needs to be made • (lit); to be at the end of a single road that suddenly divides into two or more.

EXAMPLE: I'm really **at a fork in the road**. I don't know if I should accept the job that pays less in a beautiful city, or the one that pays more in an industrial city.

TRANSLATION: I'm really **am at a critical decision point in my life**. I don't know if I should accept the job that pays less in a beautiful city, or the one that pays more in an industrial city.

"REAL SPEAK": I'm really **ad a fork 'n the road**. I dunno 'ef I should accept the job th't pays less 'n a beaudiful cidy, or the one th't pays more 'n 'n industrial cidy.

gridlock (to be in) *exp.* to be in a situation where all the roads (in a grid of intersecting streets) are so full of vehicles that none of them can move.

EXAMPLE: I'm sorry we're so late! We were **in gridlock** for two hours!

TRANSLATION: I'm sorry we're so late! We were **stuck in traffic at an intersection** for two hours!

"REAL SPEAK": I'm sorry w'r so late! We were **'n gridlock** fer two hours!

Variation: **gridlocked (to be)** *adj.* • **1.** to be stuck in traffic at an intersection • **2.** to be in a situation where no progress can be made: *We negotiated for raises with the boss for two days but neither side is willing to compromise. Now we're* **gridlocked**!; We negotiated for raises with the boss for two days but neither side is willing to compromise. Now we're **in a situation where there is no movement**!

hit and run *exp.* a traffic accident where one of the drivers does not stop and leaves the scene.

EXAMPLE: When I walked back to my car, I found it all dented! The driver who hit me didn't even leave a note. It was a **hit and run**! Now I have to pay for the damage myself!

TRANSLATION: When I walked back to my car, I found it all dented! The driver who hit me didn't even leave a note. It was a **situation where the driver at fault smashed my car and left without leaving a note**! Now I have to pay for the damage myself!

"REAL SPEAK": When I walked back ta my car, I found id all dented! The driver who hit me didn' even leave a note. It w'z a **hit 'n run**! Now I hafta pay fer the damage myself!

hitchhike (to) *v.* to travel by getting free rides from passing vehicles by raising one's thumb (which is the traditional signal in the U.S. for stopping a car on the road).

> **EXAMPLE:** My best friend and I **hitchhiked** all across the U.S. and met so many new friends! And the entire trip only cost us $100 each!

> **TRANSLATION:** My best friend and I **got free car rides** all across the U.S. and met so many new friends! And the entire trip only cost us $100 each!

> **"REAL SPEAK":** My bes' friend 'n I **hitchhiked** all across the U.S. 'n met so many new frenz! An' the entire trip only cost us a hundred dollers each!

> *Synonym 1:* **hitch a ride (to)** *exp.*

> *Synonym 2:* **thumb a ride (to)** *exp.*

in the driver's seat (to be) *exp.* to be in charge of a situation.

> **EXAMPLE:** We did everything your way, but it didn't work. Now **I'm the one in the driver's seat**!

TRANSLATION: We did everything your way, but it didn't work. Now **I'm the one in charge**!

"REAL SPEAK": We did ev'rything yer way, b'd it didn' work. Now **I'm the one 'n the driver's seat**!

"It's my way or the highway!" *exp.* "You're going to do things my way or be excluded!" • (lit); "You need to do things my way or get on the highway and drive away!"

> **EXAMPLE:** This is my project, so you need to follow my instructions. **It's my way or the highway**!

> **TRANSLATION:** This is my project, so you need to follow my instructions. **You need to do things my way or leave**!

> **"REAL SPEAK":** This 'ez my project, so ya need da follow my instructions. **It's my way 'r the highway**!

in a jam (to be stuck) *exp.* (short for **traffic jam**) to be on the road where a long line of vehicles have stopped or are moving very slowly.

> **EXAMPLE:** I missed my flight because I was **stuck in a jam** for over three hours!

> **TRANSLATION:** I missed my flight because I was **stuck on the road behind cars that were moving very slowly** for over three hours!

> **"REAL SPEAK":** I missed my flight b'cuz I w'z **stuck 'n a jam** fer over three hours!

> *Also:* **jammed up (to be)** *exp.* said of a road where cars are either stopped or moving very slowly because of heavy traffic: *The roads were **jammed up** from my house all the way to the airport!; The roads were **heavy with traffic** from my house all the way to the airport!*

jump on the bandwagon (to) *exp.* to join others in doing or supporting something.

> **EXAMPLE:** None of my friends understood how important it is to care about the environment. Now that they see the climate changing, they've all **jumped on the bandwagon**.

> **TRANSLATION:** None of my friends understood how important it is to care about the environment. Now that they see the climate changing, they've all **joined in supporting the idea**.

"REAL SPEAK": None 'a my friends understood how important it is ta care about the environment. Now th't they see the climate changing, they've all **jumped on the ban'wagon**.

kick the can down the road (to) *exp.* to delay talking about something complicated.

EXAMPLE: There's no way we're going to solve this problem today. Let's **kick the can down the road**. We can discuss it at our next meeting.

TRANSLATION: There's no way we're going to solve this problem today. Let's **talk about it later**. We can discuss it at our next meeting.

"REAL SPEAK": There's no way w'r gonna solve th's problem taday. Let's **kick the can down the road**. We c'n discuss id at 'ar next meeting.

Variation: **kick it down the road (to)** *exp.*

middle-of-the-road *adj.* not extreme and therefore acceptable to most people.

EXAMPLE: Dom's views on social issues are **middle-of-the-road**.

TRANSLATION: Dom's views on social issues are **not extreme and acceptable to most people**.

"REAL SPEAK": Dom's views on social issues 'er **middle-'a-the-road**.

off the beaten path (to be) *exp.* to be located in an isolated area, not very well known by the general public.

EXAMPLE: Why don't you follow me in your car to the hotel? It's really **off the beaten path** and I want to make sure you don't get lost.

TRANSLATION: Why don't you follow me in your car to the hotel? It's really **in an isolated area** and I want to make sure you don't get lost.

"REAL SPEAK": Why doncha follow me 'n yer car da the hotel? It's really **off the beaten path** 'n I wanna make sher ya don't get lost.

Variation: **off the beaten track (to be)** *exp.*

on the wagon (to be) *exp.* to abstain from drinking.

EXAMPLE: Ever since Ann got arrested for drunk driving, she's been **on the wagon**.

TRANSLATION: Ever since Ann got arrested for drunk driving, she has **abstained from drinking**.

"REAL SPEAK": Ev'r since Ann god arrested fer drunk driving, she's b'n **on the wagon**.

one for the road (to have) *exp.* to have one more drink before leaving.

EXAMPLE: Don't leave yet! We're having such a good time! Why don't you **have one for the road**?

TRANSLATION: Don't leave yet! We're having such a good time! Why don't you **have one more drink before leaving**?

"REAL SPEAK": Don't leave yet! W'r having such a good time! Why doncha **have one fer the road**?

put the brakes on (to) *exp.* to stop the progress of a situation or someone.

EXAMPLE: John is using the company's credit card to buy gas for his car?! I'm **going to put the brakes on that** right now!

TRANSLATION: John is using the company's credit card to buy gas for his car?! I'm **going to stop that from continuing** right now!

"REAL SPEAK": John's using the company's credit card ta buy gas fer 'is car?! I'm **gonna put the brakes on that** right now!

put the cart before the horse (to) *exp.* to do things in the wrong order.

> **EXAMPLE:** You won't know for sure whether or not you got the job until tomorrow. So why are you going to look for a house to buy today? You're **putting the cart before the horse**.

> **TRANSLATION:** You won't know for sure whether or not you got the job until tomorrow. So why are you going to look for a house to buy today? You're **doing things in the wrong order**.

> **"REAL SPEAK":** You won't know fer sher whether 'r not cha got the job 'til tamorrow. So why'er ya gonna look fer a house ta buy daday? Y'r **pudding the cart b'fore the horse**.

put the pedal to the metal (to) *exp.* a humorous way to tell the driver to hurry • (lit); to press a car's accelerator pedal to the metal floor. This expression rhymes only when using typical American pronunciation as seen below under "REAL SPEAK."

> **EXAMPLE:** My flight leaves in 30 minutes! **Put the pedal to the metal**!

> **TRANSLATION:** My flight leaves in 30 minutes! **Drive fast**!

> **"REAL SPEAK":** My flight leaves 'n thirdy minutes! **Put the pedal ta the medal**!

reinvent the wheel (to) *exp.* to waste time or effort creating something that already exists.

> **EXAMPLE:** You're going to soak your clothes in mosquito repellent? **Why reinvent the wheel** when you can easily buy clothes that have already been treated with something to repel insects?

> **TRANSLATION:** You're going to soak your clothes in mosquito repellent? **Why waste time creating something that already exists** when you can easily buy clothes that have already been treated with something to repel insects?

> **"REAL SPEAK":** Y'r gonna soak yer cloze 'n mosquido repellent? **Why reinvent the wheel** when ya c'n easily buy cloze thad've awready b'n treated w'th something ta repel insec's?

right up one's alley (to be) *exp.* to be in one's area of expertise.

> **EXAMPLE:** My friend Mike is looking to hire a graphic designer. That's **right up your alley**!

> **TRANSLATION:** My friend Mike is looking to hire a graphic designer. That's **right in your area of expertise**!

> **"REAL SPEAK":** My frien' Mike 'ez looking ta hire a graphic designer. That's **ride up yer alley**!

road rage (to have) *exp.* to have aggressive or violent behavior due to another driver's actions.

> **EXAMPLE:** Some woman kept honking at Bill for driving too slowly, so she tried to push him off the road with her car! What a terrible case of **road rage**!

> **TRANSLATION:** Some woman kept honking at Bill for driving too slowly, so she tried to push him off the road with her car! What a terrible case of **violent behavior on the road**!

> **"REAL SPEAK":** Some woman kept honking 'it Bill fer driving too slowly, so she tried da push 'im off the road w'th 'er car! Whad a terr'ble case 'ev **road rage**!

take a back seat (to) *exp.* to let someone else be in charge.

> **EXAMPLE:** I just assigned Beth as our project manager. I'm going to **take a back seat** and see how she does.
>
> **TRANSLATION:** I just assigned Beth as our project manager. I'm going to **let her be in charge** and see how she does.
>
> **"REAL SPEAK":** I just assign' Beth 'ez 'ar project manager. I'm gonna **take a back seat** 'n see how she does.

take someone for a ride (to) *exp.* to deceive or cheat someone.

> **EXAMPLE:** I hired Chris because he told me he had ten years of experience. Did he ever **take me for a ride**! I just found out this is his first job!
>
> **TRANSLATION:** I hired Chris because he told me he had ten years of experience. Did he ever **deceive me**! I just found out this is his first job!
>
> **"REAL SPEAK":** I hired Chris b'cuz 'e tol' me he had ten years 'ev experience. Did he ever **take me fer a ride**! I jus' found out this 'ez 'is firs' job!

take for a test drive (to) *exp.* to drive a car, or other vehicle, to see if it's worth buying.

> **EXAMPLE:** Look at that car over there! It's beautiful! I'm going to **take it for a test drive**.
>
> **TRANSLATION:** Look at that car over there! It's beautiful! I'm going to **drive it and see if it's worth buying**.

> **"REAL SPEAK":** Look 'it that car over there! It's beaudiful! I'm gonna **take it fer a tes' drive**.

"The squeaky wheel gets the grease!" *exp.* "The person who complains the most gets the best opportunities!"

> **EXAMPLE:** Every few months, I ask the boss for a raise and I never get it. But Greg bothers the boss almost daily about it and today he said yes! I guess it's true… **the squeaky wheel gets the grease**!
>
> **TRANSLATION:** Every few months, I ask the boss for a raise and I never get it. But Greg bothers the boss almost daily about it and today he said yes! I guess it's true… **the person who complains the most gets the best opportunities**!
>
> **"REAL SPEAK":** Ev'ry few munts, I ask the boss fer a raise an' I never ged it. B't Greg bothers the boss ahmost daily aboud it an' taday 'e said yes! I guess it's true… **the squeaky wheel gets the grease**!

Variation: **"The squeaky wheel gets the oil!"** *exp.*

throw someone under the bus (to) *exp.* to blame someone else in order to save oneself from getting in trouble.

> **EXAMPLE:** When our professor asked Andy privately why our group didn't complete the assignment on time, he **threw me under the bus**! He told her I was always late. And I was always on time! He was the one who never arrived on time!
>
> **TRANSLATION:** When our professor asked Andy privately why our group didn't complete the assignment on time, he **blamed me in order to save himself from getting in trouble**! He told her I was always late. And I was always on time! He was the one who never arrived on time!
>
> **"REAL SPEAK":** Wh'n 'ar prafesser ast Andy privately why 'ar group didn' complete the assignmen' on time, he **threw me under the bus**! He told 'er I w'z ahways late. An' I w'z ahways on time! He w'z the one 'oo never arrived on time!

SLANGMAN
Explains More
idioms & Slang for...

—ON THE ROAD—

SCAN ME!

CHAPTER 7

SCAN THE QR CODE OR GO TO: bit.ly/StreetSpeak1-Chapter7

THIS VIDEO EPISODE CONTAINS...

ASAP
- Popular initials used in everyday conversations

drive
- Popular expressions and idioms using "drive"

Idioms & slang used on TV this week plus the latest Teen Slang!
- Slangman gives you his TOP 5 LIST of the latest idioms and slang from the most popular TV shows in the U.S. plus the newest slang teens are using today!

Newest American slang just entered into the dictionary

8 AT SCHOOL

LET'S WARM UP!

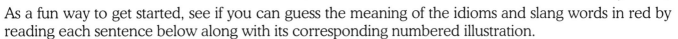

MATCH THE PICTURES *(Answers on p. 221)*

As a fun way to get started, see if you can guess the meaning of the idioms and slang words in red by reading each sentence below along with its corresponding numbered illustration.

1. Tony **cut class** yesterday and went to the movies instead.
2. My **psych** teacher is strange. I think she's neurotic!
3. I'm so excited! I **aced** the test!
4. I **pulled an all-nighter** studying! I'm exhausted.
5. The teacher surprised us all by giving us a **pop quiz**!
6. This class is too hard. I think I'm going to **drop it**.
7. My sister always gets **straight A's** without even studying!
8. If I don't pass the **final**, I'm going to be in big trouble!
9. I **bombed** my test. I'm studying harder next time!
10. What a **killer** test! It was really hard!
11. Paul **flunked** the course because he never studies.
12. I missed the test because I was sick. I hope the teacher is giving a **make-up**.
13. You forgot about the test tomorrow? You'd better **cram** for it!
14. I passed the **mid-term**! My parents will be so happy!

A. failed
B. psychology
C. perfect grades
D. surprise test
E. did extremely well on
F. middle-of-term examination
G. did extremely poorly
H. end-of-term examination
I. didn't attend class
J. stayed up all night
K. study hard in a short period of time
L. very difficult
M. second chance at taking the test
N. remove the class from my schedule

LET'S TALK!

A. DIALOGUE USING SLANG & IDIOMS

The words introduced on the previous two pages are used in the following dialogue and illustrated in the long picture above. Can you understand the conversation and find the illustration that corresponds to the slang? *Note:* The translation of the words in boldface is on the right-hand page.

— *David and Nancy are talking about Eric* —

David: I just heard Eric **flunked** our **psych** class! Is that true?

Nancy: Yeah, I can't believe it. It's never happened to him before! He always gets **straight A's** on the **pop quizzes** and he even **aced** the **mid-term**. How could he possibly **bomb** the **final**?

David: That's because he started to **cut class** all the time and stopped studying. I passed it because I **pulled an all-nighter** trying to **cram** for it.

Nancy: I've never taken such a **killer** test in my life. Unfortunately for Eric, the professor isn't allowing him to take a **make-up**.

David: He should have **dropped the class** when he had the chance!

LET'S TALK!

B. DIALOGUE TRANSLATED INTO STANDARD ENGLISH

LET'S SEE HOW MUCH YOU REMEMBER!
Just for fun, bounce around in random order to the words and
expressions in boldface below. See if you can remember their
slang equivalents without looking at the left-hand page!

— *David and Nancy are talking about Eric* —

David: I just heard Eric **failed** our **psychology** class! Is that true?

Nancy: Yeah, I can't believe it. It's never happened to him before! He always gets **perfect grades** on the **surprise tests** and he even **did extremely well on** the **mid-term examination**. How could he possibly **do extremely poorly on** the **final examination**?

David: That's because he started to **miss class intentionally** all the time and stopped studying. I passed it because I **stayed up all night** trying to **study hard** for it.

Nancy: I've never taken such a **difficult** test in my life. Unfortunately for Eric, the professor isn't allowing him to take a **re-test**.

David: He should have **removed the class from his schedule** when he had the chance!

C. DIALOGUE USING "REAL SPEAK"

The dialogue below demonstrates how the slang conversation on the previous page would *really* be spoken by native speakers!

— David 'n Nancy 'er talking aboud Eric —

David: I just heard thad Eric **flunked** 'ar **psych** class! Izat true?

Nancy: Yeah, I can't b'lieve it. It's never happen' to 'im b'fore! He always gets **straid A's** on the **pop quizzes** an' 'e even **aced** the **mid-term**. How could 'e possibly **bomb** the **final**?

Nancy: That's 'cuz 'e starded da **cut class** all the time 'n stopped studying. I passed it 'cuz I **pulled 'n all-nider** trying da **cram** for it.

Nancy: I've never taken such a **killer** test in my life. Unfortunately fer Eric, the prafesser isn' allowing 'im ta take a **make-up**.

David: He should 'a **dropped the class** when 'e had the chance!

HE = 'E   **HER = 'ER**
HIM = 'IM   **THEM = 'EM**
HIS = 'IS

The disappearing "h" in these pronouns is one of the most common reductions in English. It is used by absolutely everyone!

RULES

The **h** often disappears from the pronouns **he**, **him**, **his**, and **her** when they are not stressed in the sentence. However, the **h** <u>is</u> always pronounced when the pronoun is either stressed, begins the sentence, or follows a pause or comma.

Additionally, the **th** often disappears from the pronoun **them** when it is not stressed in the sentence. However, when **them** <u>is</u> stressed, the **th** is always pronounced. Note that the "Real Speak" pronunciation of **them** (*'em*) and **him** (*'im*) sounds the same. The distinction is made based on the context!

HOW DOES IT WORK?

I think **'e** flunked biology class.
I told **'im** he'd better cram for the test.
I hope Steve gets a good grade on **'is** final!
Kori thinks **'er** psych teacher is crazy.
Pop quizzes...I hate **'em**!

} In these examples, the **h** (or **th**) is silent because **he**, **him**, **his**, **her**, and **them** are not stressed.

Every time I see David, **he** says hello to me.
Don't tell me you're upset. Tell **him**.
That's not my pencil. It's **his**.
You invited **her** to your party?
I wasn't talking to you. I was talking to **them**.
He left for college yesterday.
Her cat ruined all the furniture.

} In these examples, the **h** (or **th**) is pronounced because the pronoun is either stressed, begins the sentence, or follows a pause or comma.

LET'S USE "REAL SPEAK!"

A. CHANGE 'EM TO REAL SPEAK *(Answers on p. 221)*

Fill in each box with the real speak version of **he ('e)**, **him ('im)**, **his ('is)**, **her ('er)**, or **them ('em)** when appropriate. But be careful! In some cases, there is no change! Most important, practice speaking the paragraph in real speak using your answers.

TRACK 55
SOUNDCLOUD

Last night I babysat my niece and nephew. You should have seen them [ ]. They're so cute!

Tessa is eight years old and her [ ] eyes look just like her [ ] mother's. When you look at

them [ ] in the sunlight, they look very dark blue. Her [ ] favorite food is ice cream and

her [ ] favorite color is red. Her [ ] brother Nicholas just had his [ ] fifth birthday.

Everyone thinks he [ ] looks just like his [ ] father but he [ ] thinks he [ ] looks like

his [ ] grandfather. Frankly, whenever I see him [ ] smile, I think he [ ] looks just like me!

After all, I'm his [ ] uncle! Both of them [ ] love to read. Yesterday, Tessa read a story to

her [ ] mother and Nicholas read one to his [ ] father. I'm glad they live so close. It's so

much fun watching them [ ] grow up!

LET'S LEARN!

SPEAKING

TRACK 56
SOUNDCLOUD

VOCABULARY

The following words and expressions were used in the previous dialogues. Let's take a closer look at what they mean.

ace a test (to) *exp.* to do extremely well on a test.

EXAMPLE:	I studied for weeks and weeks. I just know I'm going to **ace the test**!
TRANSLATION:	I studied for weeks and weeks. I just know I'm going to **do extremely well on the test**!
"REAL SPEAK":	I studied fer weeks 'n weeks. I jus' know I'm gonna **ace the test**!

NOW YOU DO IT:
(Use "ace the test" in a sentence)

bomb a test (to) *exp.* to do extremely poorly on a test.

EXAMPLE:	Steve **bombed the test** in algebra. I always thought he loved math!
TRANSLATION:	Steve **did extremely poorly on the test** in algebra. I always thought he loved math!
"REAL SPEAK":	Steve **bom' the test** 'n algebra. I always thod 'e loved math!

NOW YOU DO IT:
(Use "bombed the test" in a sentence)

cram (to) *v.* to study very hard in a short period of time.

EXAMPLE:	I should have been studying all week. Now I have to stay up and **cram** for this test tomorrow morning!
TRANSLATION:	I should have been studying all week. Now I have to stay up and **study very hard in a short period of time** for this test tomorrow morning!
"REAL SPEAK":	I should'ev been studying all week. Now I 'afta stay up 'n **cram** fer this tes' tamorrow morning!

NOW YOU DO IT:
(Use "cram" in a sentence)

cut class (to) *exp.* to miss class intentionally.

EXAMPLE: I don't feel like going to school today. Let's **cut class** and go to the movies.

TRANSLATION: I don't feel like going to school today. Let's **miss class intentionally** and go to the movies.

"REAL SPEAK": I don' feel like going ta school taday. Let's **cut class** 'n go da the movies.

NOW YOU DO IT:
(Use "cut class" in a sentence)

drop a class (to) *exp.* to remove a class from one's schedule.

EXAMPLE: You're taking eight classes this term? If you want any free time, you're going to have to **drop a class**… maybe two!

TRANSLATION: You're taking eight classes this term? If you want any free time, you're going to have to **remove a class from your schedule**… maybe two!

"REAL SPEAK": Yer taking eight classes this term? If ya wan' any free time, yer gonna hafta **drop a class**… maybe two!

NOW YOU DO IT:
(Use "drop a class" in a sentence)

final *n.* the final test that covers everything learned during the school term.

EXAMPLE: I need to study all week. If I don't pass the **final**, I won't be able to graduate!

TRANSLATION: I need to study all week. If I don't pass the **final test covering everything we learned**, I won't be able to graduate!

"REAL SPEAK": I need da study all week. If I don't pass the **final**, I won't be able da graduate!

NOW YOU DO IT:
(Use "final" in a sentence)

flunk (to) *v.* to fail a test or a subject.

EXAMPLE: I studied all night for this test! How could I have possibly **flunked**?

TRANSLATION: I studied all night for this test! How could I have possibly **failed**?

"REAL SPEAK": I studied all night fer this test! How could I'ev possibly **flunked**?

NOW YOU DO IT:
(Use "flunk" in a sentence)

killer *adj.* • **1.** extremely difficult • **2.** terrific.

EXAMPLE 1:	That was a **killer** test! I hope I didn't blow it!
TRANSLATION:	That was a **really difficult** test! I hope I didn't blow it!
"REAL SPEAK":	That w'z a **killer** test! I hope I didn't blow it!
EXAMPLE 2:	That's a **killer** dress! Where did you buy it?
TRANSLATION:	That's a **terrific** dress! Where did you buy it?
"REAL SPEAK":	That's a **killer** dress! Where'd 'ja buy it?
Note:	The difference between definitions **1.** and **2.** simply depends on the context.

NOW YOU DO IT:
(Use "killer" in a sentence)

make-up [or] **make-up test** *n.* a test that can be taken again at a later time; a re-test.

EXAMPLE:	I was sick the day the teacher gave the class the test. Luckily she's giving a **make-up**.
TRANSLATION:	I was sick the day the teacher gave the class the test. Luckily she's giving a **second chance to take it**.
"REAL SPEAK":	I w'z sick the day the teacher gave the class the test. Luckily she's giving a **make-up**.

NOW YOU DO IT:
(Use "make-up" in a sentence)

mid-term *n.* a test taken in the middle of the term which covers all the material learned up to that point.

EXAMPLE:	If I pass the biology **mid-term**, the rest of the course will be easy!
TRANSLATION:	If I pass the biology **test taken in the middle of the term**, the rest of the course will be easy!
"REAL SPEAK":	If I pass the bio **mid-term**, the rest 'a the course'll be easy!

NOW YOU DO IT:
(Use "mid-term" in a sentence)

pop quiz *n.* a surprise test (for which students aren't able to study in advance).

EXAMPLE:	My English teacher gave us a **pop quiz** today. Luckily I read all of the material last week!
TRANSLATION:	My English teacher gave us a **surprise test** today. Luckily I read all of the material last week!
"REAL SPEAK":	My English teacher gave us a **pop quiz** taday. Luckily I read all 'a the material last week!

NOW YOU DO IT:
(Use "pop quiz" in a sentence)

psych *n.* a common shortened name for "psychology."

EXAMPLE: I have to hurry. My **psych** class starts in five minutes and I don't want to be late!

TRANSLATION: I have to hurry. My **psychology** class starts in five minutes and I don't want to be late!

"REAL SPEAK": I 'afta hurry. My **psych** class starts 'n five minutes 'n I don't wanna be late!

Note: Many other school courses have shortened names such as:

bio	=	biology
chem	=	chemistry
econ	=	economics
English lit	=	English literature
home ec	=	home economics
math	=	mathematics
P.E. or phys ed	=	physical education
poli sci	=	political science
"sosh"	=	sociology
trig	=	trigonometry

NOW YOU DO IT:

(Use "psych" in a sentence)

pull an all-nighter (to) *exp.* to stay up all night studying.

EXAMPLE: I'm exhausted. I **pulled an all-nighter** studying for my chemistry final.

TRANSLATION: I'm exhausted. I **stayed up all night** studying for my chemistry final.

"REAL SPEAK": I'm exhausted. I **pulled 'n all-nider** studying fer my chemistry final.

NOW YOU DO IT:

(Use "pull an all-nighter" in a sentence)

straight A's *exp.* perfect grades (in all subjects or all of one's exams).

EXAMPLE: Did you see Nancy's report card? She got **straight A's** for the third time!

TRANSLATION: Did you see Nancy's report card? She got **perfect grades** for the third time!

"REAL SPEAK": Did'ja see Nancy's report card? She got **straid A's** fer the third time!

NOW YOU DO IT:

(Use "straight A's" in a sentence)

LET'S PRACTICE!

READING

TRACK 57
SOUNDCLOUD

A. TRUTH OR LIE (Answers on p. 221)

The students below are calling home. Read the conversation each student is having on the phone, then read their actual thoughts in the bubble. Decide if the student is telling the truth or a lie by checking the appropriate box.

B. FIND THE DEFINITION

Write the definition of the slang word(s) in boldface choosing from the word list below.

(Answers on p. 221)

TRACK 58

SOUNDCLOUD

DEFINITIONS

to study very hard in a short period of time

to stay up all night studying

a common abbreviation for "psychology"

to miss class intentionally

extremely difficult or terrific

to do extremely poorly on a test

an end-of-term test that covers everything learned during the school term

to remove a class from one's schedule

a test that can be taken again at a later time

perfect grades

a surprise test

to do extremely well on a test

1. **ace a test (to)** *exp.* _____ .

2. **bomb a test (to)** *exp.* _____ .

3. **cram (to)** v. _____ .

4. **cut class (to)** *exp.* _____ .

5. **drop a class (to)** *exp.* _____ .

6. **final** *n.* _____ .

7. **killer** *adj.* _____ .

8. **make-up / make-up test** *n.* _____ .

9. **pop quiz** *n.* _____ .

10. **psych** *n.* _____ .

11. **pull an all-nighter (to)** *exp.* _____ .

12. **straight A's** *exp.* _____ .

C. FIND-THE-WORD GRID

Fill in the blanks with the most appropriate word using the list. Next, find and circle the word in the grid below. Words may be spelled vertically or horizontally.

(Answers on p. 221)

aced	cut	flunk	pop	nighter
cram	drop	killer	psych	straight

1. I pulled an all-_____ studying for my history exam.

2. I _____ my test! I got a perfect score!

3. My sister has the highest grade point average in our school. She got _____ A's in every course!

4. I didn't see Ernie in school today. I wonder if he _____ class again.

5. If you don't start to study harder, you're going to _____ this course.

6. That was a _____ test! I hope I pass!

7. I hate when the teacher gives us _____ quizzes. I'd rather be able to prepare!

8. It's really ironic but I think our _____ teacher is crazy!

9. I'd like to go with you to the movies but I have to _____ for a big test tomorrow morning.

10. This class is so hard! I think I might _____ it and take something else.

FIND-THE-WORD GRID

T	N	W	U	F	S	A	C	E	D	G	R	R	E	W	D	W	T	M	A	T
H	O	H	T	O	E	G	R	O	A	O	O	E	D	H	S	E	O	E	M	A
V	W	Y	L	R	V	O	S	U	T	D	S	D	R	I	M	L	G	L	F	R
Y	T	S	T	R	A	I	G	H	T	I	E	A	O	C	E	L	O	U	L	V
E	H	O	W	K	N	U	R	T	N	P	S	N	P	O	P	I	H	N	U	E
I	I	T	O	O	Y	R	O	H	U	L	A	D	E	R	S	T	A	C	N	T
Q	I	T	X	R	E	F	U	C	N	E	R	V	B	E	Y	S	V	H	K	O
U	C	R	K	I	L	L	E	R	D	D	E	I	L	M	C	T	E	O	T	D
E	U	Y	W	N	R	T	H	A	E	G	R	N	I	G	H	T	E	R	O	E
I	T	T	W	D	S	H	T	M	R	E	E	L	E	N	N	M	O	I	S	A

LET'S REVIEW!

A FUN TIME WAS HAD BY ALL *(Answers on p. 222)*

Below are some slang terms and idioms you learned in previous lessons that are used to describe something fun to do in your free time. Write the number of the slang term or idiom from Column A next to its matching picture in Column B as well as next to the matching definition in Column C.

COLUMN A	COLUMN B	COLUMN C
1. to grab a bite		to take a short drive
2. to take a dip		to go eat something
3. to hit the town		to go swimming
4. to take a spin		to go to the movies
5. to catch a movie		to go into town for dinner, movie, etc.

THE SLANGMAN FILES

TRACK 60
SOUNDCLOUD

EXERCISES FOR THIS SECTION ARE IN THE WORKBOOK.

Popular Idioms, Slang & Jargon
Having to do with: SCHOOL

A for effort (to get an) *exp.* a compliment given to someone who did not succeed as expected, but who tried hard.

> **EXAMPLE:** You didn't do the assignment correctly, but you **get an A for effort**.

> **TRANSLATION:** You didn't do the assignment correctly, but you **really tried your best**.

> **"REAL SPEAK":** Ya didn' do the assignment correctly, but cha **ged 'n A fer effert**.

catch up (to) *phrV.* to hurry in order to reach the same level of knowledge as someone else.

> **EXAMPLE:** I missed a week from school because I was sick. Now I need to hurry and **catch up** with the rest of the class!

> **TRANSLATION:** I missed a week from school because I was sick. Now I need to **hurry in order to reach the same level of knowledge** as the rest of the class!

> **"REAL SPEAK":** I missed a week fr'm school b'cuz I w'z sick. Now I need da hurry 'n **catch up** w'th the rest 'a the class!

> *Variation:* **play catch up (to)** *exp.*

cheat sheet *exp.* a hidden piece of paper with notes or answers while taking an exam.

> **EXAMPLE:** I just found out that the reason Bill keeps passing all his tests is because he's been using a **cheat sheet**!

> **TRANSLATION:** I just found out that the reason Bill keeps passing all his tests is because he's been using a **hidden piece of paper with notes and answers**!

> **"REAL SPEAK":** I jus' found out th't the reason Bill keeps passing all 'is tests 'ez b'cuz 'e's been using a **cheat sheet**!

cover a lot of ground (to) *exp.* to discuss a specific subject in great detail.

> **EXAMPLE:** Today we **covered a lot of ground** on George Washington. Tomorrow we're going to be learning about Abraham Lincoln.

> **TRANSLATION:** Today we **discussed in great detail** about George Washington. Tomorrow we're going to be learning about Abraham Lincoln.

> **"REAL SPEAK":** Taday we **covered a lodda ground** on George Washington. Tamorrow w'r gonna be learning aboud Abraham Lincoln.

crack open a book (to) *exp.* to open a book (in order to study or read).

> EXAMPLE: I didn't study at all during vacation. I never **cracked open a book**!
>
> TRANSLATION: I didn't study at all during vacation. I never **open a book**!
>
> "REAL SPEAK": I didn' study ad all during vacation. I never **cracked open a book**!

crank out a paper (to) *exp.* to write an essay quickly or regularly.

> EXAMPLE: I have to **crank out a paper** by Monday morning! I guess I'll be living on coffee for a while!
>
> TRANSLATION: I have to **write an essay** by Monday morning. I guess I'll be living on coffee for a while!
>
> "REAL SPEAK": I 'afta to **crank oud a paper** by Monday morning! I guess a'll be living on coffee fer a while!

"Don't judge a book by its cover!" *exp.* "Don't form an opinion on someone or something based purely on what is seen on the surface!"

> EXAMPLE: Denise may seem shy in person, but she is the most outgoing public speaker I've ever met. **Don't judge a book by its cover**!

> TRANSLATION: Denise may seem shy in person, but she is the most outgoing public speaker I've ever met. **Don't prejudge a person only by what you see**!
>
> "REAL SPEAK": Denise may seem shy 'n person, b't she's the most outgoing public speaker I've ever met. **Don't judge a book by its cover**!

dorm *n.* (a very common shortened version of "dormitory") a large bedroom for several people in a school, camp, or other institution.

> EXAMPLE: It's not easy to study when you live in a **dorm**. There's always noise!
>
> TRANSLATION: It's not easy to study when you live in a **large bedroom for several people**. There's always noise!
>
> "REAL SPEAK": It's nod easy da study when ya live 'n a **dorm**. There's ahways noise!

draw a blank (to) *exp.* to forget something temporarily.

> EXAMPLE: I was about to introduce Steve to my professor but I **drew a blank** on his name!
>
> TRANSLATION: I was about to introduce Steve to my professor but I **temporarily forgot** his name!
>
> "REAL SPEAK": I w'z about ta inner'duce Steve ta my prafesser b'd I **drew a blank** on 'is name!

frat *n.* (a very common shortened version of "fraternity") a club for male college students that's by invitation only.

> EXAMPLE: The very first day I went to college, I was asked if I wanted to join a **frat**. They're all known for throwing great parties!
>
> TRANSLATION: The very first day I went to college, I was asked if I wanted to join a **club for male students**. They're all known for throwing great parties!
>
> "REAL SPEAK": The very firs' day I went ta college, I w'z ast 'ef I wanna join a **frat**. They're all known fer throwing great pardies!

have something down to a science (to) *exp.* to be very skilled at doing something.

> EXAMPLE: Did you see how fast they cleared out the theater when the fire alarm went off? They **have their evacuation procedure down to a science**!
>
> TRANSLATION: Did you see how fast they cleared out the theater when the fire alarm went off? They **are really skilled at their evacuation procedure**!

"REAL SPEAK": Did'ju see how fas' they cleared out the theeder wh'n the fire alarm wen' off? They **'ave their evacuation procedure down do a science**!

have one's nose in a book (to) *exp.* to be reading studiously or intently.

EXAMPLE: Nick has **had his nose in that book** for the past five hours. It must be fascinating!

TRANSLATION: Nick has **been reading that book intently** for the past five hours. It must be fascinating!

"REAL SPEAK": Nick 'ez **had 'is nose 'n that book** fer the pas' five hours. It mus' be fascinading!

hit the books (to) *exp.* to open one's books and begin studying.

EXAMPLE: We just got another homework assignment! Great . Now I have to **hit the books** on the weekend!

MORE ON... TV SLANGMAN

TRANSLATION: We just got another homework assignment! Great. Now I have to **open my books and start studying**.

"REAL SPEAK": We jus' god another homework assignment! Great. Now I 'afta **hit the books** on the weekend!

honor roll (to make) *exp.* to be on a list of students who have earned high grades in school.

EXAMPLE: My daughter **made honor roll**! I'm such a proud mom!

TRANSLATION: My daughter **got on the list of students who have earned high grades**! I'm such a proud mom!

"REAL SPEAK": My dauder **made honor roll**! I'm such a proud mom!

learn one's lesson (to) *exp.* to make a mistake through a painful experience and understand why it's important not to do it again.

EXAMPLE: See how many friends you hurt by lying? I really hope you've **learned your lesson**. It's always best to tell the truth!

TRANSLATION: See how many friends you hurt by lying? I really hope you **understand why it's important not to do it again**. It's always best to tell the truth!

"REAL SPEAK": See how many frenz ya hurt by lying? I really hope ya've **learn' jer lesson**. It's ahways bes' ta tell the truth!

Synonym: **learn something the hard way (to)** *exp.*

make the grade (to) *exp.* to succeed at something by reaching a particular standard.

EXAMPLE: Edward wanted to be a dancer, but he **couldn't make the grade**.

TRANSLATION: Edward wanted to be a dancer, but he **wasn't good enough**.

"REAL SPEAK": Edward wan'ed da be a dancer, b'd 'e **couldn' make the grade**.

old school (to be) *exp.* to be old-fashioned or traditional.

EXAMPLE: My mother is very **old school**. She prefers to write letters by hand and put them in the mail.

TRANSLATION: My mother is very **traditional**. She prefers to write letters by hand and put them in the mail.

"REAL SPEAK": My mother's very **old school**. She prafers da write ledders by hand 'n pud 'em 'n the mail.

pass with flying colors (to) *exp.* to accomplish something exceptionally well.

> **EXAMPLE:** I didn't think I'd do well on the math test, but I **passed with flying colors**!

> **TRANSLATION:** I didn't think I'd do well on the math test, but I **did exceptionally well**!

> **"REAL SPEAK":** I didn' think I'd do well on the math test, b'd I **passed w'th flying colors**!

> *Origin:* Originally a nautical expression, it used to refer to ships returning home with their "colors" (another word for "flags") flying high to show they have been victorious.

quad *n.* an outside area in a college or university, typically shaped like a **quadr**angle, with buildings on all four sides.

> **EXAMPLE:** Every day, I meet the other students in the **quad** for lunch.

> **TRANSLATION:** Every day, I meet the other students in the **outside area surrounded by buildings** for lunch.

> **"REAL SPEAK":** Ev'ry day, I meet the other stud'nts 'n the **quad** fer lunch.

quick study (to be a) *exp.* to be able to learn or memorize things very quickly.

> **EXAMPLE:** You already memorized all your lincs in the play? Wow! You're a **quick study**!

> **TRANSLATION:** You already memorized all your lines in the play? Wow! You're **able to memorize quickly**!

> **"REAL SPEAK":** Y'awready memorized all yer lines 'n the play? Wow! Y'r a **quick study**!

read something out loud (to) *exp.* to read something in a voice that can be clearly heard.

> **EXAMPLE:** Our teacher made me **read the entire story in French out loud**. I was so nervous reading in front of the class!

> **TRANSLATION:** Our teacher made me **read the entire story in a voice that could be clearly heard**. I was so nervous reading in front of the class!

> **"REAL SPEAK":** 'Ar teacher made me **read the entire story 'n French out loud**. I w'z so nervous reading 'n fronna the class!

> *Variation:* **read something aloud (to)** *exp.*

roll (to take) *exp.* (a popular shortened version of: **to take roll call**) to call out a list of names to see who is present.

> **EXAMPLE:** I'm going to **take roll**. When you hear your name called, please raise your hand.

> **TRANSLATION:** I'm going to **call out a list of names to see who is present**. When you hear your name called, please raise your hand.

> **"REAL SPEAK":** I'm gonna **take roll**. When ya hear yer name called, please raise yer hand.

school of thought *exp.* an opinion shared by a group of people.

> **EXAMPLE:** Some people think kids get confused learning other languages. Another **school of thought** is that they easily separate each language in their brains.

> **TRANSLATION:** Some people think kids get confused learning other languages. Another **opinion shared by a group of people** is that they easily separate each language in their brains.

> **"REAL SPEAK":** Some people think kids get c'nfused learning other languages. Another **school 'a thod** 'ez th't they easily seperade each language 'n their brains.

show-and-tell *exp.* a school activity for young children where a child brings an object into the class and talks about it to the other children.

> **EXAMPLE:** Today for **show-and-tell**, Sheila brought her pet frog.

> **TRANSLATION:** Today for **the activity where children bring an object into the class and talk about it to the others**, Sheila brought her pet frog.

> **"REAL SPEAK":** Taday fer **show-'n-tell**, Sheila brod 'er pet frog.

single file *exp.* a line of people or things arranged one behind the other.

> **EXAMPLE:** We had a fire drill at school today, so the teachers made sure we all walked out **single file**.

> **TRANSLATION:** We had a fire drill at school today, so the teachers made sure we all walked out **in a single line, one person behind the other**.

> **"REAL SPEAK":** We had a fire drill 'it school taday, so the teachers made sher we all walked out **single file**.

slack off (to) *phrV.* to work with less effort or energy than before.

> **EXAMPLE:** Tom never does his homework assignments anymore. He's really been **slacking off** lately.

> **TRANSLATION:** Tom never does his homework assignments anymore. He's really been **working with less and less energy** lately.

> **"REAL SPEAK":** Tom never does 'is homework assignments anymore. He's really b'n **slackin' off** lately.

tattletale *n.* an informant, especially a child, who tells someone in authority such as a teacher, that someone else has done something bad.

> **EXAMPLE:** I can't believe you told the teacher I was the one who broke her chair! What a **tattletale**!

> **TRANSLATION:** I can't believe you told the teacher I was the one who broke her chair! What an **informant**!

> **"REAL SPEAK":** I can't believe ya told the teacher I w'z'uh one 'oo broke 'er chair! Whad a **taddletale**!

> *Also:* **tattle on someone (to)** *exp.* to inform on someone.

Synonym 1: **rat on someone (to)** *exp.*

Synonym 2: **rat someone out (to)** *exp.*

Synonym 3: **snitch** *n.* / **snitch on someone (to)** *exp.*

Synonym 4: **squeal on someone (to)** *exp.*

Synonym 5: **stool pigeon** *n.*

Synonym 6: **tell on someone (to)** *exp.*

teach someone a lesson (to) *exp.* to retaliate or punish someone for doing something bad so it never happens again.

> **EXAMPLE:** Greg tried to steal away my girlfriend! I'm going to **teach that guy a lesson**!

> **TRANSLATION:** Greg tried to steal away my girlfriend! I'm going to **retaliate**!

> **"REAL SPEAK":** Greg tried da steal away my girlfriend! I'm gonna **teach that guy a lesson**!

teacher's pet *exp.* a student who is treated as a favorite by the teacher.

> **EXAMPLE:** Bill is the **teacher's pet**. Even when he comes to class late, the teacher never gets mad at him.

> **TRANSLATION:** Bill is the **favorite of the teacher**. Even when he comes to class late, the teacher never gets mad at him.

> **"REAL SPEAK":** Bill's the **teacher's pet**. Even wh'n 'e comes ta class late, the teacher never gets mad ad 'im.

SLANGMAN TV

SLANGMAN Explains More idioms & Slang for...

—AT SCHOOL—

SCAN ME!

CHAPTER 8

SCAN THE QR CODE OR GO TO: bit.ly/StreetSpeak1-Chapter8

THIS VIDEO EPISODE CONTAINS...

coffee

- Since coffee is a big part of many students' daily routine, especially when *pulling an all nighter,* Slangman presents the many ways to order the right coffee just for you at your local coffee house.

Great

- Intonation and how it can completely change the meaning of a word

Idioms & slang used on TV this week plus the latest Teen Slang!

- Slangman gives you his TOP 5 LIST of the latest idioms and slang from the most popular TV shows in the U.S. plus the newest slang teens are using today!

Newest American slang just entered into the dictionary

LET'S WARM UP!

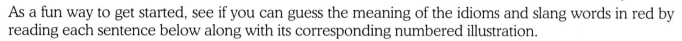

MATCH THE PICTURES (Answers on p. 222)

As a fun way to get started, see if you can guess the meaning of the idioms and slang words in red by reading each sentence below along with its corresponding numbered illustration.

1. Your skin feels very warm. I think you may be **running a fever**.
   - ❏ feverish
   - ❏ feeling energetic

2. Work has been so stressful lately! I think I need to take a **mental health day** and go to the beach.
   - ❏ day off from work in order to relax
   - ❏ day off to take care of my cold

3. Joan got dizzy and almost **passed out** in class today!
   - ❏ woke up
   - ❏ fainted

4. I missed three weeks of work because I was **as sick as a dog**.
   - ❏ feeling great
   - ❏ feeling very sick

5. After being sick for a week, I'm finally **back on my feet**.
   - ❏ in good health
   - ❏ in poor health

6. There's nothing to do here. I'm **bored out of my mind**!
   - ❏ very bored
   - ❏ very excited

7. Don't work so hard. **Take it easy**!
   - ❏ relax
   - ❏ eat something

8. If I don't get out of this house, I'll **go stir crazy**!
   - ❏ go to sleep
   - ❏ become very restless from confinement

9. My new year's resolution is to **hit the gym** every day!
   - ❏ avoid the gym
   - ❏ go to the gym

10. I can't sleep. I'm too **antsy**.
    - ❏ happy
    - ❏ nervous and agitated

11. Did your mother **pull through** after surgery?
    - ❏ get much worse
    - ❏ survive

12. You don't look well. Are you feeling **under the weather** today?
    - ❏ ill
    - ❏ healthy

13. There is no cure for a cold. You just have to let it **run its course**.
    - ❏ get better fast
    - ❏ lose strength on its own

14. I don't know what's wrong with me today. I don't really feel sick, just a little **blah**.
    - ❏ tired and lifeless
    - ❏ lively

LET'S TALK!

A. DIALOGUE USING SLANG & IDIOMS

The words introduced on the previous two pages are used in the following dialogue and illustrated in the long picture above. Can you understand the conversation and find the illustration that corresponds to the slang? *Note*: The translation of the words in boldface is on the right-hand page.

— *Karen and Janet are talking on the phone* —

Karen: Hi, Janet. I haven't heard from you in a while. How are you?

Janet: I've been **feeling under the weather**. I felt **blah** all morning. Then by the afternoon, I was **as sick as a dog**. I started **running a fever** and actually thought I was going to **pass out**! Finally I had Brad take me to the doctor who said it was a bad case of the flu that just has to **run its course**.

Karen: Well, it sounds like you'll definitely **pull through**. I'm sure you'll be **back on your feet** soon. Just try to **take it easy** for a while.

Janet: You're right, but I'm too **antsy** to just lie in bed. I get **bored out of my mind**. I can't wait to **hit the gym** again!

Karen: I know what you mean. The last time I was sick, I started to **go stir crazy**!

Janet: Well, one thing is for sure. I know that stress can make you sick. So I'm going to be sure and take a **mental health day** more often!

LET'S TALK!

B. DIALOGUE TRANSLATED INTO STANDARD ENGLISH

LET'S SEE HOW MUCH YOU REMEMBER!
Just for fun, bounce around in random order to the words and
expressions in boldface below. See if you can remember their
slang equivalents without looking at the left-hand page!

— Karen and Janet are talking on the phone —

Karen: Hi, Janet. I haven't heard from you in a while. How are you?

Janet: I've been **feeling sick**. I felt **lifeless** all morning. Then by the afternoon, I was **extremely sick**. I started **getting a fever** and actually thought I was going to **faint**! Finally I had Brad take me to the doctor who said it was a bad case of the flu that just has to **lose strength on its own**.

Karen: Well, it sounds like you'll definitely **survive**. I'm sure you'll be **back in good health** soon. Just try to **relax** for a while.

Janet: You're right, but I'm too **restless** to just lie in bed. I get **extremely bored**. I can't wait to **go to the gym** again!

Karen: I know what you mean. The last time I was sick, I started to **become very restless from being confined to one place**!

Janet: Well, one thing is for sure. I know that stress can make you sick. So I'm going to be sure and take a **day off from work in order to relax** more often!

C. DIALOGUE USING "REAL SPEAK"

The dialogue below demonstrates how the slang conversation on the previous page would *really* be spoken by native speakers!

— *Karen 'n Janet 'er talking on the phone* —

Karen: Hi, Janet. I haven't heard fr'm ya in a while. How are ya?

Janet: I've been **feeling under the weather**. I felt **blah** all morning. Then by the afternoon, I w'z **ez sick ez a dog**. I starded **running a fever** 'n akshelly thod I w'z gonna **pass out**! Fin'lly I had Brad take me da the doctor who said it w'z a bad case 'a the flu that just hasta **run its course**.

Karen: Well, it sounds like you'll definitely **pull through**. I'm sher you'll be **back on yer feet** soon. Jus' try da **take id easy** fer a while.

Janet: Yer right bud I'm too **antsy** da jus' lie 'n bed. I get **bored oudda my mind**! I can't wait ta **hit the gym** again!

Karen: I know what'cha mean. The las' time I w'z sick, I starded ta **go stir crazy**!

Janet: Well, one thing's fer sher. I know th't stress c'n make ya sick. So I'm gonna be sure 'n take a **men'al health day** more often!

YOU=YA • YOUR=YER
YOU'RE=Y'R • YOURS=YERS

The reduction of **you** to **ya** is so common, you'll probably hear it within your first five minutes of being in the U.S.!

RULES

The **ou** sound in words like **you**, **your**, **you're**, and **yours** typically involves puckering the lips. However in everyday speech, Americans tend to pronounce this with no puckering of the lips at all, creating the reductions **ya**, **yer**, **y'r** and **yers**.

STANDARD ENGLISH		"REAL SPEAK"
Do **you** feel under the weather? **You** look really happy today!	**you**=*ya*	Do *ya* feel under the weather? *Ya* look really happy today!
Is that **your** sister? **Your** brother is going to pull through.	**your**=*yer*	Is that *yer* sister? *Yer* brother is going to pull through.
You're my best friend. **You're** right!	**you're**=*y'r*	*Y'r* my best friend. *Y'r* right!
Is that computer **yours**? I love my PC, but **yours** is my favorite.	**yours**=*yers*	Is that computer *yers*? I love my PC, but *yers* is my favorite.

BUT!

When **you** is stressed (indicated by the voice rising), it is <u>not</u> reduced to **ya**:

–How are **ya**, Bill? –I'm fine, Ted. How are **you**?

LET'S USE "REAL SPEAK!"

D. UNSCRAMBLE *(Answers on p. 222)*

Step 1: Unscramble the word tiles and write the sentence below in box 1.

Step 2: Rewrite the sentence replacing **you**, **your**, **you're**, and **yours** with their "Real Speak" equivalents in box 2.

WHAT GET DID YOU YOUR BIRTHDAY FOR ?

1.
2.

GOING ARE YOU TO ? HOUSE MOTHER'S YOUR

1.
2.

YOU YOUR MONEY GAVE ALL YOUR BROTHER TO ?

1.
2.

YOU BEST KNOW MY YOU ARE . FRIEND

1.
2.

CAR WASHED TO GET TODAY YOU ARE GOING ? YOUR

1.
2.

LET'S LEARN!

SPEAKING

TRACK 63
SOUNDCLOUD

VOCABULARY

The following words and expressions were used in the previous dialogues. Let's take a closer look at what they mean.

antsy (to be) *adj.* to be restless.

EXAMPLE:	The movie was three hours long. After two hours, I started getting **antsy**.
TRANSLATION:	The movie was three hours long. After two hours, I started getting **restless**.
"REAL SPEAK":	The movie w'z three hours long. After two hours, I starded gedding **antsy**.
Synonym:	**ants in one's pants (to have)** *exp.*
Note:	Both expressions conjure up an image of ants crawling all over someone causing that person to squirm around and fidget.

NOW YOU DO IT:
(Create a sentence using "antsy")

back on one's feet (to be) *exp.* to be enjoying good health again.

EXAMPLE:	My father is feeling much better. He's finally **back on his feet** again.
TRANSLATION:	My father is feeling much better. He's finally **enjoying good health** again.
"REAL SPEAK":	My dad's feeling much bedder. He's fin'lly **back on 'is feed** again.
Synonym:	**bounce back (to)** *PhrV.*

NOW YOU DO IT:
(Create a sentence using "back on my feet")

blah (to feel) *adj.* to feel lifeless, generally a little tired and unfocused.

EXAMPLE:	Thank you for inviting me to go with you, but I think I'm just going to stay home tonight. I'm feeling a little **blah**.
TRANSLATION:	Thank you for inviting me to go with you, but I think I'm just going to stay home tonight. I'm feeling a little **tired and unfocused**.
"REAL SPEAK":	Thanks fer inviding me da go with ya, b'd I think I'm jus' gonna stay home tanight. I'm feeling a liddle **blah**.
Synonym 1:	**out of it (to feel)** *exp.*
Synonym 2:	**out of sorts (to feel)** *exp.*
Synonym 3:	**to be oneself (not)** *exp.*

NOW YOU DO IT:
(Create a sentence using "blah")

bored out of one's mind (to be) *exp.* to be very bored.

EXAMPLE: I was **bored out of my mind** during the lecture! I couldn't wait for it to end!

TRANSLATION: I was **terribly bored** during the lecture! I couldn't wait for it to end!

"REAL SPEAK": I w'z **bored oudda my min'** during the lecture! I couldn' wait fer it ta end!

Synonym 1: **bored out of one's skull (to be)** *exp.*
Synonym 2: **bored stiff (to be)** *exp.*

NOW YOU DO IT:
(Create a sentence using "bored out of one's mind")

hit the gym (to) *exp.* to go to the gym.

EXAMPLE: I'm starting to gain weight! It guess it's time for me to **hit the gym**!

TRANSLATION: I'm starting to gain weight! It guess it's time for me to **go to the gym**!

"REAL SPEAK": I'm starding da gain weight! It guess it's time fer me da **hit the gym**!

Variation: **hit the weights (to)** *exp.* to work out with machines, dumbbells, and barbells.

NOW YOU DO IT:
(Create a sentence using "hit the gym")

mental health day (to take a) *exp.* to take a day off from work in order to relax.

EXAMPLE: After this stressful week at work, tomorrow I'm **taking a mental health day**! Maybe I'll just read a book at the beach all day!

TRANSLATION: After this stressful week at work, tomorrow I'm **taking a day off from work to relax**! Maybe I'll just read a book at the beach all day!

"REAL SPEAK": Afder th's stressful week 'it work, tamorrow I'm **takin' a men'al health day**! Maybe a'll jus' read a book 'it the beach all day!

NOW YOU DO IT:
(Create a sentence using "bounce back")

pass out (to) *phrV.* to faint.

EXAMPLE: Jody **passed out** after working out at the gym. I think he exercised too hard!

TRANSLATION: Jody **fainted** after working out at the gym. I think he exercised too hard!

"REAL SPEAK": Jody **passed oud** after working oud at the gym. I think 'e exercised too hard!

NOW YOU DO IT:
(Create a sentence using "pass out")

pull through (to) *phrV.* to survive.

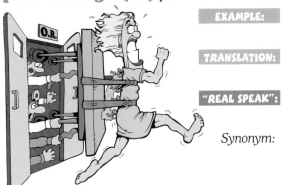

> **EXAMPLE:** Don't worry. I'm sure Debbie will **pull through**. The doctors say she's getting better every day.
>
> **TRANSLATION:** Don't worry. I'm sure Debbie will **survive**. The doctors say she's getting better every day.
>
> **"REAL SPEAK":** Don't worry. I'm sher Debbie'll **pull through**. The docters say she's gedding bedder ev'ry day.
>
> *Synonym:* **make it (to)** *exp.*

NOW YOU DO IT:

(Create a sentence using "pull through")

run a fever (to) *exp.* to have a high body temperature, to be feverish.

> **EXAMPLE:** If you start to **run a fever**, you should go see your doctor right away.
>
> **TRANSLATION:** If you start to **get a high body temperature**, you should go see your doctor right away.
>
> **"REAL SPEAK":** If ya start ta **run a fever**, you should go see yer docter ride away.

NOW YOU DO IT:

(Create a sentence using "run a fever")

run its course (to) *exp.* said of an illness that will lose strength on its own over time.

> **EXAMPLE:** Unfortunately, there's no treatment for the common cold yet. It just has to **run its course**.
>
> **TRANSLATION:** Unfortunately, there's no treatment for the common cold yet. It just has to **lose strength on its own over time**.
>
> **"REAL SPEAK":** Unfortunately, there's no treatment fer the common cold yet. It just hasta **run its course**.

NOW YOU DO IT:

(Create a sentence using "run its course")

sick as a dog (to be as) *exp.* to be extremely sick.

> **EXAMPLE:** Usually I never get sick. But last week I was **as sick as a dog**! Luckily, I'm doing a lot better now.
>
> **TRANSLATION:** Usually I never get sick. But last week I was **extremely sick**! Luckily, I'm doing a lot better now.
>
> **"REAL SPEAK":** Usually I never get sick. B't last week I w'z **'ez sick 'ez a dog**! Luckily, I'm doing a lot bedder now.

NOW YOU DO IT:

(Create a sentence using "sick as a dog")

stir crazy (to go) *exp.* to become very restless from being confined to one place.

EXAMPLE:	I wish it would stop raining so I could go outside. I've been locked up in this house for almost a week and I'm starting to **go stir crazy**!
TRANSLATION:	I wish it would stop raining so we could go outside. I've been locked up in this house for almost a week and I'm starting to **become very restless from being confined to one place**!
"REAL SPEAK":	I wish it'd stop raining so we could go outside. I' been locked up 'n this house fer almost a week 'n I'm starding ta **go stir crazy**!
Synonym:	**cabin fever (to have)** *exp.*

NOW YOU DO IT:
(Create a sentence using "stir crazy")

take it easy (to) *exp.* to relax.

EXAMPLE:	Ralph works so hard all the time. I'm worried that if he doesn't start to slow down and **take it easy**, he's going to get sick!
TRANSLATION:	Ralph works so hard all the time. I'm worried that if he doesn't start to slow down and **relax**, he's going to get sick!
"REAL SPEAK":	Ralph works so hard all the time. I'm worried thad if 'e doesn' start ta slow down 'n **take id easy**, he's gonna get sick!
Synonym 1:	**chill (to)** *v.* • short for **chill out (to)** *v.* • *Why don't you come to my house and we'll watch some movies and **chill**?*
Synonym 2:	**cool off (to)** *phrV.* to relax after being angry • *You're so upset! You need to sit down, watch some TV, and **cool off**.*
Synonym 3:	**loosen up (to)** *phrV.* to relax after being stiff and tense • *When you dance, you look like a robot! You need to **loosen up** and move with the music!*
Synonym 4:	**mellow out (to)** *phrV.* to relax especially after being tense • *After a long day at work, I like to **mellow out** by listening to classical music.*

NOW YOU DO IT:
(Create a sentence using "take it easy")

under the weather (to feel) *exp.* to feel sick.

MORE ON...
SLANGMAN

EXAMPLE:	Hi, Richard. You look a little tired today. Have you been **feeling under the weather**?
TRANSLATION:	Hi, Richard. You look a little tired today. Have you been **feeling sick**?
"REAL SPEAK":	Hi, Richard. You look a liddle tired taday. Have you been **feeling under the weather**?

NOW YOU DO IT:
(Create a sentence using "feel under the weather")

LET'S PRACTICE!

WRITING

TRACK 64
SOUNDCLOUD

A. THE UNFINISHED CONVERSATION *(Answers on p. 223)*

Read the conversations then fill in the last line with your own words in response to what you've just read. Make sure to use the suggested words in your response. Your response can be in the form of a question or statement.

1

Jodi: Would you like to go to the movies tonight?

Angela: I'd like to but I've been **feeling a little under the weather**. Maybe I'd better just stay home.

Jodi: [   ]

use: **stir crazy**

2

Steve: Where have you been? I haven't seen you at school.

Al: I was **as sick as a dog**. I was **running a high fever** all week!

Steve: [   ]

use: **run its course**

3

Kim: I can't stand biology class. I don't know how I'm going to be able to dissect frogs today. I hope I don't get dizzy and **pass out**!

Doug: Just **take it easy**. You'll **pull through** just fine.

Kim: [   ]

use: **as sick as a dog**

4

Nick: The doctor said you have to **take it easy** until the flu **runs its course**.

Tessa: But I'm so **antsy** being inside all day! I'm **bored out of my mind**!

Nick: [   ]

use: **back on your feet**

5

Carl: Good to see you again. Have you **bounced back** from that virus?

Sandy: Yeah, I'm feeling much better. I was **going stir crazy** lying in bed all day long. I hope you didn't catch it.

Carl: [   ]

use: **feel blah**

B. CHOOSE THE RIGHT WORD

Underline the appropriate word that best completes the phrase.
(Answers on p. 223)

TRACK 65
SOUNDCLOUD

1. My mother caught the flu last week and was sick as a (**cat**, **giraffe**, **dog**).

2. I haven't gone outside for three days because I've been sick. I'm starting to go stir (**happy**, **hungry**, **crazy**)!

3. I've been cold all day and it's the middle of summer! I wonder if I'm (**skipping**, **walking**, **running**) a fever.

4. I'm feeling a little (**under**, **over**, **behind**) the weather today. I hope I'm not catching a cold. I have to go to work tonight!

5. You really don't need to worry at all. The surgeon said Monica will (**pull**, **push**, **lift**) through just fine.

6. Let's go to the movies. I want to do something fun. I've been bored out of my (**brain**, **mind**, **eyes**) all day!

7. Unfortunately, there's no cure for a virus. You just have to let it (**run**, **jog**, **walk**) its course.

8. I was sick for two weeks but I'm finally back on my (**hands**, **head**, **feet**)!

9. I don't feel sick or anything. I just feel kind of (**blue**, **blond**, **blah**).

10. I've never seen you so stressed out before! For your own good, I think you need to take a (**cerebral**, **mental**, **metal**) health day tomorrow!?

11. I feel like I'm going to pass (**up**, **in**, **out**). I need to sit down.

12. Why are you (**antsy**, **fancy**, **sick as a dog**) today? You need to calm down!

13. You're working too hard. You really need to take it (**hard**, **easy**, **simple**).

14. After a few days of rest, I'll be ready to (**punch**, **slap**, **hit**) the gym again.

C. COMPLETE THE STORY (Answers on p. 223)

Use the illustrations to help you fill in the blanks with the correct slang term or expression.

Today I took a _____, so I could take care of my sister

because she's been feeling a little _____. She said she

was feeling _____ last night, then later she started to

_____. She'll _____ just fine but for now,

she's _____. I totally understand it! I'm

sure I'd go completely _____ being _____

and stuck in the house all day. But I told her not to worry. In just a few days, she'll be able to

_____ again! For now, it has to

_____. She just needs to _____ and

get plenty of rest and drink plenty of liquids. Then she'll certainly be back

_____ in just a few days!

LET'S REVIEW!

THE NIGHT SHIFT *(Answers on p. 224)*

In previous lessons, you have learned some idioms and slang terms iused to describe something that happens at night. Write the number of the slang term or idiom from Column A next to its matching picture in Column B as well as next to the matching definition in Column C.

ZOOM!!

COLUMN A	COLUMN B	COLUMN C
1. rush hour		give someone a place to stay for the night
2. to pull an all-nighter		the time when most drivers are on the road
3. to stay up till all hours of the night		to stay up all night
4. red-eye		overnight flight
5. to put up for the night		to stay up all night studying

 **THE SLANGMAN FILES**

 **TRACK 67** SOUNDCLOUD

 **EXERCISES FOR THIS SECTION ARE IN THE WORKBOOK.**

Popular Idioms, Slang & Jargon
Having to do with: **HEALTH**

alive and kicking (to be) *exp.* to be alive and well.

> **EXAMPLE:** I was in the market today and saw my first elementary school teacher! I was so glad to see he's still **alive and kicking**!

> **TRANSLATION:** I was in the market today and saw my first elementary school teacher! I was so glad to see he's still **alive and well**!

> **"REAL SPEAK":** I w'z 'n the market taday 'n saw my first element'ry school teacher! I w'z so glad da see 'e's still **alive 'n kicking**!

as pale as a ghost (to look) *exp.* said of someone's complexion that is very light in color or almost white due to fright or sickness.

> **EXAMPLE:** I visited Lee in the hospital today. **She looked as pale as a ghost**.

> **TRANSLATION:** I visited Lee in the hospital today. **Her complexion was extremely light in color**.

> **"REAL SPEAK":** I visided Lee 'n the hospid'l taday. **She looked 'ez pale 'ez a ghost**.

> *Variation:* **as white as a ghost (to look)** *exp.*

> *Synonym:* **as white as a sheet (to be)** *exp.*

at death's door (to be) *exp.* to be close to dying.

> **EXAMPLE:** I had no idea how sick Trevor was! When I saw him today, he looked like he was **at death's door**!

> **TRANSLATION:** I had no idea how sick Trevor was! When I saw him today, he looked like he was **close to dying**!

> **"REAL SPEAK":** I had no idea how sick Trevor was! Wh'n I saw 'im taday, he looked like 'e w'z **'it death's door**!

 MORE ON... SLANGMAN

bacne *n.* a humorous way to refer to acne on one's back (*Note:* Instead of calling this condition "acne of the back," this humorous combination of the words "**back**" and "**acne**" [pronounced *back-nee*] is commonly used.)

> **EXAMPLE:** When I was a teenager, I had horrible **bacne**. I hated puberty!

> **TRANSLATION:** When I was a teenager, I had horrible **acne on my back**. I hated puberty!

> **"REAL SPEAK":** Wh'n I w'z a teenager, I had horr'ble **bacne**. I haded puberdy!

black out (to) *phrV.* to faint.

> **EXAMPLE:** What happened? I must have **blacked out** from not eating today!

> **TRANSLATION:** What happened? I must have **fainted** from not eating today!

> **"REAL SPEAK":** What happened? I must'a **blacked out** fr'm nod eading taday!

break out in a cold sweat (to) *exp.* to begin sweating due to nervousness or fright.

> **EXAMPLE:** Every time I have to do any public speaking, I get so nervous. Just talking about it makes me **break out in a cold sweat**!

> **TRANSLATION:** Every time I have to do any public speaking, I get so nervous. Just talking about it makes me **begin sweating from fear**!

> **"REAL SPEAK":** Ev'ry time I hafta do any public speaking, I get so nervous. Jus' talking about it makes me **break oud 'n a cold sweat**!

break out in (to) *phrV.* said of one's skin when a rash, or some other unpleasant condition, develops.

> **EXAMPLE:** Whenever I eat grapefruit, my face **breaks out** in little red bumps. It must be an allergy.

> **TRANSLATION:** Whenever I eat grapefruit, my face **develops** little red bumps. It must be an allergy.

> **"REAL SPEAK":** Wh'never I eat grapefruit, my face **breaks oud** 'n liddle red bumps. It mus' be 'n allergy.

> *Also:* **outbreak** *n.* a sudden rise in the incidence of a disease such as *an* **outbreak** *of measles.*

burn oneself out (to) *phrV.* to exhaust oneself (like a lightbulb that eventually burns out).

> **EXAMPLE:** You need to stop working and get some rest. You're going to **burn yourself out**!

> **TRANSLATION:** You need to stop working and get some rest. You're going to **exhaust yourself**!

> **"REAL SPEAK":** Ya need da stop working 'n get s'm rest. Y'r gonna **burn yerself out**!

> *Also:* **burned out (to be)** *adj.* to be exhausted.

catch one's death of cold (to) *exp.* to become extremely sick.

> **EXAMPLE:** If you go outside dressed like that, you're going to **catch your death of cold**. It's freezing out there!

> **TRANSLATION:** If you go outside dressed like that, you're going to **become extremely sick**. It's freezing out there!

> **"REAL SPEAK":** If ya go outside dressed like that, y'r gonna **catch yer death 'a cold**. It's freezing out there!

> *Variation:* **catch one's death (to)** *exp.*

Charley horse (to get a) *exp.* to get a muscle spasm or cramp.

> **EXAMPLE:** I woke up in the middle of the night with the worst **Charley horse** in my thigh! I had to get up and walk until the muscles relaxed.

> **TRANSLATION:** I woke up in the middle of the night with the worst **muscle cramp** in my thigh! I had to get up and walk until the muscles relaxed.

> **"REAL SPEAK":** I woke up 'n the middle 'a the night w'th the wors' **Charley horse** 'n my thigh! I had da get up 'n walk 'til the muscles relaxed.

checkup *n.* a detailed examination, especially a medical or dental one.

> **EXAMPLE:** It's really important to get a yearly **checkup** by your doctor. That way you can avoid a lot of health problems!

> **TRANSLATION:** It's really important to get a yearly **detailed examination** by your doctor. That way you can avoid a lot of health problems!

"REAL SPEAK": It's really impordant ta ged a yearly **checkup** by yer docter. That way ya c'n avoid a lodda health problems!

clean bill of health (to get a) *exp.* to receive a report by a doctor that you are fit and healthy.

> **EXAMPLE:** My grandfather is 90 years old and always gets a **clean bill of health** every time he gets a *checkup*!

> **TRANSLATION:** My grandfather is 90 years old and always gets a **report from his doctor that he is fit and healthy** every time he gets a *checkup*!

> **"REAL SPEAK":** My grampa's nindey years old 'n ahways gets a **clean bill 'a health** ev'ry time 'e gets a *checkup*!

come down with (to) *exp.* to develop a specific illness.

> **EXAMPLE:** In the middle of our vacation, I **came down with** the flu. Luckily it only lasted 24 hours!

> **TRANSLATION:** In the middle of our vacation, I **developed** the flu. Luckily it only lasted 24 hours!

> **"REAL SPEAK":** In the middle 'ev 'ar vacation, I **came down w'th** the flu. Luckily id only lasted twen'y four hours!

draw blood (to) *exp.* to take blood from a person's body for medical reasons.

> **EXAMPLE:** As part of my yearly checkup, they always **draw blood** to make sure I don't have any diseases.

> **TRANSLATION:** As part of my yearly checkup, they always **take my blood** to make sure I don't have any diseases.

"REAL SPEAK": As part 'a my yearly checkup, they ahways **draw blood** da make sher I don't have any diseases.

drop dead (to) *exp.* to die suddenly and unexpectedly.

> **EXAMPLE:** John **dropped dead** while he was working on his car. No one even knew he had a heart problem.

> **TRANSLATION:** John **died suddenly and unexpectedly** while he was working on his car. No one even knew he had a heart problem.

> **"REAL SPEAK":** John **dropped dead** while 'e w'z working on 'is car. No one even knew 'e had a heart problem.

flare-up *n.* a sudden return of a medical condition.

> **EXAMPLE:** Every time I eat chocolate, I get a **flare-up** of acne all over my entire face.

> **TRANSLATION:** Every time I eat chocolate, I get a **sudden return** of acne all over my face.

> **"REAL SPEAK":** Ev'ry time I eat chocolate, I ged a **flare-up** 'ev acne all over my entire face.

> *Also:* **flare up (to)** *phrV.* For example: *After I eat chocolate, my acne* **flares up**; After I eat chocolate my acne **returns**.

foot-in-mouth disease (to have) *exp.* to have a tendency to make remarks that are embarrassingly wrong or inappropriate.

> **EXAMPLE:** I accidentally called my new girlfriend by my ex-girlfriend's name! I sure do have **foot-in-mouth disease**!

TRANSLATION: I accidentally called my new girlfriend by my ex-girlfriend's name! I sure do **have a tendency to make remarks that are embarrassingly inappropriate**!

"REAL SPEAK": I accident'ly called my new girlfrien' by my ex-girlfrien's name! I sher do have **foot-'n-mouth disease**!

Original: This idiom is actually a variation of the idiom: **to put one's foot in one's mouth**. For example: *I really **put my foot in my mouth** this time! I accidentally called my new girlfriend by my ex-girlfriend's name!*

get over something (to) *exp.* to recover from something.

    EXAMPLE: If you get a lot of rest, you'll **get over** your cold faster.

    TRANSLATION: If you get a lot of rest, you'll **recover from** your cold faster.

    "REAL SPEAK": If ya ged a lodda rest, you'll **ged over** yer cold faster.

give someone a dose of one's own medicine (to) *exp.* to give someone the same bad treatment that they have given to others.

    EXAMPLE: Bill never invites me to his parties. So I'm going to **give him a dose of his own medicine** and not invite him to my birthday dinner.

    TRANSLATION: Bill never invites me to his parties. So I'm going to **give him the same bad treatment he gives me** and not invite him to my birthday dinner.

"REAL SPEAK": Bill never invites me to 'is pardies. So I'm gonna **give 'im a dose 'ev 'is own medicine** an' nod invide 'im ta my birthday dinner.

Variation: **give someone a taste of one's own medicine (to)** *exp.*

huff and puff (to) *exp.* to breathe heavily from exhaustion.

    EXAMPLE: What a long hike! I **huffed and puffed** my way to the top of the mountain, but at least I did it!

    TRANSLATION: What a long hike! I **was breathing heavily from exhaustion** on my way to the top of the mountain, but at least I did it!

    "REAL SPEAK": Whad a long hike! I **huffed 'n puffed** my way da the top 'a the mountain, b'd at least I did it!

kick the habit (to) *exp.* to overcome an addiction to something.

    EXAMPLE: I'm not going to smoke ever again. Now that we're expecting a baby, I've decided to **kick the habit**.

    TRANSLATION: I'm not going to smoke ever again. Now that we're expecting a baby, I've decided to **overcome that addiction**.

    "REAL SPEAK": I'm not gonna smoke ever again. Now th't w'r expecting a baby, I've decided da **kick the habit**.

kink in one's neck (to get a) *exp.* to get a cramp in one's neck.

    EXAMPLE: I got a **kink in** my neck from sitting in front of the computer all day. I need to start taking more breaks and stretch!

    TRANSLATION: I got a **cramp in** my neck from sitting in front of the computer all day. I need to start taking more breaks and stretch!

    "REAL SPEAK": I god a **kink 'n** my neck fr'm sidding 'n fronna the c'mpuder all day. I need da start taking more breaks 'n stretch!

nothing but skin and bones (to be) *exp.* to be extremely skinny (to the point of looking unhealthy).

> **EXAMPLE:** I was shocked when I saw Mindy at the market. She used to be really overweight. Now she's **nothing but skin and bones**!
>
> **TRANSLATION:** I was shocked when I saw Mindy at the market. She used to be really overweight. Now she's **extremely skinny**!
>
> **"REAL SPEAK":** I w'z shocked wh'n I saw Mindy 'it the market. She usta be really overweight. Now she's **nothing b't skin 'n bones**!

nurse someone back to health (to) *exp.* to care for a sick person until good health returns.

> **EXAMPLE:** After your surgery, I'll stay with you and **nurse you back to health**.
>
> **TRANSLATION:** After your surgery, I'll stay with you and **take care of you until you're healthy again**.
>
> **"REAL SPEAK":** Afder yer surgery, a'll stay w'th ya 'n **nurse ya back ta health**.

on the mend (to be) *exp.* to recover from an illness or surgery.

> **EXAMPLE:** Greg has been sick for the past month. I'm glad to hear he's finally **on the mend**!
>
> **TRANSLATION:** Greg has been sick for the past month. I'm glad to hear he's finally **getting better**!
>
> **"REAL SPEAK":** Greg's been sick fer the past month. I'm glad da hear 'e's fin'lly **on the mend**!

one foot in the grave (to have) *exp.* to be close to death.

EXAMPLE: Butch is such a hypochondriac. He always acts like he **has one foot in the grave**.

TRANSLATION: Butch is such a hypochondriac. He always acts like he **is about to die**.

"REAL SPEAK": Butch 'ez such a hypac'ondriac. He ahways ac's like 'e **'as one foot 'n the grave**.

Note: In the previous illustration, you'll notice **RIP** (pronounced R-I-P), which means "**R**est **I**n **P**eace," a common acronym on tombstones.

out of shape (to be) *exp.* to be in poor physical condition or overweight.

> **EXAMPLE:** I can't believe how hard it was for me to climb those stairs! I'm really **out of shape**!

> **TRANSLATION:** I can't believe how hard it was for me to climb those stairs! I'm really **in poor physical condition**!
>
> **"REAL SPEAK":** I can't believe how hard it was fer me da climb those stairs! I'm really **oudda shape**!

pass away (to) *phrV.* to die.

> **EXAMPLE:** Did you hear the sad news? Jay's father **passed away** last night. I didn't even know he was sick!
>
> **TRANSLATION:** Did you hear the sad news? Jay's father **died** last night. I didn't even know he was sick!
>
> **"REAL SPEAK":** Did'ja hear the sad news? Jay's father **passed away** las' night. I didn' even know 'e w'z sick!

Synonym: **pass on (to)** *phrV.*

pass out (to) *phrV.* to faint.

> **EXAMPLE:** When Jenn found out she won the award, she **passed out** from excitement!
>
> **TRANSLATION:** When Jenn found out she won the award, she **passed out** from excitement!

"REAL SPEAK": Wh'n Jenn found out she won the award, she **passed out** fr'm excitement!

pick up a bug (to) *exp.* to catch a cold.

EXAMPLE: I'm not feeling well. I think I may have **picked up a bug** from my sister's children. They were both sick when I visited.

TRANSLATION: I'm not feeling well. I think I may have **caught a cold** from my sister's children. They were both sick when I visited.

"REAL SPEAK": I'm not feeling well. I think I may'ev **picked up a bug** fr'm my sister's children. They were both sick wh'n I visided.

recharge one's batteries (to) *exp.* to rest in order to feel energetic again.

EXAMPLE: This was the most difficult week I've ever had at work! I really need to **recharge my batteries**!

TRANSLATION: This was the most difficult week I've ever had at work! I can't wait for the weekend! I really need to **rest in order to feel energetic again**!

"REAL SPEAK": This w'z the mos' difficult week I' ever had 'it work! I can't wait fer the weekend! I really need da **recharge my badderies**!

rub salt in the wound (to) *exp.* to make another person's bad or painful situation worse.

EXAMPLE: You and Janet are breaking up? I don't mean to **rub salt in the wound** but I heard she was dating another guy the entire time you were together.

TRANSLATION: You and Janet are breaking up? I don't mean to **make your situation more painful** but I heard she was dating another guy the entire time you were together.

"REAL SPEAK": You 'n Janed 'er breaking up? I don' mean da **rub salt 'n the wound** b'd I heard she w'z dading another guy the entire time ya were dagether.

run down (to feel) *exp.* to feel tired or a little sick.

EXAMPLE: I've been working nonstop for the past three days. I **feel so run down**!

TRANSLATION: I've been working nonstop for the past three days. I **feel so tired**!

"REAL SPEAK": I' been working nonstop fer the pas' three days. I **feel so run down**!

run some tests (to) *exp.* to administer medical tests to look for possible health problems.

EXAMPLE: I don't know why I've been feeling so tired lately. The doctor **ran some tests**, so I should be getting the results tomorrow.

TRANSLATION: I don't know why I've been feeling so tired lately. The doctor **did some medical tests**, so I should be getting the results tomorrow.

"REAL SPEAK": I dunno why I' been feeling so tired lately. The docter **ran s'm tes's**, so I should be gedding the results tamorrow.

shrink *n.* a professional in the mental health field such as a psychiatrist, psychologist, or psychotherapist.

EXAMPLE: I don't need a **shrink** to help me solve my problems. I can fix them on my own.

TRANSLATION: I don't need a **professional in the mental health field** to help me solve my problems. I can fix them on my own.

"REAL SPEAK": I don' need a **shrink** ta help me solve my problems. I c'n fix th'm on my own.

sick day (to take a) *exp.* to take a day off from work, with pay, because of illness.

EXAMPLE: I think I'm getting sick. I'd better **take a sick day** tomorrow and get some rest.

TRANSLATION: I think I'm getting sick. I'd better **take a day off from work with pay** tomorrow and get some rest.

"REAL SPEAK": I think I'm gedding sick. I' bedder **take a sick day** damorrow 'n get s'm rest.

splitting headache (to have a) *exp.* to have severe head pain.

EXAMPLE: Hearing all that construction going on all day has given me a **splitting headache**!

TRANSLATION: Hearing all that construction going on all day has given me a **severe headache**!

"REAL SPEAK": Hearing all that construction going on all day 'ez given me a **splidding headache**!

Synonym: **crushing headache (to have a)** *exp.*

swole (to be) *adj.* to be very muscular.

EXAMPLE: Wow! Have you been *hitting the gym* more often? I can't believe how **swole** you are!

TRANSLATION: Wow! Have you been *going to the gym* more often? I can't believe how **muscular** you are!

"REAL SPEAK": Wow! You been *hittin'* the gym more often? I can't b'lieve how **swole** you are!

take a turn for the worse (to) *exp.* to get worse, often quickly or suddenly.

EXAMPLE: The patient was doing well after surgery but **took a turn for the worse** overnight.

TRANSLATION: The patient was doing well after surgery but **suddenly got worse** overnight.

"REAL SPEAK": The patient w'z doing well afder surgery b't **took a turn fer the worse** overnight.

Synonym: **go downhill (to)** *exp.*

under the knife (to go) *exp.* to undergo surgery.

EXAMPLE: Jeff was **under the knife** for six hours! The surgery must have been more complicated than they originally thought!

TRANSLATION: Jeff was **in surgery** for six hours! The surgery must have been more complicated than they originally thought!

"REAL SPEAK": Jeff w'z **under the knife** fer six hours! The surgery must'a been more complicaded th'n they originally thought!

up and about (to be) *exp.* to be out of bed after an illness and able to live a normal life.

EXAMPLE: After Leon's heart surgery, he was **up and about** in just a few weeks!

TRANSLATION: After Leon's heart surgery, he was **out of bed and able to live a normal life** in just a few weeks!

"REAL SPEAK": After Leon's heart surgery, he w'z **up 'n about** 'n just a few weeks!

Slangman Explains More Idioms & Slang for...

—TO YOUR HEALTH—

SCAN ME!

CHAPTER 9

SCAN THE QR CODE OR GO TO: bit.ly/StreetSpeak1-Chapter9

THIS VIDEO EPISODE CONTAINS...

under the weather
- Slangman presents idioms having to do with the weather

sick
- Slangman presents some of his favorite idioms and slang terms for "sick"

swole (to be)
- Popular slang and idioms used at the gym

Idioms & slang used on TV this week plus the latest Teen Slang!
- Slangman gives you his TOP 5 LIST of the latest idioms and slang from the most popular TV shows in the U.S. plus the newest slang teens are using today!

Newest American slang just entered into the dictionary

LET'S WARM UP!

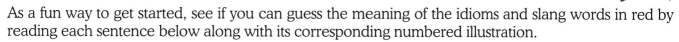

MATCH THE PICTURES *(Answers on p. 224)*

As a fun way to get started, see if you can guess the meaning of the idioms and slang words in red by reading each sentence below along with its corresponding numbered illustration.

1. They're not old enough to know true love. It's just **puppy love**.
   Definition: "immature love"
   ☐ True   ☐ False

2. Cathy's smiling at you. Maybe she has a **crush on** you!
   Definition: "dislike for"
   ☐ True   ☐ False

3. That's your wife? When did you **tie the knot**?
   Definition: "get married"
   ☐ True   ☐ False

4. There are **no strings attached** to my invitation. I don't expect anything in return.
   Definition: "hidden motives"
   ☐ True   ☐ False

5. My boyfriend **dumped** me for another girl!
   Definition: "rejected"
   ☐ True   ☐ False

6. If you don't want to go out with Bill, **turn him down**.
   Definition: "decline his offer"
   ☐ True   ☐ False

7. John is definitely not a *hunk*. He's the biggest **nerd**!
   Definition: "athlete"
   ☐ True   ☐ False

8. Ted was late, but he finally **showed up**.
   Definition: "appeared"
   ☐ True   ☐ False

9. Tessa is **drop-dead gorgeous**! Is she a model?
   Definition: "very beautiful"
   ☐ True   ☐ False

10. I waited an hour for him. He **stood me up**!
    Definition: "finally arrived"
    ☐ True   ☐ False

11. When I met your father, it was **love at first sight**.
    Definition: "instant love"
    ☐ True   ☐ False

12. If you want a date with Jennifer, just **ask her out**!
    Definition: "ask her on a date"
    ☐ True   ☐ False

13. I heard you went out on a **blind date** last night! Did you know what he looked like before you met him?
    Definition: "date with someone you know well"
    ☐ True   ☐ False

14. If you don't really like Martin, don't go out with him. You're just **leading him on**!
    Definition: "making him falsely think you're interested in him"
    ☐ True   ☐ False

15. Leonard and I planned on having dinner together last night, but he had **to break our date**.
    Definition: "to cancel our date"
    ☐ True   ☐ False

LET'S TALK!

A. DIALOGUE USING SLANG & IDIOMS

The words introduced on the previous two pages are used in the following dialogue and illustrated in the long picture above. Can you understand the conversation and find the illustration that corresponds to the slang? *Note*: The translation of the words in boldface is on the right-hand page.

— Susan is telling Melanie about her date —

Melanie: You have to tell me about your **blind date**. How was it? Was he **drop-dead gorgeous**? Was it **love at first sight**?

Susan: Hardly! First of all, I waited for an hour before he finally picked me up. I just assumed that he **stood me up**. Then when he finally did **show up**, I opened the door to find the biggest **nerd** standing there! By the end of the evening, he told me that he had a **crush on** me and then started talking about **tying the knot**!

Melanie: On the first date?! It was probably just **puppy love**. Listen, my advice to you is that the next time he **asks you out**, just **turn him down** and run in the opposite direction! Whatever you do, you certainly don't want to **lead him on**.

Susan: I'm supposed to go out with another guy next week, but I've decided to **break our date**. I just can't go through this again.

Melanie: Now, don't **dump** him before you even meet him! He may be a great guy for you. Just make sure there are **no strings attached** before you go out.

Susan: Fine. *You* go out with him.

LET'S TALK!

B. DIALOGUE TRANSLATED INTO STANDARD ENGLISH

LET'S SEE HOW MUCH YOU REMEMBER!
Just for fun, bounce around in random order to the words and
expressions in boldface below. See if you can remember their
slang equivalents without looking at the left-hand page!

— *Susan is telling Melanie about her date* —

Melanie: You have to tell me about your **date with the person you've never met before**.
How was it? Was he **extremely attractive**? Was it **immediate love when you saw
him for the first time**?

Susan: Hardly! First of all, I waited for an hour before he finally picked me up. I just assumed that he
intentionally didn't arrive for our date. Then when he finally did **arrive**, I opened
the door to find the biggest **social misfit** standing there! By the end of the evening, he told
me that he had an **infatuation with** me and then started talking about **getting married**!

Melanie: On the first date?! It was probably just **immature love between young people**. Listen,
my advice to you is that the next time he **invites you to go on a date**, just **decline** and
run in the opposite direction! Whatever you do, you certainly don't want to **make him
falsely think that you're interested in him**.

Susan: I'm supposed to go out with another guy next week, but I've decided to **cancel the date**.
I just can't go through this again.

Melanie: Now, don't **end the relationship** with him before you even meet him! He may be a
great guy for you. Just make sure there are **no hidden motives** before you go out.

Susan: Fine. _You_ go out with him.

C. DIALOGUE USING "REAL SPEAK"

The dialogue below demonstrates how the slang conversation on the previous page would *really* be spoken by native speakers!

— Susan's telling Melanie aboud 'er date —

Melanie: Ya hafta tell me about cher **blin' date**. How was it? Was 'e **drop-dead gorgeous**? Was it **love 'it firs' sight**?

Susan: Hardly! First of all, I waided fer 'n hour b'fore 'e fin'lly picked me up. I just assumed th'd I w'z being **stood up**. Then when 'e fin'lly did **show up**, I open' the door da fin' the bigges' **nerd** standing there! By the end 'a the ev'ning, he told me thad 'e had a **crush on** me an' then starded talking about **tying the knot**!

Melanie: On the firs' date?! It w'z prob'ly jus' **puppy love**. Listen, my advice ta you is that the nex' time 'e **asks you out**, jus' **turn 'im down** an' run 'n the opposite direction! Whadever ya do, ya certainly don't wanna **lead 'im on**.

Susan: I'm sapposta go out with another guy next week, b'd I've decided ta **break 'ar date**. I jus' can't go through this again.

Melanie: Now, don't **dump** 'im b'fore ya even meed 'im! He may be a great guy fer you. Jus' make sher there'er **no strings attached** b'fore ya go out.

Susan: Fine. *You* go out with 'im.

HAVE TO = HAFTA
HAS TO = HASTA

In the above dialogue in "Real Speak," **have to** became **hafta**. This is an extremely common reduction used by everyone!

RULES

Rule 1: When **have** is followed by **to**, the combination is commonly pronounced **hafta**.
Rule 2: When **has** is followed by **to**, the combination is commonly pronouced **hasta**.

__I have to break our date.__

HOW DOES IT WORK?

I ha**ve** to break our date.
↓
I ha**f** to break our date.
}
In the phrase **have to**, the **e** is silent and the **v** sound changes to **f**.

I haf t**o** break our date.
↓
I haf t**uh** break our date.
}
Many unstressed vowels (such as the **o** in **to**) are commonly pronounced **uh**.

↓   ↓

I *hafta* break our date.

This reduced version of **have to** is so common in everyday speech that it is often seen written in magazines and newspapers when quoting spoken language.

THE HAFTA / HASTA CHART

	SINGULAR		PLURAL				SINGULAR		PLURAL	
1st person	I	*have to*	We	*have to*		1st person	I	*hafta*	We	*hafta*
2nd person	You	*have to*	You	*have to*		2nd person	You	*hafta*	You	*hafta*
3rd person	He She It }	*has to*	They	*have to*		3rd person	He She It }	*hasta*	They	*hafta*

LET'S USE "REAL SPEAK!"

A. NOW YOU HAFTA DO A "HAFTA" EXERCISE

Fill in each box deciding when to use "hafta" and when to use "hasta." Most important, practice speaking the paragraph in "Real Speak" using your answers.

(Answers on p. 225)

TRACK 69
SOUNDCLOUD

THE ABSOLUTE BEST CHOCOLATE SOUFFLÉ RECIPE IN THE WORLD!

When making a chocolate soufflé, you ⬜ start with fresh ingredients. The eggs ⬜ be room temperature and the chocolate ⬜ be the dark or bittersweet kind. Believe it or not, all you ⬜ buy at the store is two large packages of chocolate chips, eight eggs, and a cup of whipping cream. All you ⬜ do is heat up the cream and pour it over the chocolate chips and stir until it's all combined. The cream ⬜ be hot enough to melt the chocolate, but make sure the cream doesn't boil! Beat the eggs in a bowl and add the chocolate mixture, continuing to beat until it's all nice and creamy. You don't even ⬜ separate the eggs for this soufflé, which makes it really easy! Pour the mixture into a soufflé bowl and carefully put it in a pre-heated 350-degree oven. The soufflé ⬜ cook for one hour....and POOF! You'll have the lightest and most chocolaty soufflé you've ever tasted!

LET'S LEARN!

VOCABULARY

The following words and expressions were used in the previous dialogues. Let's take a closer look at what they mean.

ask someone out (to) *exp.* to invite someone to go on a date.

> **EXAMPLE:** Don't be so scared. Just **ask her out**. The worst thing she could say is no.
>
> **TRANSLATION:** Don't be so scared. Just **invite her to go on a date with you**. The worst thing she could say is no.
>
> **"REAL SPEAK":** Don't be so scared. Just **ask 'er out**. The wors' thing she could say is no.
>
> **NOW YOU DO IT:**
>
> *(Create a sentence using "ask someone out")*

blind date *exp.* • **1.** a date with someone you have never met in person • **2.** a person you are going on a date with that you have never seen in person.

> **EXAMPLE 1:** Tonight I'm going on a **blind date**. I hope he's better than the last one. He was so horrible!
>
> **TRANSLATION:** Tonight I'm going on a **date with someone I've never met before**. I hope he's better than the last one. He was so horrible!
>
> **"REAL SPEAK":** Tanight I'm going on a **blin' date**. I hope 'e's bedder th'n the last one. He w'z so horrible!
>
> **EXAMPLE 2:** Did you see Tina's **blind date**? He's gorgeous!
>
> **TRANSLATION:** Did you see Tina's **date that she's never seen in person before**? He's gorgeous!
>
> **"REAL SPEAK":** Did'ja see **Tina's blin'** date? He's gorgeous!
>
> *Note:* The difference between definitions **1.** and **2.** simply depends on the context.
>
> **NOW YOU DO IT:**
>
> *(Create a sentence using "blind date")*

break  **a date (to)** *exp.* to cancel a date.

> **EXAMPLE:** I'm sorry but I'm going to have to **break our date**. I need to go out of town on business.
>
> **TRANSLATION:** I'm sorry but I'm going to have to **cancel our date**. I need to go out of town on business.
>
> **"REAL SPEAK":** I'm sorry bud I'm gonna hafta **break 'ar date**. I need ta go oudda town on business.
>
> **NOW YOU DO IT:**
>
> *(Create a sentence using "break a date")*

crush on someone (to have a) *exp.* to have an infatuation with someone.

> **EXAMPLE:** I think Betty has a **crush on** me. She keeps following me everywhere!
>
> **TRANSLATION:** I think Betty has an **infatuation with** me. She keeps following me everywhere!
>
> **"REAL SPEAK":** I think Betty has a **crush on** me. She keeps following me ev'rywhere!
>
> **NOW YOU DO IT:**
> *(Create a sentence using "have a crush on someone")*

drop-dead gorgeous *exp.* extremely beautiful.

> **EXAMPLE:** Nancy's children are **drop-dead gorgeous**! It wouldn't surprise me if they became movie stars.
>
> **TRANSLATION:** Nancy's children are **extremely beautiful**! It wouldn't surprise me if they became movie stars.
>
> **"REAL SPEAK":** Nancy's children 'er **drop-dead gorgeous**! It wouldn't saprise me if they b'came movie stars.
>
> *Synonym:* **babe (to be a)** *n.*
>
> **NOW YOU DO IT:**
> *(Create a sentence using "drop-dead gorgeous")*

dump someone (to) *v.* to end a relationship with someone.

> **EXAMPLE:** My boyfriend just **dumped me** because he saw me with another man and that man was my brother!
>
> **TRANSLATION:** My boyfriend just **ended our relationship** because he saw me with another man and that man was my brother!
>
> **"REAL SPEAK":** My boyfrien' just **dumped me** cuz 'e saw me with another man an' that man w'z my brother!
>
> **NOW YOU DO IT:**
> *(Create a sentence using "dump someone")*

lead someone on (to) *exp.* to make someone falsely think that there is mutual interest.

> **EXAMPLE:** You have to be honest and stop **leading him on**. Just tell him that you're not interested in him.
>
> **TRANSLATION:** You have to be honest and stop **making him think you like him when you don't**. Just tell him that you're not interested in him.
>
> **"REAL SPEAK":** Ya hafta be honest 'n stop **leading 'im on**. Jus' tell 'im that ch'r nod int'rested in 'im.
>
> **NOW YOU DO IT:**
> *(Create a sentence using "lead someone on")*

love at first sight *exp.* instant love when seeing someone for the first time.

> **EXAMPLE:** When I met your father twenty years ago, it was **love at first sight**.
>
> **TRANSLATION:** When I met your father twenty years ago, it was **instant love upon seeing him**.
>
> **"REAL SPEAK":** When I met ch'r father twen'y years ago, it w'z **love 'it firs' sight**.
>
> **NOW YOU DO IT:**
>
> *(Create a sentence using "love at first sight")*

nerd *n.* a social misfit, someone who is out-of-date in appearance and unsophisticated.

> **EXAMPLE:** I've never met anyone who is so boring! And you should have seen the way he dresses. What a **nerd**!
>
> **TRANSLATION:** I've never met anyone who is so boring! And you should have seen the way he dresses. What a **social misfit**!
>
> **"REAL SPEAK":** I've never med anyone who's so boring! An' you should'ev seen the way he dresses. Whad a **nerd**!
>
> **NOW YOU DO IT:**
>
> *(Create a sentence using "nerd")*

no strings attached *exp.* with no hidden expectations, no hidden motives.

> **EXAMPLE:** Would you like to go to the movies tonight? **No strings attached**.
>
> **TRANSLATION:** Would you like to go to the movies tonight? **No hidden motives**.
>
> **"REAL SPEAK":** Would'ja like ta go da the movies tanight? **No strings attached**.
>
> **NOW YOU DO IT:**
>
> *(Create a sentence using "no strings attached")*

puppy love *exp.* immature love between young people or children.

> **EXAMPLE:** I think my little son likes your little daughter. **Puppy love** is so sweet!
>
> **TRANSLATION:** I think my little son likes your little daughter. **Immature love between young children** is so sweet!
>
> **"REAL SPEAK":** I think my liddle son likes yer liddle daughter. **Puppy love** is so sweet!
>
> **NOW YOU DO IT:**
>
> *(Create a sentence using "puppy love")*

show up (to) *phrV.* to arrive.

EXAMPLE: You won't believe what time Noah finally **showed up**... two o'clock in the morning!

TRANSLATION: You won't believe what time Noah finally **arrived**... two o'clock in the morning!

"REAL SPEAK": You won't b'lieve what time Noah fin'lly **showed up**... two a'clock 'n the morning!

NOW YOU DO IT:
(Create a sentence using "show up")

stand someone up (to) *exp.* to fail to arrive for a date.

EXAMPLE: Greg was supposed to meet me at seven o'clock for dinner, but he never arrived! This is the last time he's going to **stand me up**!

TRANSLATION: Greg was supposed to meet me at seven o'clock for dinner, but he never arrived! This is the last time he's going to **fail to arrive for a date with me**!

"REAL SPEAK": Greg w'z sapposta meet me 'it seven a'clock fer dinner, bud 'e never arrived! This is the las' time 'e's gonna **stan' me up**!

NOW YOU DO IT:
(Create a sentence using "stand someone up")

tie the  knot (to) *exp.* to get married.

EXAMPLE: I heard you and Nicholas **tied the knot** last month! Congratulations!

TRANSLATION: I heard you and Nicholas **got married** last month! Congratulations!

"REAL SPEAK": I heard'ju 'n Nicholas **tied the knot** las' month! C'ngradjalations!

NOW YOU DO IT:
(Create a sentence using "tie the knot")

turn someone down (to) *exp.* to decline someone's offer of going on a date.

EXAMPLE: I never should have listened to you. When I asked Sally out, she **turned me down**!

TRANSLATION: I never should have listened to you. When I asked Sally out, she **declined my offer**!

"REAL SPEAK": I never should'a listen' da you. When I asked Sally out, she **turn' me down**!

NOW YOU DO IT:
(Create a sentence using "turn someone down")

LET'S PRACTICE!

A. CREATE YOUR OWN STORY (Part 1) (Answers on p. 225)

Follow the instructions below and write down your answer in the space provided. When you have finished answering all the questions, transfer your answers to the story on the opposite page. Make sure to match the number of your answer with the numbered space in the story.

1. Write down a "thing" (pencil, potato, toothbrush, etc.):

   _____

2. Write down a "man's name":

   _____

3. Write down a "body part":

   _____

4. Write down an "adjective" (big, small, pretty, etc.):

   _____

5. Write down "something you eat":

   _____

6. Write down "any kind of liquid":

   _____

7. Write down another "kind of liquid":

   _____

8. Write down a "thing":

   _____

9. Write down another "thing":

   _____

10. Write down a "body part":

    _____

11. Write down a "mode of transportation":

    _____

12. Write down a "thing":

    _____

13. Write down another "thing":

    _____

14. Write down another "thing":

    _____

B. CREATE YOUR OWN STORY *(Part 2)*

Once you've filled in the blanks, read your story aloud. If you've done Part 1 correctly, your story should be hilarious!

THE WEEKLY

Cupid Gazette

THE WEEKLY NEWSPAPER THAT PROVES LOVE IS ALWAYS IN THE AIR

"Dear Gabby..."

by Gabby Blabber
Advice Columnist

Dear Gabby...

Today, I went out on a blind date with a ___1.___ named ___2.___. At first I thought I was being stood up because he showed up late. But when I took one look at his ___3.___, it was love at first sight! He took me to a ___4.___ restaurant that serves large portions of ___5.___ covered in ___6.___. We even drank an expensive bottle of ___7.___ with dinner. Everything was going great until a drop-dead gorgeous ___8.___ suddenly walked into the room wearing an extremely tiny ___9.___. He just couldn't take his ___10.___ off her. I'm sure he had a crush on her that was more than just puppy love. I was so mad that I dumped him right there and went home by ___11.___. Yesterday, he called me on the ___12.___ and apologized for being such a ___13.___. In fact, he even asked me out again. When I turned him down, he kept begging me to give him one more ___14.___. What should I do?

signed... Confused

C. WHAT WOULD YOU DO IF SOMEONE SAID...?

What would you do in response to the words in white italics?
Choose your answer by placing an "X" in the box.

(Answers on p. 225)

1.	*Oh, darling! I love you so much. Let's tie the knot!*	I would... ☐ a. bend down and tie my shoe ☐ b. make wedding plans ☐ c. get some rope
2.	*I've been waiting here for an hour. I was beginning to think you stood me up!*	I would... ☐ a. offer an apology ☐ b. offer to hold them upright for an hour ☐ c. offer to fix her car
3.	*I can't hide my feelings any longer. I have a crush on you.*	I would... ☐ a. crush that person back ☐ b. put that person in a headlock ☐ c. tell the person my true feelings
4.	*My aunt is in the hospital. I'm afraid I'm going to have to break our date.*	I would... ☐ a. get a broom to clean up the mess ☐ b. try to make plans for a later time ☐ c. offer to help break it
5.	*Where did you get those clothes? You dress like such a nerd!*	I would... ☐ a. thank the person for the compliment ☐ b. run out and buy new clothing ☐ c. buy more clothing in the same style
6.	*There's Karen. She's drop-dead gorgeous!*	I would... ☐ a. quickly try to revive her ☐ b. call an ambulance ☐ c. agree and explain that she's a model
7.	*My girlfriend just dumped me. What should I do?*	I would... ☐ a. offer to pick him back up ☐ b. offer to get him a bandage ☐ c. offer advice
8.	*I think you're very nice. I'd like to ask you out for Saturday night.*	I would... ☐ a. accept and suggest going to a movie ☐ b. accept but insist on staying indoors ☐ c. accept and go stand outside
9.	*Thank you for inviting me to the party but I have to turn you down.*	I would... ☐ a. tell her that I'll see her there ☐ b. tell her that I'm disappointed ☐ c. tell her to take the elevator instead
10.	*Let's go out tonight and just have fun. No strings attached.*	I would... ☐ a. suggest that chains really are stronger ☐ b. agree to go ☐ c. argue that violins are better than horns

LET'S REVIEW!

SOME OPPOSITES DO ATTRACT! *(Answers on p. 225)*

Now that you've learned almost 200 slang terms and idioms, this review exercise should be a piece of cake (which means "easy" in slang)! Match the picture in Column A with the picture in Column B that has the opposite meaning by connecting the dots next to each picture.

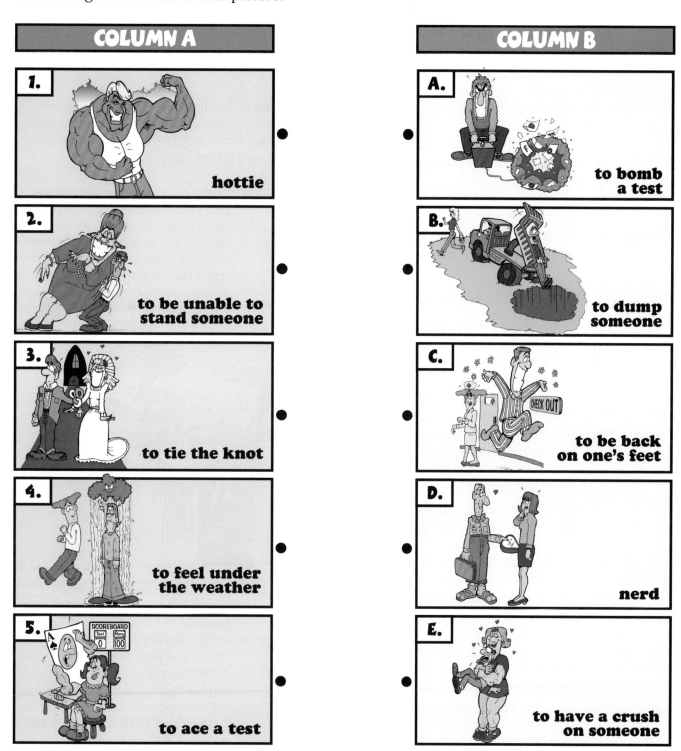

TRACK 72
SOUNDCLOUD

EXERCISES FOR THIS SECTION ARE IN THE WORKBOOK.

Popular Idioms, Slang & Jargon
Having to do with: **DATING**

For more, see *The Slangman Guide to STREET SPEAK 3*, Chapters 1-3.

---

ask for someone's hand in marriage (to) *exp.* to propose to someone.

> EXAMPLE: Mr. Burke, I would like to **ask for your daughter's hand in marriage**.

> TRANSLATION: Mr. Burke, I would like to **propose to your daughter**.

> "REAL SPEAK": Mr. Burke, I'd like ta **ask fer yer dauder's hand 'n marriage**.

bride-to-be *n.* a woman who is soon to be married; fiancée.

> EXAMPLE: Steve started getting nervous when his **bride-to-be** didn't arrive at the wedding ceremony.

> TRANSLATION: Steve started getting nervous when his **fiancée** didn't arrive at the wedding ceremony.

> "REAL SPEAK": Steve starded gedding nervous wh'n 'is **bride-da-be** didn' arrive 'it the wedding ceremony.

> *Antonym:* **groom-to-be / groom / bride-groom** *n.* a man who is soon to be married; fiancé.

call off the wedding (to) *exp.* to cancel the wedding.

> EXAMPLE: Mindy **called off her wedding** because she caught Victor cheating with another woman!

> TRANSLATION: Mindy **cancelled her wedding** because she caught Victor cheating with another woman!

> "REAL SPEAK": Mindy **called off 'er wedding** b'cuz she caught Victer cheading w'th another woman!

catfishing *n.* the deceptive action of Internet predators who fabricate online identities to trick people into emotional relationships and sending money / **catfished** *adj.* victimized from catfishing.

> EXAMPLE: Craig was a victim of **catfishing**. He met this beautiful girl online and fell in love with her. Then he started sending her money. Unfortunately, when he tried to have a voice conversation with her, she disappeared! I can't believe he got **catfished** like that!

> TRANSLATION: Craig was a victim of **being tricked into believing a phony profile**. He met this beautiful girl online and fell in love with her. Then he started sending her money. Unfortunately, when he tried to have a voice conversation with her, she disappeared! I can't believe he got **tricked into believing she existed** like that!

"REAL SPEAK": Craig w'z a victim 'ev **catfishing**. He met th's beaudiful girl online 'n fell 'n love w'th 'er. Then 'e starded sending 'er money. Unforch'nately, wh'n 'e tried da have a voice conversation w'th 'er, she disappeared! I can't believe 'e got **catfished** like that!

chemistry (to have) *exp.* to have a strong emotional connection with someone.

EXAMPLE: Jack and Irene have been married for fifty years! I've never seen a couple with better **chemistry**!

TRANSLATION: Jack and Irene have been married for fifty years! I've never seen a couple with a better **emotional connection**!

"REAL SPEAK": Jack 'n Irene'ev been married fer fifdy years! I've never seen a couple w'th bedder **chemistry**!

cold feet (to get) *exp.* to feel too nervous and scared to do something you had planned to do.

EXAMPLE: At the wedding ceremony, Christopher **got cold feet** at the last second and ran off!

TRANSLATION: At the wedding ceremony, Christopher **got nervous and scared** at the last second and ran off!

"REAL SPEAK": At the wedding ceremony, Christopher **got cold feet** 'it the las' second 'n ran off!

Synonym: **lose one's nerve (to)** *exp.* For example: *At the wedding ceremony, Christopher **lost his nerve** at the last second and ran off!*

date night *exp.* a night that two people reserve each week to do something fun together.

EXAMPLE: Thank you for the invitation to go to the play with you on Friday night. Unfortunately, I can't. Every Friday is **date night** with Susan.

TRANSLATION: Thank you for the invitation to go to the play with you on Friday night. Unfortunately, I can't. Every Friday is **reserved to do something fun at night** with Susan.

"REAL SPEAK": Thanks fer the invitation ta go da the play w'th ya on Friday night. Unforchu'nately, I can't. Ev'ry Friday 'ez **date night** w'th Susan.

deal-breaker *n.* something that discourages someone from dating another person.

EXAMPLE: I'm going out tonight with a guy I met online. I forgot to ask him if he smokes. If he does, it's a **deal-breaker**.

TRANSLATION: I'm going out tonight with a guy I met online. I forgot to ask him if he smokes. If he does, it's **the last time we're going out on a date**.

"REAL SPEAK": I'm going out tanight w'th a guy I med online. I fergot ta ask 'im 'ef 'e smokes. If 'e does, it's a **deal-breaker**.

double date (to go on a) *exp.* to go on a social outing with someone along with another couple.

EXAMPLE: I'm dying for you to meet Steve. Why don't we go on a **double date** this weekend?

TRANSLATION: I'm dying for you to meet Steve. Why don't we go on a **social outing with you and the person you're dating** this weekend?

"REAL SPEAK": I'm dying fer you da meet Steve. Why don' we go on a **double date** th's weekend?

get serious (to) *exp.* to get involved in a relationship on a deep level.

EXAMPLE: Tonight I'm meeting Diane's parents for the first time. It's really **getting serious** between us!

TRANSLATION: Tonight I'm meeting Diane's parents for the first time. It's really **becoming a committed relationship** between us!

"REAL SPEAK": Tanide I'm meeding Diane's parents fer the firs' time. It's really **gedding serious** b'tween us!

have a thing for something (to) *exp.* to have a strong attraction or liking for something.

EXAMPLE: Jerry **has a thing for** blonds. He only dates women with light-colored hair.

TRANSLATION: Jerry **has a strong attraction for** blonds. He only dates women with light-colored hair.

"REAL SPEAK": Jerry **has a thing fer** blon's. He only dates women w'th light-colored hair.

jilt someone (to) *v.* to suddenly abandon a lover.

EXAMPLE: Tony **jilted** Bonnie for another woman!

TRANSLATION: Tony **abandoned** Bonnie for another woman!

"REAL SPEAK": Tony **jilted** Bonnie fer another woman!

Variation: **get jilted (to)** *adj.* For example: *I can't believe I got **jilted**! I was on a date with this new guy, I turned around to say hello to someone, and the next thing I knew, he was dancing with another woman!*

joined at the hip (to be) *exp.* to be inseparable.

EXAMPLE: Chuck never goes anywhere without Sharon. Those two are **joined at the hip**!

TRANSLATION: Chuck never goes anywhere without Sharon. Those two are **inseparable**!

"REAL SPEAK": Chuck never goes anywhere w'thout Sharon. Those two'er **joined 'it the hip**!

leave someone at the altar (to) *exp.* to abandon one's fiancé(e) at the wedding ceremony.

EXAMPLE: I felt so sorry for Brad! Barbara **left him at the altar**. Everyone felt so bad for him they told him to keep all the wedding gifts.

TRANSLATION: I felt so sorry for Brad! Barbara **abandoned him at the wedding ceremony**. Everyone felt so bad for him they told him to keep all the wedding gifts.

"REAL SPEAK": I felt so sorry fer Brad! Barb'ra **left 'im 'it the altar**. Ev'ryone felt so bad fer 'im they told 'im da keep all the wedding gif's.

Variation: **leave someone standing at the altar (to)** *exp.*

Also: **runaway bride** *exp.* a bride-to-be who runs away from a wedding shortly before the ceremony.

Note: An *altar* (also spelled *alter*) is a platform where religious ceremonies are held.

makeover (to get a) *exp.* to undergo a transformation of a person's hairstyle, makeup, or clothes.

EXAMPLE: Before my wedding day, I'm going to get a complete **makeover**.

TRANSLATION: Before my wedding day, I'm going to get a complete **transformation of my hairstyle and makeup**.

"REAL SPEAK": B'fore my wedding day, I'm gonna ged a complete **makeover**.

make up (to) *phrV.* to reconcile and become friends again.

> **EXAMPLE:** I didn't think the wedding was going to happen because of Anne and Craig's argument. Fortunately they **made up** a day before the wedding!
>
> **TRANSLATION:** I didn't think the wedding was going to happen because of Anne and Craig's argument. Fortunately they **reconciled** a day before the wedding!
>
> **"REAL SPEAK":** I didn' think the wedding w'z gonna happen b'cuz 'ev Anne 'n Craig's argument. Forch'nately they **made up** a day b'fore the wedding!

Mister Right (to look for) *exp.* to look for a potential husband.

> **EXAMPLE:** Laura has been looking for a relationship for a long time. She goes to a different party every weekend looking for **Mister Right**.

> **TRANSLATION:** Laura has been looking for a relationship for a long time. She goes to a different party every weekend looking for **a potential husband**.
>
> **"REAL SPEAK":** Laura's b'n looking fer a relationship fer a long time. She goes do a diff'rent pardy ev'ry weeken' looking fer **Mister Right**.
>
> *Variation:* **Mister Right Now (to look for)** *exp.* to look for the perfect relationship but only for the moment.
>
> *Synonym:* **Ms. or Miss Right (to look for)** *exp.* to look for a wife.
>
> *Variation:* **Ms. or Miss Right Now** *exp.* (see directly above)

past one's sell-by date (to be) *exp.* to be past one's point of being attractive • (lit); to be older than the expiration date on a food product.

> **EXAMPLE:** Just because you're older doesn't mean you'll never find a girlfriend! You'll never be **past your sell-by date** if you stay in shape and keep a positive attitude.

> **TRANSLATION:** Just because you're older doesn't mean you'll never find a girlfriend! You'll never be **past the point of being attractive** if you stay in shape and keep a positive attitude.
>
> **"REAL SPEAK":** Jus' b'cuz y'r older doesn' mean you'll never find a girlfriend! You'll never be **past yer sell-by dade** 'ef ya stay 'n shape 'n keep a posidive additude.

player *n.* a man who dates more than one person at a time.

> **EXAMPLE:** You're going on a date with Randy? Haven't you heard about his reputation? The guy's a total **player**! He's definitely not interested in a serious relationship.
>
> **TRANSLATION:** You're going on a date with Randy? Haven't you heard about his reputation? The guy **dates more than one person at a time**! He's definitely not interested in a serious relationship.

"REAL SPEAK": Y'r goin' on a date w'th Randy? Haven'cha heard aboud 'is reputation? The guy's a todal **player**! He's def'nitely nod int'rested 'n a serious relationship.

Note: You may often see this word spelled **playa** (pronounced: *play-ah*) which is from African-American Vernacular English. This is a dialect of some working- and middle-class African Americans particularly in urban communities, and commonly heard in rap music.

seeing each other (to be) *exp.* to be dating each other.

EXAMPLE: Ben and Julie have **been seeing each other** now for two years. I wonder if they'll get married some day.

TRANSLATION: Ben and Julie have **been dating each other** now for two years. I wonder if they'll get married some day.

"REAL SPEAK": Ben 'n Julie 'ev **been seeing each other** now fer two years. I wonder 'ef they'll get married some day.

settle down (to) *phrV.* to begin to live a steady life by getting married, getting a regular job, maybe having children, etc.

EXAMPLE: Doug used to be such a player. Now he's finally decided to **settle down** and have a family.

TRANSLATION: Doug used to be such a player. Now he's finally decided to **live a steady life, get married, get a regular job** and have a family.

"REAL SPEAK": Doug usta be such a player. Now 'e's fin'lly decided da **seddle down** 'n have a fam'ly.

thrill of the chase (the) *exp.* the excitement of trying to find someone with whom to have a romantic relationship.

EXAMPLE: Josh has been trying to date me for months. The moment I said yes, he disappeared! Some guys are only interested in **the thrill of the chase**.

TRANSLATION: Josh has been trying to date me for months. The moment I said yes, he disappeared! Some guys are only interested in **the excitement of trying to find someone with whom to have a romantic relationship**.

"REAL SPEAK": Josh 'ez b'n tryin' da date me fer munts. The momen' I said yes, he disappeared! Some guys 'er only int'rested 'n **the thrill 'a the chase**.

walk down the aisle (to) *exp.* to get married.

EXAMPLE: I never thought Ted would be the first one to **walk down the aisle**. He used to say he'd never get married!

TRANSLATION: I never thought Ted would be the first one to **get married**. He used to say he'd never get married!

"REAL SPEAK": I never thought Ted'd be the firs' one da **walk down the aisle**. He usta say 'e'd never get married!

SLANGMAN TV

Slangman Explains More idioms & Slang for...

—ON A DATE—

SCAN ME!

CHAPTER 10

SCAN THE QR CODE OR GO TO: bit.ly/StreetSpeak1-Chapter10

THIS VIDEO EPISODE CONTAINS...

dating

- Slangman presents a 3-part video on dating slang
  - The *Pick Up*
  - The *Rocky* Relationship
  - The *Break Up*

Idioms & slang used on TV this week plus the latest Teen Slang!

- Slangman gives you his TOP 5 LIST of the latest idioms and slang from the most popular TV shows in the U.S. plus the newest slang teens are using today!

Newest American slang just entered into the dictionary

ANSWERS TO LESSONS 1-10

LESSON ONE - AT THE PARTY

LET'S WARM UP!

1. get control of your emotions
2. came to my party uninvited
3. what's wong with
4. negative person at parties
5. lover of parties
6. muscular man
7. that's impossible
8. kidding me
9. having a great time
10. look at
11. really dislike
12. stop nagging me

LET'S USE "REAL SPEAK"
A. WHA'DID THEY SAY?

1. b
2. a
3. a
4. a
5. a
6. a

LET'S PRACTICE!
A. CONTEXT EXERCISE

1. makes sense
2. makes sense
3. doesn't make sense
4. doesn't make sense
5. makes sense
6. makes sense
7. doesn't make sense
8. makes sense
9. doesn't make sense

B. CHOOSE THE RIGHT WORD

1. upset
2. muscular
3. messing
4. blast
5. up
6. out
7. animal
8. mean
9. bugs
10. No

C. COMPLETE THE PHRASE

1. what's up
2. get a grip
3. messing with me
4. bugs me
5. blast
6. can't stand
7. no way
8. pooper
9. hottie

D. IS IT "YES" OR IS IT "NO?" (POSSIBLE ANSWERS)

1. Yes. He's a hottie.
2. No. I can't stand her.
3. No. I crashed a party.
4. No. I'm messing with you.
5. Yes. He needs to get a grip.
6. Yes. It bugs me that she gives us so much homework!.
7. Yes. I checked it out the moment I walked in.
8. No. No way!
9. Yes. I had a blast!
10. Yes. What's up with his eye?

LESSON TWO - AT THE MARKET

LET'S WARM UP!

1. C
2. A
3. E
4. G
5. F

6. J
7. I
8. D
9. H
10. B

LET'S USE "REAL SPEAK"

A. "T" PRONOUNCED LIKE "D"

1. Wha**t** a beau**t**iful swea**t**er! Did you ge**t** it when you went shopping last Sa**t**urday?

2. My parents ordered a bo**tt**le of champagne for their anniversary.

3. My laptop comp**u**ter is ba**tt**ery-opera**t**ed.

4. Wha**t** a great car! Is **it** an au**t**oma**t**ic?

5. Let's go **t**o the par**t**y la**t**er. Be**tt**y said there's going to be a lo**t** of good food there.

6. What ci**t**y do you live in?

7. Would you like a soft drink or a bo**tt**le of wa**t**er?

8. Did you invite that pre**tt**y girl to your house for a li**tt**le dinner?

9. I just bough**t** a po**tt**ed plant. It's a beau**t**iful bonsai tree.

10. Wha**t** a pi**t**y about your li**tt**le sister's babysi**tt**er. I heard she go**t** into a car accident!

LET'S PRACTICE!

A. TV COMMERCIAL

1. In the produce department, they have veggies.
2. You won't have to wait in line because there are ten checkers waiting to ring up your order.
3. The announcer suggests that you pick up lemon cake from the bakery.
4. They are lowering prices of vegetables at David's Market.
5. The lemon sponge cake is to die for!
6. Yes, the market has everything I need to make a wonderful dessert from scratch.

B. YOU'RE THE AUTHOR

Joe: We need to **pick up** some **veggies** like lettuce, cucumber, and tomatoes for our salad tonight. You're going to love this store. They **carry** the best organic products and they've **slashed** their prices on everything this week.

Kim: You're right! I've never seen such **rock**-bottom prices. At my store, everything is so expensive. Yesterday I paid five dollars for bread! What a **rip-off**!

Joe: You're not kidding! Hey, I have an idea. Instead of buying dessert, let's make one from **scratch**...something with chocolate. I have a recipe that's **to die for**!

Kim: You're making my **mouth water**! Let's buy the ingredients quickly so we can have the **checker** ring **up** our order before I faint from hunger!

C. TRUE OR FALSE

1. False
2. True
3. False
4. True
5. False
6. False
7. True
8. False
9. False
10. True

D. CROSSWORD PUZZLE

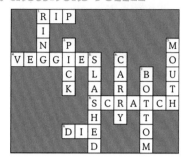

LESSON THREE - AT THE MOVIES

LET'S WARM UP!

1. False
2. False
3. False
4. False
5. True
6. True
7. True
8. True
9. True
10. True
11. True
12. False

LET'S USE "REAL SPEAK"

A. SHOULD'A, COULD'A, WOULD'A, MUST'A

1. must'a
2. should'a
3. must'a
4. would'a
5. would'a / couldn'a
6. would'a
7. shouldn'a
8. must'a / wouldn'a

LET'S PRACTICE!

A. I KNOW THE ANSWER, BUT WHAT'S THE QUESTION?

1. Why did Henry volunteer to give a speech in front of all those people?
2. Were you able to get tickets for the play?
3. Do we have time to eat something before we leave?
4. Do you want to see the new musical *Felines*?
5. The movie made a fortune, didn't it?
6. Look at the long line! I thought you said this movie wasn't popular.

C. IMAGINE THAT...

In this section, you could have many possible answers. Remember, respond to each situation by making a complete sentence using one of the groups of words in the word list AND using each group only once. Be as creative as you'd like!

B. FIND YOUR PERFECT MATCH

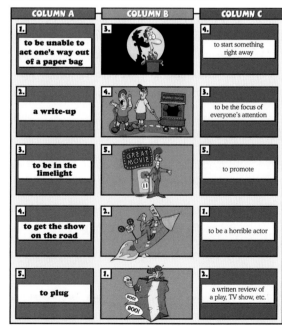

LESSON FOUR - ON VACATION

LET'S WARM UP!

1. go to the movies
2. relax and do nothing
3. hotel with bed and breakfast
4. go swimming
5. sunbathing
6. go into town
7. completely filled
8. to accommodate us
9. take a taxicab
10. stayed awake until very late
11. visiting some interesting places
12. sleeping late

LET'S USE "REAL SPEAK"

A. PUT THE PAIRS BACK TOGETHER

1. queen
2. out
3. down
4. right
5. fork
6. pepper
7. butter
8. bad
9. jelly
10. white
11. bottom
12. cold
13. day
14. take
15. son
16. brother
17. wife
18. socks
19. ears
20. wrong
21. eggs
22. dogs

LET'S PRACTICE!

A. FIND THE MISSING WORDS

Tom: This **B&B** has so much more charm than the hotel we stayed at last night.

Becky: It's a good thing they were able to **put us up** for the night. It was the only vacancy in the entire city! All the other places were booked **solid**.

Tom: We really got lucky. It's so quiet here. It was hard to **sleep** in at the other hotel because of all the noise. So, what do you want to do tonight?

Becky: Let's go hit the **town**!

Tom: Good idea. We could go **catch** a movie.

Becky: Actually, I thought it would be fun to go **sightseeing** and explore a little. We could **grab** a cab and be there in a few minutes.

Tom: After we visit the sights, we could get something to eat at that great restaurant around the corner and then go dancing till all **hours of the night**.

Becky: That's perfect! Then tomorrow we can relax all day. It would be so nice to wake up late then **hang out** by the pool and **soak up** some sun. We could even take a **dip** if it's gets too hot!

B. MATCH THE SENTENCES

1. F
2. J
3. D
4. I
5. A
6. B
7. E
8. G
9. H
10. K
11. L
12. C

LESSON FIVE - AT THE AIRPORT

LET'S WARM UP!

1. I
2. K
3. C
4. J
5. A
6. F

7. D
8. H
9. L
10. B
11. E
12. G

LET'S USE "REAL SPEAK"

A. "ACROSS" WORD PUZZLE

1. Will you go to the market to get me something to eat?
2. I have to try to find a present to give to my wife.
3. You need to know how to drive in order to buy a car.
4. If I need you to help me move tomorrow, I'll ask.
5. It's really too cold to go to the beach this morning.

B. "TA BE" OR NOT "TA BE..."

1. I went **ta** the market **ta** pick up some bread.
2. Can you tell me how **da** get **ta** the post office from here?
3. Steve wanted **da** go **da** the park but I wanted **da** go shopping instead.
4. I'd love **da** join you but I have work **ta** do.
5. On the way **da** the airport, I had **ta** stop **ta** get gas.
6. We need **da** close the windows before it starts **ta** rain.
7. I don't like **ta** go **da** the dentist.

LET'S PRACTICE!

A. COMPLETE THE FAIRY TALE

Once upon a time, there was a young girl named Cinderella who lived way out in the **boonies** and wanted something fun to do. So one day, she decided to use her frequent **flyer** miles and get a free ticket to somewhere exciting. She made an appointment to sell her script to a big producer in Hollywood. She always thought that her life story would make a good movie or even a musical!

Later that day, taking only a **carry**-on, she left for the airport. She always believed in **traveling** light. Unfortunately, when she arrived at the airport, she got **bumped** because she was late. So, she was put on **standby** for the next available flight. Finally, several hours later and completely wiped **out**, she was put on the **red** eye for Hollywood, California!

The flight was so bumpy she started to feel airsick and feared that she might have to use the **barf** bag. Fortunately, just then the plane made a landing in Denver. After a two-hour **layover**, she was once again on her way to Hollywood, the land of fame and fortune.

By the time she arrived, she was so **wired** that she couldn't sleep and stayed up till all **hours** of the night. Unfortunately, the combination of no sleep and jet **lag** caused her to **sleep** in late and miss her appointment with the producer!

She was so disappointed that she decided to take the next flight back home. However, as fate would have it, she found herself sitting in the airplane next to Howard, a very handsome young man, formerly known as Prince.

B. CONTEXT EXERCISE

1. K	5. G	9. F
2. E	6. J	10. B
3. A	7. D	11. L
4. C	8. I	12. H

C. COMPLETE THE PHRASE

Steve: I'm sorry we're so late. We had an unexpected two-hour **layover** some place way out in the **boonies**. You know, I almost missed the flight entirely because of all the traffic! So I arrived late and got **bumped**. Luckily they agreed to put me on **standby**. All I had was a **carry-on** so it was easy.

Karen: It's a good thing you travel **light**. Well, with the jet **lag**, I imagine you're pretty wiped **out**.

Steve: Actually, I'm pretty **wired** after all that traveling. At least I got a free ticket for being a frequent **flyer**!

Karen: So, how was it traveling on the red **eye**?

Steve: It got a little bumpy for a while. Luckily, I never had to use the barf **bag**!

LESSON SIX - AT A RESTAURANT

LET'S WARM UP!

1. eat less
2. an additional order of
3. omit
4. pay separately
5. passion for sweets
6. You believe you can eat more than you can
7. remaining food
8. is going to be paid for by me
9. get something to eat
10. chocolate lover
11. ate in excess
12. bag to carry food home

LET'S USE "REAL SPEAK"

A. NOW YOU'RE GONNA DO A "GONNA" EXERCISE

1. I'm so hungry! I'm **gonna** pig out tonight!
2. This restaurant serves such big portions. I'm **gonna** need a doggie bag.
3. I'm starting to get fat. I'm **gonna** have to cut down on desserts.
4. I'd like a hamburger but I'm **gonna** skip the fries.
5. I'm having lunch with Irene today, but we're **gonna** go Dutch.
6. If David is anything like his mother, he's **gonna** be a chocaholic when he grows up.
7. We have a lot of extra food from the party. Steve is **gonna** take home the leftovers.
8. I'm hungry. I'm **gonna** go grab a bite.

B. IS IT GONNA OR GOING TO?

Janet and I are **going to** a great French restaurant tonight and we're **gonna** pig out! I'm probably **gonna** need a doggie bag because they serve so much food. After dinner, we're **going to** my mother's house and I'm **gonna** bring her the leftovers. In fact, I'm **gonna** order an extra chocolate dessert that I'm **gonna** surprise her with. I know that's **gonna** make her happy because she's a bigger chocaholic than I am!

LET'S PRACTICE!

A. CHOOSE THE RIGHT WORD

1. Dutch
2. doggie
3. down
4. bite
5. skip
6. tooth
7. on
8. pig
9. eyes
10. side
11. overs
12. chocolate

C. MATCH THE COLUMN

1. B
2. F
3. I
4. A
5. J
6. D
7. H
8. C
9. K
10. G
11. L
12. E

B. CROSSWORD PUZZLE

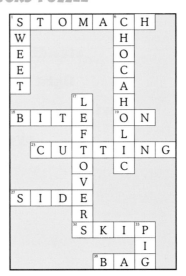

LET'S REVIEW! - THE GOOD, THE BAD, AND THE...

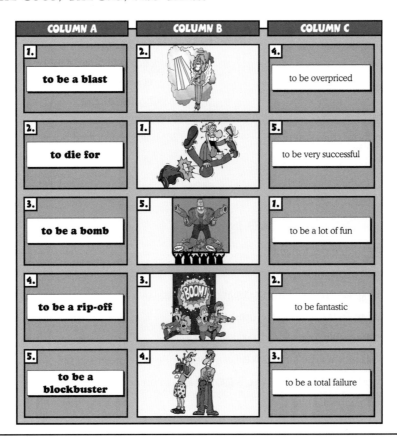

COLUMN A	COLUMN B	COLUMN C
1. to be a blast	2.	4. to be overpriced
2. to die for	1.	5. to be very successful
3. to be a bomb	5.	1. to be a lot of fun
4. to be a rip-off	3.	2. to be fantastic
5. to be a blockbuster	4.	3. to be a total failure

LESSON SEVEN - ON THE ROAD

LET'S WARM UP!

1. flat tire
2. destroyed
3. drove through a red light
4. drive
5. accelerate suddenly
6. minor car accident
7. the time when everyone is driving on the road
8. get in
9. arrested
10. heavy traffic
11. police officer
12. defective car
13. car
14. tendency to drive fast

LET'S USE "REAL SPEAK"

A. WANNA OR WANSTA

1. Yes. I **wanna** see a comedy.
2. He **wansta** pig out on pizza.
3. Everybody **wansta** order hamburgers and a side of fries.
4. Yes. He **wansta** take home the leftovers in a doggie bag.
5. Yes. I **wanna** take a spin to the beach.
6. She **wansta** eat at a French restaurant.
7. Nobody **wansta** play cards tonight. Everyone **wansta** watch TV.
8. No. The cat **wansta** sleep on the sofa.

LET'S PRACTICE!

A. CORRECT OR INCORRECT

1. incorrect
2. incorrect
3. correct
4. incorrect
5. incorrect
6. correct
7. incorrect
8. incorrect
9. correct
10. correct
11. correct
12. incorrect

B. BLANK-BLANK

1. bumper-to-bumper traffic
2. go for a spin
3. ran a light
4. lead foot
5. punch it
6. fender-bender
7. hop in
8. totaled
9. lemon
10. blowout
11. cop
12. rush hour
13. wheels
14. hauled in

C. TRUE OR FALSE

1. true
2. false
3. false
4. true
5. true
6. false
7. true
8. false
9. true
10. true
11. false
12. true
13. true
14. false

LET'S REVIEW! - IN OTHER WORDS...SYNONYMS!

1. flat
2. yank someone's chain
3. dirt cheap
4. smash hit
5. dud
6. grand opening
7. piece of junk
8. pull oneself together
9. buzzed
10. jaunt
11. pork out
12. grab

LESSON EIGHT - AT SCHOOL

LET'S WARM UP!

1. I
2. B
3. E
4. J
5. D
6. N
7. C

8. H
9. G
10. L
11. A
12. M
13. K
14. F

LET'S USE "REAL SPEAK"

A. CHANGE 'EM TO REAL SPEAK

Last night I babysat my niece and nephew. You should have seen **'em**. They're so cute! Tessa is eight years old and **'er** eyes look just like **'er** mother's. When you look at **'em** in the sunlight, they look very dark blue. **Her** favorite food is ice cream and **'er** favorite color is red. **Her** brother Nicholas just had **'is** fifth birthday. Everyone thinks **'e** looks just like **'is** father but **'e** thinks **'e** looks like **'is** grandfather. Frankly, whenever I see **'im** smile, I think **'e** looks just like me! After all, I'm **'is** uncle! Both of **'em** love to read. Yesterday, Tessa read a story to **'er** mother and Nicholas read one to **'is** father. I'm glad they live so close. It's so much fun watching **'em** grow up!

LET'S PRACTICE!

A. TRUTH OR LIE

1. lie
2. lie
3. lie

4. truth
5. truth
6. truth

B. FIND THE DEFINITION

1. to do extremely well on a test
2. to do extremely poorly on a test
3. to study very hard in a short period of time
4. to miss class intentionally
5. to remove a class from one's schedule
6. an end-of-term test that covers everything learned during the school term

7. extremely difficult or terrific
8. a test that can be taken again at a later time
9. a surprise test
10. a common abbreviation for "psychology"
11. to stay up all night studying
12. perfect grades

C.

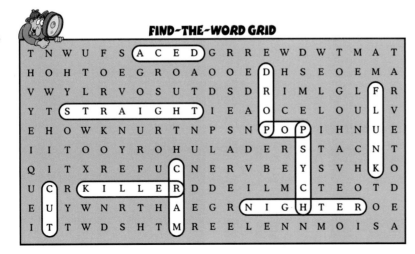

FIND-THE-WORD GRID

LET'S REVIEW! – A FUN TIME WAS HAD BY ALL

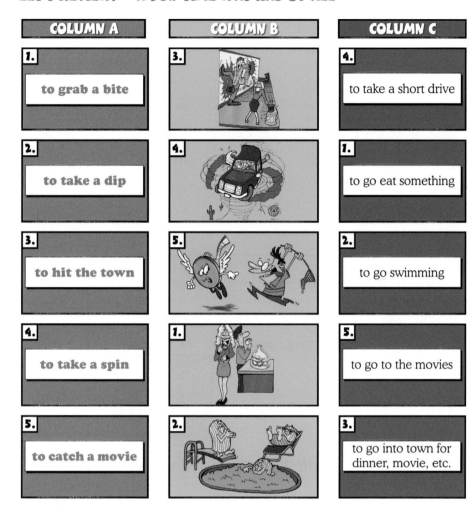

COLUMN A	COLUMN B	COLUMN C
1. to grab a bite	**3.**	**4.** to take a short drive
2. to take a dip	**4.**	**1.** to go eat something
3. to hit the town	**5.**	**2.** to go swimming
4. to take a spin	**1.**	**5.** to go to the movies
5. to catch a movie	**2.**	**3.** to go into town for dinner, movie, etc.

LESSON NINE - TO YOUR HEALTH

LET'S WARM UP!

1. feverish
2. day off from work in order to relax
3. fainted
4. feeling very sick
5. in good health
6. very bored
7. relax
8. become very restless from confinement
9. full of energy
10. nervous and agitated
11. survive
12. ill
13. lose strength on its own
14. tired and lifeless

LET'S USE "REAL SPEAK"

A. UNSCRAMBLE

1. What did you get for your birthday?
   What did **ya** get for **yer** birthday?

2. Are you going to your mother's house?
   Are **ya** going to **yer** mother's house?

3. You gave all your money to your brother?
   Ya gave all **yer** money to **yer** brother?

4. You know you are my best friend.
   Ya know **yer** my best friend.

5. Are you going to get your car washed today?
   Are **ya** going to get **yer** car washed today?

LET'S PRACTICE!

A. THE UNFINISHED CONVERSATION

In this exercise, be as creative as you'd like. Make sure to use the slang and idioms provided.

B. CHOOSE THE RIGHT WORD

1. dog
2. crazy
3. running
4. under
5. pull

6. mind
7. run
8. pink
9. blah
10. mental

11. out
12. antsy
13. easy
14. go

C. COMPLETE THE STORY

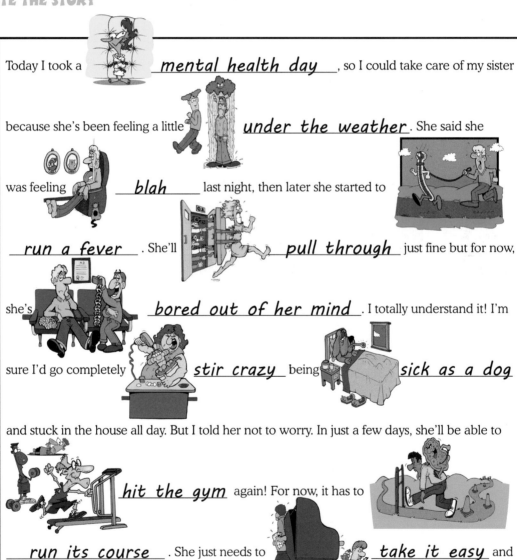

Today I took a *mental health day*, so I could take care of my sister

because she's been feeling a little *under the weather*. She said she

was feeling *blah* last night, then later she started to

run a fever. She'll *pull through* just fine but for now,

she's *bored out of her mind*. I totally understand it! I'm

sure I'd go completely *stir crazy* being *sick as a dog*

and stuck in the house all day. But I told her not to worry. In just a few days, she'll be able to

hit the gym again! For now, it has to

run its course. She just needs to *take it easy* and

get plenty of rest and drink plenty of liquids. Then she'll certainly be back

on her feet in just a few days!

LET'S REVIEW! - THE NIGHT SHIFT

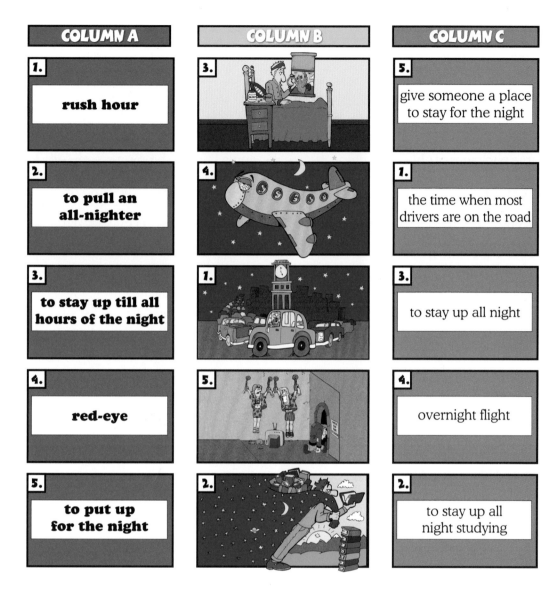

COLUMN A	COLUMN B	COLUMN C
1. rush hour	**3.**	**5.** give someone a place to stay for the night
2. to pull an all-nighter	**4.**	**1.** the time when most drivers are on the road
3. to stay up till all hours of the night	**1.**	**3.** to stay up all night
4. red-eye	**5.**	**4.** overnight flight
5. to put up for the night	**2.**	**2.** to stay up all night studying

LESSON TEN - ON A DATE

LET'S WARM UP!

1. True
2. False
3. True
4. True
5. True
6. True
7. False
8. True
9. True
10. False
11. True
12. True
13. False
14. True
15. True

LET'S USE "REAL SPEAK"

A. NOW YOU HAFTA DO A "HAFTA" EXERCISE

THE ABSOLUTE BEST CHOCOLATE SOUFFLÉ RECIPE IN THE WORLD

When making a chocolate soufflé, you **hafta** start with fresh ingredients. The eggs **hafta** be room temperature and the chocolate **hasta** be the dark or bittersweet kind. Believe it or not, all you **hafta** buy at the store is two large packages of chocolate chips, eight eggs, and a cup of whipping cream. All you **hafta** do is heat up the cream and pour it over the chocolate chips and stir until it's all combined. The cream **hasta** be hot enough to melt the chocolate but make sure the cream doesn't boil! Beat the eggs in a bowl and add the chocolate mixture, continuing to beat until it's all nice and creamy. You don't even **hafta** separate the eggs for this soufflé, which makes it really easy! Pour the mixture into a soufflé bowl and carefully put it in a pre-heated 350-degree oven. The soufflé **hasta** cook for one hour....and POOF! You'll have the lightest and most chocolaty soufflé you've ever tasted!

LET'S PRACTICE!

A. & B. CREATE YOUR OWN STORY (PARTS 1 & 2)

Create your own word list. Be as creative as you can!

C. WHAT WOULD YOU DO IF SOMEONE SAID...

1.	b	6.	c
2.	a	7.	c
3.	c	8.	a
4.	b	9.	b
5.	b	10.	b

LET'S REVIEW! ~ SOME OPPOSITES DO ATTRACT!

1.	D	4.	C
2.	E	5.	A
3.	B		

INDEX

SLANGMAN PUBLISHING

CONTACT SLANGMAN

I hope you enjoyed the first book in my series on American idioms & slang!

*If you want to contact me with your questions, ideas, suggestions, or to place an order, I'd love to hear from you! Here are a few ways to **get in touch with me** ("contact me")!*

 @TheRealSlangman

 facebook.com/TheRealSlangman

 (website) **www.slangman.com**

 orders@slangman.com

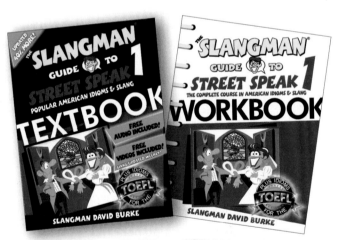

COMING SOON!